Hair and Beauty Business Management

Other books on hairdressing from Addison Wesley Longman

Colouring - A Salon Handbook
Second edition
Lesley Hatton, Phillip Hatton and Alisoun Powell
0-582-28759-6

Hygiene - A Salon Handbook
Second edition
Phillip Hatton
0-582-29454-1

Perming and Straightening - A Salon Handbook
Second edition
Lesley Hatton and Phillip Hatton
0-632-03316-9

Cutting and Styling – A Salon Handbook
Lesley Hatton and Phillip Hatton
0-582-29044-9

Afro Hair - A Salon Handbook
Phillip Hatton
0-632-02285-X

Foundation Hairdressing
Lesley Hatton and Phillip Hatton
0-632-02613-8

Setting up your own Salon
National Hairdressers' Federation
0-632-03889-6

How to win Clients and Interpret their Needs
A Hairdressers Guide
Ian Mistlin
0-632-03891-8

HAIR AND BEAUTY
BUSINESS MANAGEMENT

Second Edition

Annette Mieske

 LONGMAN

Addison Wesley Longman Limited,
Edinburgh Gate, Harlow,
Essex CM20 2JE, England
and Associated Companies throughout the world

First edition published 1990
under the title Hairdressing Business Management
Reprinted 1992
Second edition published 1994
Reprinted by Longman Group Limited 1995
Reprinted by Addison Wesley Longman Limited 1997

British Library Cataloguing in Publication Data
A catalogue entry for this title is available from the British Library

ISBN 0-582-29453 3

Produced through Longman Malaysia, PP

For my parents and daughter Kate
whose encouragement, support and
love make all things possible –
even this book!

Contents

Preface to the Second Edition

As we move towards the end of the century our environment and the way in which we work or, indeed, want to work is changing. This raises issues for the future of the hair and beauty industry for which, being labour-intensive, costs will continue to rise as people's expectations with regard to training, recognised qualifications and financial rewards continue to grow.

For many years clients and colleagues have said that not enough information about hair and beauty business management is available for the people who actually work in hair and beauty or who wish to enter the industry.

When you first thought about becoming a hairdresser or beauty therapist you were probably attracted to the industry because of your creative ability or because you liked the idea of meeting and helping people. One of the other skills that is needed to be a good hairdresser or beauty therapist is an eye for detail. If you wish to progress further or learn more about hair or beauty business management, this book will show you how important it is to be analytical in your approach to running a salon whether it is to promote the business, recruit the right staff, train and develop them as well as to make a profit. The skills required are 80 per cent analysis and 20 per cent instinct or intuition.

The ability to analyse can sound very boring but, just as a hairdresser or therapist needs an eye for detail to create a high quality hair cut or to complete a comprehensive beauty or skin care programme for a client, that same skill can be adapted successfully to run a salon.

This book has been written from many years' experience of working with and advising salons and companies within the hair and beauty industry in all aspects of managing, marketing and training and being able to show them how to successfully apply basic business concepts within the industry.

It is essential reading for all those who wish to increase their knowledge and confidence by qualifying as professional hairdressers or beauty therapists at NVQ levels 1, 2 and 3 or the Management Charter Initiative level 1 and 2 which is equivalent to NVQ 4 and 5.

Acknowledgements

This book has been possible because of the support of many people in the hair and beauty industry – people who believed in me and my views on the future of business management in hair and beauty, and how tried and tested management and business skills could successfully apply to hair and beauty businesses.

Along the way, these people were prepared to take the 'risk', as they saw it, of trying new approaches in managing their businesses and to be open to new ideas requiring flexible thinking. It is impossible to name them all but I shall be forever grateful to Felicity Green and Philip Rogers who first introduced me to the world of hairdressing, Remy, Steve Ellis, Derek Green, Patrick Hare, Philip McCarthy, the late Brian Jarvis and Kevin Arkell who were prepared to try new things.

Female workers represent 80 per cent of the industry. Many of them not only run, but own, successful hairdressing businesses as well as look after their homes and families. Their energy and stamina are a constant inspiration to me and special mention must be made of Frances Urwin, Shelley Daly and Denise Gibbs.

Annette Mieske

Chapter One
Marketing and Promotions

1.1 Introduction

This chapter covers the crucial area of marketing and promotions. It develops the major marketing concepts and applies these to hairdressing and beauty businesses. It examines the whole area of promotions and how to make these effective.

Many salon owners spend enormous amounts of time and money in opening a salon but frequently forget that the research required *prior* to selecting a salon is essential if the new venture is to be successful.

Secondly, time and money must be allocated to market and promote the business so that the public, the community, suppliers and potential staff know of its existence.

1.2 What is marketing?

In today's climate of increased competition many salon owners realise the need to constantly promote their business. Most would agree that the purpose of promotion is to attract new clients into the salon. But is it? Modern marketing theory would suggest that for a hairdresser, promotion in all its forms including advertising has at least six objectives:

- To inform clients of the services offered
- To attract new clients to the business
- To persuade old clients to come back to the business
- To remind clients that they are doing the right thing by using your business
- To attract new staff and motivate current staff
- To promote your image to competitors, staff, clients etc

Research has shown that all these objectives can be achieved by effective promotional and marketing strategy.

But what is promotion? Is it advertising? Special offers? Shows? Model nights? Yes, all of these and more.

Promotion is one part of a whole approach or philosophy towards the way you run your business. This has sometimes been called the *marketing concept*.

In this book we will adopt a disciplined approach to managing promotion where, as far as possible, myths, hunches or intuition are eliminated or at least tempered with reasoned judgement based on carefully prepared information and statistics – in other words obtaining the facts and analysing

Our recommended approach hinges on six main steps:

- Analyse
- Define
- Propose
- Evaluate
- Choose
- Execute

Let us now look at these steps in more depth.

1.3 A systematic approach

1.3.1 Analyse

We must analyse the situation within the business as it is at the present time by collecting as much information as possible in order to give a clear picture.

Client base

We show you in Exercise 1.1 how to do a simple analysis in two ways to test what percentage of clients are regular visitors. *The key to any successful business is regular clients*: they are the easiest to sell to and your staff can build up rapport and develop a profitable relationship. Research has shown many reasons why people change salons. There are those who 'always try the new salon' or 'want a change' but often the reasons are simpler:

- The staff aren't rude
- They do a professional job
- The salon is clean
- It has a friendly atmosphere
- They don't keep you waiting
- They don't rip you off with all those *extras* on the bill
- You get treated properly there

We will examine these 'buying reasons', as they are called, in later sections.

Exercise 1.1 Assessing client loyalty

Method 1
Examine one month's bookings. Count the following categories:

- Clients for the first time
- Clients who have been 1–5 times before
- Clients who have been 6+ times before (or for over a year)

If you do not know all this just use two simple categories, i.e. new and repeats.

Express these as percentages, i.e.

$$\% \text{ new clients} = \frac{\text{no. of new clients}}{\text{total clients}} \times 100$$

If the salon is not very new or has not recently been expanded, then the higher the percentage of new clients the more concern you need have.

Method 2

Only use if you have proper client record cards – (which you should have!). Take every tenth card and calculate how many months the client has been coming to you by completing the table below. If the first card shows 8 months you put a tick in the 7–12 months row, i.e.

	Ticks	Nos	%
1 month or less			
1–3 months			
4–6 months			
7–12 months			
More than a year			

TOTAL _____

$$\text{Note } \% = \frac{\text{no.}}{\text{total}} \times 100$$

You can check it has been done correctly if the totals of % come to about 100. The more clients you have had for a long time, the healthier your business is (and the more stable).

If you do not have a proper record system then setting this up should be one of the items to put into *action now*!

Client knowledge

In order to correctly meet client needs you must have a clear idea of:

- Who your clients are and how many there are
- Why they come to your salon (instead of competitors)
- What the market potential is in your area for your kind of client
- Your own business strengths and weaknesses and your advantages/ disadvantages over your competitors

Meeting business targets

The third aspect of analysing where you are now is assessing your financial performance. After all, you must want to make money too unless you are running a hairdressing salon because you love clients or as an ego trip! There are three quick measures to see if you are on target:

- Return on capital employed – around 20 per cent
- Gross profit – about 40–50 per cent
- Net profit – about 12–20 per cent

Exercise 1.2 Stylist's client analysis form

Branch ....   Week ending ....

Stylist's name

Day	Rev £ p	Client	Rev £ p	Client	Rev £ p	Client	Rev £ p	Client	Rev £ p	Client	Total Rev £ p	Clients New	Clients Reg	Total
Mon														
Tues														
Wed														
Thur														
Fri														
Sat														
Total														
Average														
New														
Reg														

Absentees:

	Holidays:
Mon	
Tues	
Wed	
Thurs	
Fri	
Sat	

Customer complaints: ....

Manager's notes: ....

Manager's signature: ....

If you cannot answer the above questions then contact your accountant *now* and ask him the following or read Chapter 2 on Understanding money:

(1) What are my figures for the salon this year?
(2) Have they improved/worsened/stayed the same?
(3) How do they compare with the competition?
(4) Why did he not tell you all this without asking?

Client services

You need to know not only how many new and regular clients your salon takes per week or month but which of your staff have the most regular clients and which are booked with the new clients. You need to know that 50 per cent of all *new* clients are being converted over 8–10 weeks to regular clients by individual stylists (see Exercise 1.2 Stylist's client analysis form).

You also need to know which of your services are most used by clients, e.g. cuts, perms, colours, so that you have evidence of what most of the salon and individual's time is devoted to. This subject will be covered in more depth in section 1.8 Pricing.

Client satisfaction

You must aim to provide what the client wants. The client is 'boss', not the owner or manager. Too many hairdressers treat clients as something to be tolerated or endured. But how can you tell if you are satisfying your clients?

- Ask them about service
- Analyse client base

Ask clients about the service

If you wish to find out what your clients want then you must ask them in such a way that does not embarrass them and by using questioning techniques which will require their honest opinion as opposed to a straightforward yes/no answer.

Exercise 1.3 gives an example of a client satisfaction survey.

Do bear in mind that some clients may be more generous than others in their praise of the salon – so it's never wise to be complacent!

To summarise, marketing is concerned with providing client satisfaction at a profit and requires a knowledge of what clients want and a determination to provide it in a better way than competitors.

These ideas are developed further in later sections where marketing theory is examined and applied to the hairdressing industry.

Exercise 1.3 Client satisfaction survey

We are constantly trying to improve our service and would be grateful if you could help by telling us where we are good and where we can improve. All your answers will be treated in confidence but will be considered. Thank you for taking the time to complete this survey.

Please ring the number which indicates how you felt about each aspect below. Ring 1 if you felt it was very poor, 2 = poor; 3 = acceptable; 4 = good; 5 = very good/excellent. Please add comments or write overleaf if you wish to say more. Leave an item blank if you do not wish to or cannot answer.

		Score			
(1) Telephone manner	1	2	3	4	5
(2) Pricing policy	1	2	3	4	5
(3) Welcome by receptionist and staff	1	2	3	4	5
(4) Decoration	1	2	3	4	5
(5) Comfort: (a) Cleanliness	1	2	3	4	5
(b) Temperature	1	2	3	4	5
(6) Lighting	1	2	3	4	5
(7) Music: (a) Choice of music	1	2	3	4	5
(b) Volume of music	1	2	3	4	5
(c) Lack of music	1	2	3	4	5
(8) Availability of appointments	1	2	3	4	5
(9) Efficiency of service (not kept waiting etc.)	1	2	3	4	5
(10) Friendliness of staff	1	2	3	4	5
(11) Quality of service (hairdressing)	1	2	3	4	5
(12) Were the staff informative about our services and products?					
(a) Colour	1	2	3	4	5
(b) Perms	1	2	3	4	5
(c) Home hair care products	1	2	3	4	5
(13) Treatment when settling up bill	1	2	3	4	5

Is this your first visit to this salon? ....

Will you come again   YES ☐   NO ☐   If NO, why not?

What things do you like about this salon? ....

What do you think could be improved? ....

What did you have done today? ....

Which member(s) of staff served you? ....

Thank you for completing this survey

1.4 Who are my clients and what do they want?

Many staff do not stop and think 'what type of clients do I have and where do they come from?' Ask a stylist the reasons why a client visits and they will tend to be very different from the client's reasons. If you are to establish your salon's strengths and weaknesses you need as many facts as possible. Marketing men seem almost obsessed with the answers to the question

Fig. 1.1 Some reasons why women go to hairdressers (*Street Research* 1982).

(1) To make them feel good.
(2) To make them look beautiful and/or younger.
(3) To get some peace and quiet from the kids.
(4) To look fashionable.
(5) To be able to talk to a sympathetic ear.
(6) To have a nice young man/woman looking after them.
(7) To get out of the house.
(8) To spoil themselves – a special treat.
(9) To make their hair easy-to-manage.
(10) To get a good rest.

'what business are we in?' You would probably answer 'hairdressing'. But are you? If you think hard you will see that the President of Revlon who said 'in the factory we make cosmetics, in the drug store we sell hope' has relevance to the hairdressing industry. Our research has shown that the real reasons that people go to hairdressers are varied and there are no general reasons. If you look at Fig. 1.1 showing some reasons why women go to hairdressers then clearly the choice of salon is directly connected with the reasons and your ability to meet the client's requirements.

If you are to analyse the business you are in, you need to define the three kinds of service that a hairdressing salon offers. These are:

(1) *Tangible service* – the obvious thing you offer – cutting/styling/perming, etc.
(2) *Extended service* – the whole range of interlinked services you offer, e.g. products, fashion advice, hair care and beauty aids, etc.
(3) *Generic service* – the real (often unstated) benefit that the client actually wants from coming to the salon.

The first two kinds of service seem reasonably straightforward but it is the third area, the generic service, which is most volatile and *rapidly changes as a client's needs change*. Marketing research has identified that during the next decade customers' needs will change and it is up to a salon to decide how some of these needs can be met through the services that are offered.

Fig. 1.2 New aspects of consumer needs and wants in the 1990s.

(1) More casual lifestyles.
(2) Desire for elegance and individualism.
(3) Flexibility of roles, e.g. women's liberation.
(4) More 'instant gratification' as lifestyle.
(5) Readier acceptance of credit etc.
(6) New work ethic ('work to live' not 'live to work').
(7) Consumerism (quality and value for money is a *right*).
(8) Shrinking world (acceptance of ethnic groups etc.).
(9) Rejection of big business ('small *is* beautiful').
(10) Pleasure is good and not immoral.
(11) More leisure time.
(12) Energy conservation/ecology/environmental issues.
(13) Changing morality about all things.
(14) Concern about appearance and health.
(15) Novelty, change and escapism fashionable.
(16) Desire for natural things now important.

For example more people are now increasingly concerned about their health, i.e. health food, preservatives in food, anti-smoking, what is contained in hair and beauty products. Thus any promotion stressing the positive factors will appeal to people who have these kinds of needs. Young people in particular are very concerned about the environment and health. You may like to think through the implications of some of the other consumer needs and wants for the 1990s for yourself (see Fig. 1.2).

1.5 Market segmentation – a key concept

Many hairdressers try to be 'all things to all people' and have a wide range of clients. You can compare this with the small corner shop which sold everything. But few people ever 'got rich quick' in a corner shop (and had time to enjoy the fruits of their labours) and those that did copied the ideas of supermarkets by attracting a particular group of clients and tailoring their image to meet those clients' needs. Market segmentation or *client group identification* is a key concept for promotional success.

The market for each type of product or service is unique, e.g. cars, perms or clothing. This individuality is caused by variations in many characteristics, e.g. size of market, pricing structure, characteristics of customers, buying habits etc.

It is essential to analyse the market in which the organisation is interested, in order to establish its characteristics, prior to the formulation of any objectives and plans. The issues that need to be covered include:

(1) What do the clients in the market buy, i.e. what type of product/service and how much of it, how often etc.?
(2) Why does the client buy it, i.e. for what purpose is it purchased and for what reason, e.g. reliability, status, cheapness?
(3) Who purchases the product/service and who does the buying, e.g. in a family is it the wife or husband?
(4) What is the person's buying procedure, e.g. walk-ins, appointments, impulse visits, perms or colour correction, occasional appointments?
(5) When is the purchase made, e.g. half-yearly, once a week during a shopping trip, on holiday, at a particular time of year, when hair is unmanageable?
(6) Where is the product purchased, e.g. retail shops, mail order, superstores, supermarkets, at exhibitions etc.?

Answers to the questions listed above will provide an outline of the market concerned and reveal that there is often more than one answer to each question. This is because clients buying a certain category of product will be very different in their characteristics including buying behaviour and the use to which the product is put.

Market segmentation – a definition

Market segmentation involves recognition that every market is made up of distinguishable groups consisting of buyers with different needs, methods of buying and responses to variations of what the seller offers. No single item, product or service offered to the market will meet the needs of all buyers. The process of identifying these groups is 'market segmentation'.

The uses of segmentation

(1) Identification of market opportunities available, i.e. what needs and whose needs. There will be several segments in each market.

(2) Evaluation of opportunities offered by each segment on a logical basis against the firm's objectives, resources and capability. An aid in the selection of which group of buyers to serve, which of their needs and with what offering.

(3) As a basis for planning, executing and monitoring the firm's offering to buyers.

(4) To provide competitive advantage if the firm can identify segments not adequately served by competitors, e.g. a small firm may be able to service a large share of a small specialised segment of the market, which would be uneconomic for a large rival. This may avoid direct confrontation witth powerful competitors in the larger segments. The largest segment does not always offer the greatest opportunity.

To summarise, the stages in developing market segmentation are:

- Identify clear leader segments (or groups) whom you wish to aim at
- Examine the characteristics of those groups in detail and in particular their needs and preferences
- Tailor your whole approach to them
- Promote directly to these segments and sell to them and reap the benefits
- Be constantly aware of changing needs of new segments and act accordingly

See Fig. 1.3 Market segmentation and Fig. 1.4 Five possible segments to exploit.

It is not just in the biggest segment that money is to be made. Ford sell more cars per day than BMW per week, but BMW make more profit. Any segment can be profitable if you (a) identify it and (b) sell to it correctly.

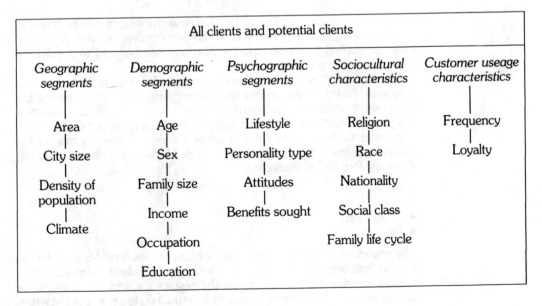

Fig. 1.3 Market segmentation.

Fig. 1.4 Five possible segments to exploit.

> (1) *Ethnic groups*
>   'Black' or 'Asian' styles
>
> (2) *Trends*
>   'Punk' or 'Mod' styles
>
> (3) *Age*
>   Young teenagers
>   OAPs
>   Middle aged
>   Mothers
>
> (4) *Sex*
>   Men
>   Unisex
>   Women
>
> (5) *Personality type*
>   Beauty-conscious type. Offer complete service e.g. sunbed, manicure, beauty advice etc.
>   Price up-market

It is not just large companies that do it. The difference between those that make it and those that don't is (a) recognising it and (b) doing it.

You can segment a market in a large number of ways. For example, Fig. 1.3 shows the various segmenting categories and Fig. 1.4 lists a number of segments you might consider as possibilities for marketing and promotional approach.

1.6 The marketing mix

In this section we examine one of the most powerful weapons in any business – the marketing mix. This is one of the hardest concepts to understand but it can be applied to almost any situation and can be used to predict the implications of any course of action.

The concept of the marketing mix is simple in that you see the business as a system sitting in an environment competing with other businesses attempting to attract clients from that market – in other words, a salon sitting in a place competing with other hairdressing salons to attract clients.

In order to do this you need to adopt the right marketing mix for the particular segment to which you wish to sell. Marketing experts usually talk about the four 'Ps' of marketing:

- Price
- Place
- Promotion
- Product

The important thing to remember is that you cannot consider any of these four in isolation. Hairdressers who increase or indeed decrease prices without considering the effects on the rest of the mix are likely to be unsuccessful either by losing clients or by attracting too many of the wrong type, e.g. unprofitable ones. But how do you choose the right mix? There are

Fig. 1.5
Marketing mix.

(1) *Product factors (services)*
Product planning (new products/lines) (new styles)
Market segments aimed for – who? what? where? how many?
Innovation (attitudes to)
Expertise of staff

(2) *Price factors*
Competitive prices (in same segments)
Specific price ranges and structures (e.g. higher prices on weekends/holidays?)
Nature and type of discounts (client loyalty discounts)
Pricing policies – how many prices? (Are they too complicated, are they inclusive of conditioners/styling aids?) e.g. school-leaver/OAPs/unemployed
How often are prices reviewed?
Differential pricing on key services (higher prices for blow-dries, lower prices for perms)
Attitudes to credit or accounts etc.

(3) *Promotion*
Sales training for staff
Promotional methods to be used
Amount of money to be spent on all forms of advertising/promotion
Image to be maintained/enhanced
Merchandising/promotion of products where stocked (display material)
Packaging/own branding (where products are sold in quantity)
Competitors' activities

(4) *Place (distribution)*
Location of salon (can it be found?)
Stock control of key items
Parking facilities/transport availability

no definite answers. There are a large number of factors, however, which affect the mix.

Figure 1.5 shows in detail the four categories of the marketing mix. What must be done, however, is to analyse clients and their segments together with a detailed profit analysis to identify where turn-over and profit is obtained. In other words, finding out what are your most profitable services and an examination in detail of all of your promotional activities.

1.7 Selecting the right image

Selecting an image for a salon sounds to many stylists and salon owners like the fun side of starting up a business. In fact, many of them select an image by their own personal taste or style – this can often be a costly mistake.

What is an image?

The word 'image' means different things to different people. *The Oxford Dictionary* describes it as a 'likeness, reproduction in the memory of the sensation of sight, hearing and smell'. You should use this interpretation as a useful guideline and consider how you can create an image using sensations of 'sight, hearing and smell' that meet the needs of the majority of your clients with the *segment you wish to attract*.

Let's take each of the senses in turn:

Sight   What can be seen?
Sound   What can be heard, e.g. what kind of atmosphere? How are we greeted? What kind of conversation goes on in the salon?
Smell   What smells invade the salon?
Touch   How is our sense of touch affected?
Taste   What do we eat/drink in the salon?

1.7.1 Sight

What can we see with our eyes?

Accessibility

The position of the salon is the first item to consider.

Ground floor – can be seen by potential passing trade. The external appearance would be essential. Many salons alienate their clients by an 'up-market' appearance even though their prices are much lower than the appearance of the salon. Tinted glass, net curtains and blinds all create visual images that can enhance or detract from the image you wish to create.

First floor salons – when walking down your local high street how often do you look up to another floor or even notice the architecture of the buildings? Even the most outstanding architecture becomes commonplace when you shop in the same town regularly. Ensuring a visual impact on the first floor can be difficult from the outside. This is where concentration on other 'image' factors should be used.

Salons in side streets – immediate accessibility is difficult. Other 'visual' image methods need to be adopted, e.g. promotions, advertising and public relations.

Colour schemes

When fitting out the salon how did you select the colours? How much thought did you really give to this? Did you think it should be ultra-modern or did you look at other salons in the area first to see if your ideas coincided? The drawback of selecting your favourite colours is that they may be fine for you, but what about the impact they have on your clients and the *segments* that you wish to attract?

Psychologists tell us that certain colours have different effects on mood and behaviour. Think about the effects of sitting in a grey room. Does it make you feel depressed? Is it a soft grey which can be relaxing or a hard blue grey which can be cold and clinical? What effect does red have on you? Does it cheer you up – or make you feel claustrophobic and aggressive? When selecting colours decisions need to be made about the atmosphere as well as the visual impact that colours can have upon your clients and, just as important, the effect they will have upon your staff who have to work in the salon every day. So give some thought to colours and the effect they can have and how they help create a backcloth for the mood and atmosphere of your business.

Hairdressers often think that if they are creating fashionable styles salon fitments should be up-to-the-minute in design, but consider how quickly a salon dates by having orange or brown backwashes – these can be very expensive to re-vamp. There are many ways of making salons modern, by changing the colour of the walls, lighting and easily removed fittings, without having to change the essentials such as flooring, styling positions and styling chairs. It is often possible to tell when a salon was opened by the colour schemes and fitments – unless the owner had the foresight to be aware of future colour trends.

When selecting a colour scheme it should be used or co-ordinated within gowns, towels and stationery such as appointment cards and price lists. Otherwise the image created confuses not only the public but potential employees whom you will also need to attract.

Printing

Hairdressers fall too easily into the trap of thinking they should be experts in everything. Some salon owners have tremendous talent for design and visual impact, but do not consider the nitty-gritty like the quality of the printing. Printing and typesetting should be left to other professionals but beware of back street printers who imply that the more expensive printers are ripping off their clients. This is not always the case. There are exceptions in every business but it is usual to get what you pay for. Bear in mind that selecting unusual colours for the interior of the salon, equipment and printing could escalate the production cost in all these items.

Salon names and logos

Selecting a name needs considerable thought. These are the guidelines to follow:

- Keep it timeless. These examples indicate different decades:

  Maison Fred
  Cut and Blow
  Curl Up and Dye
  Head Shavers

  Old-fashioned names do not encourage new clients

- Tell clients what you offer, e.g. hair cutting, colouring, perming, dressing, service, products, expertise.
- Don't let the name of the salon grow old like the salon owner unless it is synonomous with success, e.g. Vidal Sassoon or Mister Michael, John Thomas etc.
- Select a name consistent with the image you wish to adopt for the client segment you want to attract, e.g.

  Barnetts!
  Coiffure!
  Hair!

- Think about how the name can be written in an attractive form to remind people of who you are.

- Use a 'pay-off line' or slogan in advertising or promotional material, e.g. 'Philip's Hair Studio – We Care More'.
- Use the logo and pay-off line in all your sales/advertising material to get your message across, e.g. 'Beanz Meanz Heinz'.

Advertising/sales material

Play on the theme and image you have created whenever and wherever possible:

- Appointment cards
- Letter headings
- Price lists
- Staff tee-shirts
- Company cars
- Products
- Gowns/towels
- Coffee/tea cups
- Magazine folders
- Hair care leaflets
- Advertising space
- Job vacancies
- Model posters

Look at the classified ads at the back of the trade press – which ones would attract you to apply for a job? When advertising use the following guidelines:

- Don't overcrowd – white space says a lot about your image.
- Use only one or two typefaces and not several, which confuse the message.
- Lay it out attractively.
- Remember *who will be reading it* and give them the information that will make them contact you.
- Keep the message simple.
- Don't try to achieve too many things.

The staff

There is no point spending time and money on a coherent image if your staff do not reflect it in terms of:

- Appearance – clothes and hair
- Manner/behaviour to each other and to the clients
- Standards of work
- Standards of service

Encompass all of the above – *your staff are your image. Train them to get it right.*

Products

Products can enhance or detract from your image so choose carefully, particularly a retail range.

(1) Manufacturers
   Check out the following:

   - Packaging
   - Support material/hair care leaflets/show cards
   - Training support
   - Price – ask yourself if they reflect your image

(2) Own brand

- Will the labelling and packaging complement your image or conflict? Is the product better than a manufacturer's range or the same? (or worse?)
- What price should be charged? The same as a manufacturer, cheaper or more expensive? (Consider the effects of selling very cheap products in an up-market salon.)
- Will staff believe in them? If they don't how will you sell them?
- Consider the capital outlay of packaging and purchasing of stock.

Photographs

Do the photographs displayed in the salon emphasise the type of work covered – commercial, avante garde – or are they just pretty pictures to fill up the window? Photographs and display material quickly discolour and should be changed regularly. Unless tatty display material reflects your image!

1.7.2 Sound

What can be heard?

Atmosphere

It is hard to measure atmosphere but clients and staff know when they feel comfortable with the sounds in the salon.

- *Music.* What type of music? Does it suit the clients or staff? What image does it create?
- *Conversation.* The dialogue between staff and clients – is it happy and bubbly or stressful and aggressive? Are clients included in the conversation? Is the conversation informative or flotsam? 'How were your hols Mrs Smith?' or 'How did you get on with your perm Mrs Smith?' Which conversation will be most fruitful to the business? The flotsam may be necessary as a 'warm-up' conversation but how the client copes with her hair and products is more constructive to both parties.
- *Silence.* Silence can be positive or negative. Think about the effect on clients when stylists don't talk to them.
- *Noise.* Noise can be disruptive and for many clients it is uncomfortable when they do not hear what the stylist is saying.
- *Listening.* You may ask how listening can reflect the image of the salon. If we do not listen to what a client says how can we find out her needs? More salons lose clients by not listening to what the client wants than probably any other area of the business. You must learn to listen by asking open questions and checking you have understood and agreed a course of action. Read Section 4.2 Communication.

Answering the telephone

You should never underestimate the value of how the telephone is answered – indeed, who does answer it? Is it the youngest, most inexperienced trainee or someone who has been trained properly to answer the telephone? If the salon does not have a receptionist then it is essential that all staff are trained in how to answer the telephone and the range of questioning techniques that can be used to extract information from people as well as make them feel welcome.

Welcome!

When clients walk into a salon how are they greeted? Do the staff look at the client as if they are an interruption to the work they are already carrying out? Or are they greeted with a smile and by name? Are they helped with their coat and gown? How many salons offer consultation prior to having their hair shampooed at the backwash? Remember, it is the first impression that counts, particularly with new clients visiting the salon. It is the new clients that see the salon as it really is.

Client interest

What kind of conversation goes on in the salon? Is the conversation about holidays and what everyone saw on the TV the night before or, is it about how the client copes with her hair? What products does she use on her hair? How does she dry it? How does she cope with it? How has she handled her hair since the last perm, colour or treatment? The business that you are really in is not hairdressing but the business of offering knowledge and information so that clients can cope with their hair between salon visits. An interesting concept and anathema to many people in the hairdressing industry!

1.7.3 Smell

What smells invade the salon? How can smell reflect our image? The smell of products, people and equipment can be attractive to clients. Check the following:

- Adequate heating and ventilation to ensure a comfortable atmosphere
- Cleanly laundered gowns and towels – not dried-off towels smelling of perm solution and the give-away musty smell of re-dried towels!
- Pleasant-smelling products – more people today are concerned with the use of chemicals than at any other time;
- Sweet-smelling staff – at the backwash and particularly those staff who have a taste for alcohol, garlic and curries!

1.7.4 Touch

How is our sense of touch affected when we are in a hairdressing salon?

- Gowns – do they feel pleasant to touch?
- Surfaces – do they feel clean or sticky?
- Products – are we allowed to touch the products? Are they available to be touched at a styling position? .
- Client contact – do we touch our clients in a friendly, reassuring way? When does the touch become a grope or sexual overture? The line is a fine one and we need to train staff in body contact and body signals in order that they understand clients' responses.

1.7.5 *Taste*

What is eaten or drunk in the salon? If you are going to offer drinks to your clients then ensure that the coffee tastes of coffee, that the tea tastes of tea and that it is served in cups that do not taste of washing-up liquid or another client's lipstick.

Consumer trends for the 1990s indicate healthy, natural and preservative-free food and drink wherever possible. Does the salon offer herbal teas, decaffeinated coffee, fresh orange juice and bottled water? If sandwiches are offered, are they on wholemeal bread – in other words, are clients given a wider choice than just standard tea or coffee? More importantly, when the food or drink is served does it taste good?

In conclusion, image is definable and measurable if you consider all the points raised above. By being aware of these things you can ensure you remain in control of what can so easily slip from our grasp.

1.8 Pricing

Pricing is probably one of the most important factors of running any hairdressing or beauty salon – and the one with which most people in the hair and beauty industry have problems. From my own experience in working in consultancy within the industry for a number of years, pricing is the one area that the vast majority of salons get wrong. Yet it is the one, if calculated properly, that is the key to success and profitability and makes marketing and promoting the salon easier.

The factors you need to consider in deciding your prices are many and include:

- Competition
- Market acceptance
- Your own costs
- Your image
- What you wish to achieve by your pricing strategy

Research shows that hairdressers in particular are reluctant to price up, in case they lose clients. Yet, given a higher profit on each price, it is possible to lose clients and still emerge eventually better off in profit terms. But how do you balance all of these factors? You need to examine each of them in turn.

The following factors covering pricing are just as relevant to beauty salons with the exception of beauty salon costs which are different than those which apply to hairdressing salons.

Beauty salon pricing

Prices will depend upon the services a beauty salon offers. For example, waxing and electrolysis will tend to be offered by most competitive salons and therefore the prices for these services will tend to be comparable. Those salons who offer skin and make-up care will find that wage costs must be kept within 25–30 per cent of turnover due to the high cost of products. Stock costs will be 45–55 per cent of turnover.

Beauty salons tend to work on a one-to-one basis due to the very personal nature of the services which cannot be handed over to support staff. This means that a realistic price per hour for all services is crucial.

Example

£25.50 per hour is equivalent to 3 × 20 minute appointments @ £8.50 per service

Clients cannot usually be left to 'process' or be handed over to a trainee. The beauty space is occupied, meaning the number of clients which can be handled on an hourly basis is limited. Many beauty salons underprice their services and are forced to work on a volume basis contradictory to the concept of beauty salon services.

Retail sales in beauty are an essential part of the service. Therapists quickly realise that without them there is insufficient profit in the business. One should aim for the following ratio of beauty salon business to retail sales:

60 per cent beauty salon services: 40 per cent retail sales

Retail beauty products tend to be costly with a stock cost of about 60–70 per cent of turnover but because of the labour-intensive nature of in-salon services these must be on sale to increase turnover and profit.

Salons without a high volume of retail sales will find that the net profit will be low at about 5 per cent of turnover. This raises the issue regarding the mix of services offered to clients. Whilst salons need to offer services such as waxing, electrolysis, manicures, eye-lash tinting, providing a range of higher priced services such as facials, make-up and aromatherapy needs considerable thought.

To aim for a ratio of 50 per cent low price services to 50 per cent high price services makes sound business sense. It is the high price facials and skin care programmes which also will generate the majority of add-on retail sales. Ratios of 50 per cent low price and 50 per cent high price services, and 40 per cent retail sales will generate a net profit in the region of 20 per cent.

Example

	Number of services	Percentage of services		Cost		Revenue
Waxing	30	55	×	£6	=	£180
Electrolysis	12	22	×	£7	=	£84
Manicure	6	11	×	£8	=	£48
Facials	4	7	×	£25	=	£100
Make-up	3	5	×	£12.50	=	£37.50
				Total revenue	=	£449.50

In this example 48 services representing 88% of the beauty salon business, are low price services which require a minimum of 15–20 minutes allocated appointment time but generate 69 per cent of turnover. The higher price services – facials and make-up sessions – represent 12 per cent of services but generate 29 per cent of turnover.

If a salon has the mix of services illustrated in our example, the following problems can arise:

(1) Competition may force waxing and electrolysis prices down.

(2) The more the salon concentrates on volume, low price services, the greater the difficulty of generating retail sales.

(3) There is a maximum volume of clients beauty therapists can handle, and this will limit potential income.

1.8.1 Competition

Clearly you wish to be competitive but you must ensure that you are comparing 'like with like'. If you are up-market, giving a good service and extras to clients, then you may be able to command a higher price in the market place, e.g. compare Tesco and Marks and Spencer! You can check competition both in terms of price and service either by visiting or 'sending in' someone to find out for you. This 'military intelligence' approach is common in other types of business and can provide useful information. You can look at other aspects while you are there. Some hairdressers use wives, girlfriends, friends or relatives to do this. What is essential is that a hairdresser, particularly the salon owner, does not analyse or visit competitors' salons. The reason for this is that hairdressers are always biased against other hairdressers and their services. They very rarely judge the services objectively and are often very critical of each other's services and hairdressing. Clients who are not hairdressers judge services by the way they are treated upon a visit and the standard of the hairdressing is judged by the following:

(1) Whether it was what the client wanted

(2) Whether he/she can manage it at home

(3) The knowledge and advice they were given to help keep their hair in the same style and condition in between salon visits

To analyse competitors in a simple way see Fig. 1.6.

Fig. 1.6
Checking out your competitors.

Item	Us	Competitor 1	Competitor 2	Competitor 3
(1) Telephone manner				
(2) Prices				
(3) Opening hours				
(4) Image (external)				
(5) Image (internal)				
(6) Extras – coffee, tea, styling aids				
(7) Types of client in the salon at time of visit				
(8) Overall impression (cleanliness, atmosphere, appearance of staff)				
(9) Quality of work				
(10) Any other comments				

1.8.2 Market acceptance

This is clearly a key factor. In a poor area you cannot command the high prices that central town salons do and in areas of high unemployment high prices would make for difficulties. However, many segments will still pay more than others and various kinds of differential pricing are worth considering, e.g.:

(1) Charging more at holiday times, weekends and other busy times
(2) Charging less on quiet days
(3) Special categories, e.g. school leavers, OAPs, unemployed etc.
(4) Offering a special 'Rolls Royce' service

So what is an acceptable price for hairdressing services in your locality? The key is *to increase prices to the maximum level the market will bear but the effect must be monitored carefully to see any changes of client usage.* Measure this by the following criteria:

(1) Are clients spreading out their visits from 8 weeks to 10 weeks?
(2) Are clients spending less on retail products (although this can often be due to the barrier the staff create in thinking clients cannot afford any more!)?
(3) Are clients opting for cutting only instead of the 'finished' effect?
(4) Are less technical services asked for?
(5) Is there a reduction in regular clients using the salon?
(6) Are clients selecting lower price stylists?
(7) Is there a change in the market segment, e.g. age group, sex, occupations?

1.8.3 Your own costs

The problem here is two-fold:

(1) Determining your costs properly
(2) Interpreting the cost data in a meaningful way so as to lead to realistic pricing

Costing is described more fully in Chapter 2 Understanding money but suffice it to say here that there are a number of different kinds of cost which are confusingly similar in definition. Two useful ones are *unit cost* and *full cost.* For this you need to understand and calculate the following information explained more fully in Chapter 2:

- Gross profit which should ideally be 40–48 per cent
- Net profit – in the hairdressing industry, usually 10–15 per cent
- Return on capital employed

In calculating pricing you must understand the idea of contribution, e.g.

Contribution = selling price – variable costs

In the hairdressing business, variable costs are made up of two main elements:

(1) Wages/salaries including employer's National Insurance contributions
(2) Consumables – stock, coffee/tea included in the price, supply of laundry per client etc.

If you look at Fig. 1.7 you will see that this business has a 43 per cent gross

Fig. 1.7 Income statement.

Income statement	Company XYZ	Period 1994

(1) Sales (turnover) excl. VAT   £100,000

(2) Cost of sales
     Materials   7,000
     Wages/salaries   50,000   £57,000
                                 ───────
                                 £57,000   Gross profit   £43,000
                                                                          ───────
                                                                          (43%)

(3) Expenses
     Salon operating
        Rent, rates and water   10,000
        Repairs and renewals   2,000
        Light and heat   800
        Insurances   200   £13,000

     Salon administration
        Telephone   600
        Accountancy and audit   800
        Stationery and postage   500
        Advertising/promotion   3,500   £5,400

     Motor vehicle costs
        Running expenses   2,400
        Leasing/hire   4,000   £6,400

     Financial charges
        Bank interest and charges 1,600   £1,600

     Depreciation   5,000   £5,000   £31,400

     n.b. Capital = 10,000   Net profit   £11,600
                                                              ───────
                                                              (11.6%)

These figures are exemplary only.

profit, a 11.6 per cent net profit and that wages and materials amount to 57 per cent of turnover. Wages, including employer's National Insurance contributions, should never be higher than 53 per cent and within the range of 40–53 per cent. If the figure is much lower then this means one of three things:

(1) Staff are underpaid
(2) Staff are being paid 'under the table' or cash-in-hand
(3) The owner or manager of the business is working harder than anyone else generating turnover (takings) in order to pay the wages of the staff!

Break-even

We must now introduce another new concept, that of break-even volume where we define

$$\text{Break-even} = \frac{\text{Total fixed costs}}{\text{Contribution}} \text{ (or Expenses)}$$

which in this case amounts to

$$\frac{£31\,400}{0.43} = £73\,023$$

Break-even means the turnover that you must make to cover your costs, which in our example gives us £73 023. We call the difference between actual turnover and break-even turnover the 'margin of safety', i.e.

$$£100\,000 - £73\,023 - £26\,977$$

Sales can fall by £26 977 before actually losing money. The higher the margin, the less vulnerable one is to competition. If prices are increased then the break-even goes down and it is possible to estimate what sales are needed to equate new and old profit levels. This is the basis of 'contribution or break-even' pricing.

Example
Suppose XYZ Company increased its prices by 10 per cent (exclusive of VAT) without changing its costs.

	Before price increase	10% price increase
Sales	£100 000	?
Contribution (per £)	0.43	0.53
Fixed costs	£31 400	£31 400
Net profit	£11 600	?
Break-even	£73 023	£59 245

Thus break-even has fallen because more contribution has been made per sale.

1.8.4 *Your image*

You must price according to the image you are putting forward, e.g. if you are up-market then you need to price accordingly. In fact, some research in the USA has indicated that many clients perceive a higher price to indicate a higher standard for the same product within a 10–15 per cent range. Thus by pricing a service too low people may actually believe it to be inferior to a higher priced equivalent service. This, we feel, is a hairdresser's major mistake and reduces profits. Consumers' perceptions of price come from various sources but a number of factors do affect 'what consumers will pay' and their concept of 'value for money':

(1) The image of the salon including:

  - Appearance/decor/ambience
  - Comfort and furnishings
  - Quality of product – cuts, perms etc.
  - Staff dress standards etc.

(2) Staff attitudes/professionalism and friendliness, i.e. quality of total services offered. Time spent on *them* is also an important factor – time spent by the stylist and not the most junior member of staff who is

Fig. 1.8 Uses of pricing.

(1) Launching or promoting a new style or product (*initial pricing*) or to a new segment e.g. OAPs.

(2) 'Killing off' a style or product ('*sell off*').

(3) Promoting your image, i.e. setting the right price for your particular market and the particular image you wish to put across.

(4) 'Skimming or creaming' policy. This is where one uses a high price initially (to maximise profit) and then reduces price when competitors come in or sales fall off.

(5) 'Penetration pricing'. A low price initially to attract high volume or to *compete strongly*, i.e. eliminate competitors. Then when well established allow price to drift up and profit percentages to improve.

(6) 'Charm pricing'. An approach where prices have a certain 'charm' e.g. £9.99 not £10.00, £7.75 not £8.00 etc. These are more 'attractive' than natural prices.

(7) 'Responsive pricing'. Responding to competition and competitors' prices (see Fig 1.9).

(8) 'Irritation pricing'. Moving prices about may cause competition great problems and particularly if discounts or vouchers are readily given, it may cause confusion among competition. It needs to be watched carefully because it must not irritate clients as well.

allocated to shampoo, neutralise perms and apply tints! Many clients are unhappy with being passed around on a production line basis from one so-called 'specialist' to another.

(3) Amount of advertising/promotion. Promotion offsets the negative effects of price and reinforces the image. If the salon only advertises its business when it is offering discounts on prices or colours then this is the only image that the public will have of that particular salon. Promotions reinforcing the image are much more powerful than offering discounts.

(4) Things included in price:

- Drinks
- Conditioners/styling aids
- Leaflets on haircare advice
- Free samples of retail products

(5) If your salon is up-market then you should avoid having 'scruffy' clientele or staff around the place. It is no coincidence that 'up-market' stores, e.g. Harrods etc. have high standards for all aspects of their business.

1.8.5 *What you wish to achieve by your pricing strategy*

The owner or manager of the business must think through the consequences of a pricing strategy and we list below the different types of pricing strategy and the effect that these can have upon a salon. We have listed details in Fig. 1.8 but we examine two examples below:

(1) Differential pricing – certain days are always more busy than others. One can use differential pricing to:

- Attract clients to quiet days, e.g. discount
- Detract clients from busy days by premium prices, e.g. increases; or
- Both

Differential pricing is a powerful technique generally ignored by hairdressers and one which clearly is advantageous in maximising profit and adjusting demand to supply.

(2) 'Skimming' or 'creaming' – a possible approach here is to identify a new segment and to prepare a product-package at a premium price with promotion until competition responds with a lower price, then subsequently reduce the price to lower levels (after you have recouped your investment), e.g. a new, exciting style.

The effect of price changes on competitors is interesting. Research has shown that clients may perceive price decreases in terms of:

(1) Product or service is outmoded
(2) Product or service is defective and is not selling well
(3) The business has financial problems
(4) Price will come down further if we wait
(5) Quality has been reduced

They may perceive price increases as:

(1) Product or service was exceptionally good value and is now reasonable
(2) Product or service is 'burning' and may only be available for a short time
(3) Product or service has been improved
(4) Inflation increases only

Competitors' response is variable too. Many competitors will move only in case of a reduction. Others automatically follow. Clearly where there is less competition there may be little problem. In some areas hairdressers have agreed collectively to raise prices where profits are low or the market is poor.
So how do you respond when a competitor increases his prices? It is a complex process but we offer a model, shown in Fig. 1.9, containing possible guidelines. Ask the questions:

(1) Why has he increased prices?

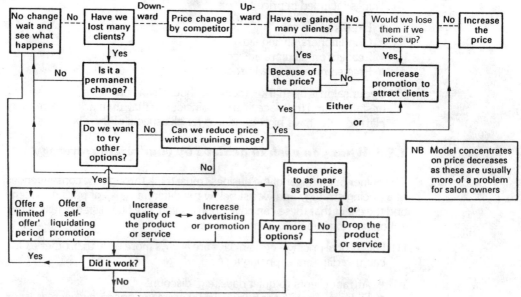

Fig. 1.9 Price change model – competitive response.

(2) Is it temporary or permanent?

(3) What are other competitors doing?

(4) Have many clients switched to us as a result? Evidence shows that 'regulars' do tend to be loyal!

(5) Has the service/image changed?

(6) What are my preferences in response?

It is important to try to understand his motives before responding. Is he losing money?

When considering what the owner or manager is trying to achieve with his/her pricing strategy, we must also consider how long the salon owner, in particular, wishes to remain in business. Does the salon owner intend to get rich quick – which is perfectly possible within a three-year time span – and sell the business and move into other industries outside hairdressing? Alternatively, does the salon owner wish to have a business that will grow over a long period of time with an increased reputation for being fair and professional but also one that will attract staff and clients who wish to be associated with the salon? What is essential is to understand that it is not possible to 'have one's cake and eat it'!

1.8.6 User-friendly pricing

During the 1980s and beginning of the 1990s there has been a growth in complex pricing in many hairdressing salons.

In my opinion this is a mistake. Those adopting complex pricing systems try to be all things to all people. The price list ceases to be 'user-friendly' and becomes another barrier to prevent clients from using the salon. Pricing should be simple and easy for the client to understand, and should be used as a *marketing tool* to enhance the business, not confuse the customer.

Many salons allow the staff and pay structure to dictate prices instead of what the business wishes to achieve. Below is a range of five examples of *unfriendly pricing*:

(1) Multi-tiered pricing

A salon may offer several different prices, depending on who is to cut the hair – whether it is a young stylist or the Artistic Director. Different prices may sometimes be offered to pacify the egos of staff or to reward them by improving their salaries.

In one salon I know, the price of a hair cut can vary from £3.50 to £20.00. This can make it difficult to justify to clients paying the higher price when, from the client's viewpoint, a hair cut is just a hair cut no matter who is doing it. Other clients will avoid young stylists as they regard them as inexperienced, making it difficult for younger staff to build a client base. The price differentials can then become self-defeating.

Those salons that try to be all things to all people, e.g. offering low prices for price-conscious clients, high prices for image-conscious clients, cheaper prices at the beginning of the week, expensive prices at the end of the week, etc., are giving the client mixed messages – rather like a supermarket trying to offer something for everyone.

The following section (1.9) on Competitive marketing strategies will explain in more detail why this approach can be confusing.

(2) Cuts and finishes

Should the 'core' service of a hair cut have a higher value compared to shampooing and finishing? Price lists often show a cut to have the same value as a finish or blow dry, e.g. a cut at £5.00 and a cut and blow dry at £10.00. Some salons argue that this is based upon time cost, calculated at a rate per stylist per hour. Clients, however, perceive the cost of a hair cut compared with a blow dry or finish differently from how the industry sees it.

Market research shows that clients wash their hair more frequently compared to 10 years ago, so charging for shampooing and drying is seen as expensive when compared to a cut which will last longer!

Many salons charge for short, medium and long hair cutting. But when does a short hair cut become a medium one or a medium one become a long one, and who decides?

I have discovered that clients are usually charged at the short length price, whatever the hair length, as the staff find it difficult to justify the additional cost for a medium or long hair cut, thereby creating confusion and hassle for everyone.

Another area of misunderstanding is between prices for trims, cuts and re-styles. When does a trim become a cut, or a re-style? Re-styles generally tend to be charged to new clients, who will always be a small proportion of the client base compared to regular customers. Staff have difficulty in justifying the difference in price to frequent visitors.

(3) Perming

Perming prices can be a mystery to clients! How many request a perm by its brand name, yet think of the number of times that brand names are itemised on a price list, as if this justifies the price difference. Technical jargon such as 'acid balance' can confuse the customer because their interpretation of it means 'burn for danger' creating a further barrier for the stylist to overcome.

For different prices to be justified, the price list needs to illustrate either the use of a perm for a particular hair type, e.g. specialist perm for tinted, porous or fine hair; or selling the finished effect or benefit, e.g. style support for movement and volume. The range of perms the salon chooses to use is one of preference for the owner and not the client who visits the salon to be given expert knowledge regarding suitability

(4) Colouring

Colouring prices in many salons discourage their use by being cloaked in jargon. As with perms, colouring prices should state the finished result.

It is unnecessary to state the method or technique by which they are achieved – after all, root regrowth, paint-on colours, fringe or crown colouring are all partial colouring techniques. Colouring prices could be simplified by basing them on the time the treatment takes. Thus, partial colouring takes 30–45 minutes to mix and apply, so the price could be based on this cost. Adding 50p or £1 to various techniques makes the price list read like a holiday brochure!

(5) Children

Are your prices children- and family-friendly? Today's children are tomorrow's teenagers and adults, and serving children should encourage their parents to use the salon too. Prices could reflect the times of the day, and the days of the week you may wish to encourage children, e.g. half price service from Monday to Wednesday, or free hair cuts if booked with an adult on less busy days.

Many salons actively discourage children from using their salons because the staff do not like cutting children's hair, but positive marketing and pricing would encourage the whole family to use the salon's services.

1.8.7 *How to rationalise your pricing policy*

(1) Analyse the usage now. If you offer multi-tiered pricing, does it work?
(2) Which services are used most by clients, e.g. wet cuts, dry cuts, finishes and re-styles?
(3) What proportion of clients have short, medium or long length hair cuts?
(4) Which stylists are busy and why?
(5) How is multi-tiered pricing handled on the telephone?
(6) Which perm prices are used most? Why?
(7) Which colouring techniques are used most? Why?
(8) Do the prices reflect your image or confuse it? For example, offering discounts in upmarket salons confuses the client.

Profitable pricing

Collecting facts and data abolishes the guesswork. First, analyse the gross profit margins by deducting

(1) Percentage stock usage
(2) Percentage wage cost of all 'productive staff', e.g. stylists, and support staff who help to apply tints and perms (available in your year end accounts)
(3) Consumables, e.g. cleaning of towels, and refreshments if offered as part of the service

Do this for every price available on the price list! A mammoth task for those with multi-tiered pricing, e.g. Young Stylist to Artistic Director prices. Find out the gross profit for all services – cutting, colouring, perming. Expect to be shocked by how little gross profit there really is. Don't forget that from the gross profit all your operating and fixed costs have to be paid – an even more depressing thought! At this stage, you will probably be thinking that perming is the most profitable service but an accurate cost must include how long the service takes before you decide on the right prices for your salon (see section 2.3.1).

This information can be obtained by one or the other following methods but not both:

(1) How much time is allocated in the appointment book for each service?
(2) How much time is actually spent working on the client?

Don't be fooled by the idea that if a trainee does the support work you are making more money. Now it is possible to calculate the gross profit on your prices per hour. Only then will you know which services make you money and those that cost you money unless you use them to sell on other services.

For those who are defeated by this method other options are available:

(1) Buy a hairdressing software package to do the job for you on your computer

(2) Go on a pricing course run by your friendly manufacturer

(3) Get a consultant to do the analysis for you

1.9 Competitive marketing strategies

Many salon owners, particularly in the spring, start to think about boosting business with special offers or discounts on technical services. How often do you give any thought to whether you are using the best marketing strategies to suit your individual business and the local market place?

We have already mentioned that promotions should be a thought through, analytical process based upon the way you wish to run your business. This means obtaining facts about your business, the customers, the competition, and the local market place, then analysing what they tell you.

Haphazard promotions that may have worked in the past, hunches or gut feelings merely provide a way of spending a lot of money, time and heartache for very little return. We have already stressed the problem earlier in this chapter of salons that try to be all things to all people. Identifying the marketing strategy suitable for your business means planned promotions and clearly focusing the direction of your business.

There are three key marketing strategies:

(1) Price leadership

This means becoming the low cost producer of the service by concentrating the business on volume, i.e. 'bums on seats'. This approach is based upon a 'no frills' standardised service where extras such as coffee are charged separately. Price leadership means producing the service at a cheaper rate than the local competition.

Price leadership can be achieved by the following approach:

- Time restraints, e.g. 15-minute hair cuts, 30-minute cut and finish as opposed to 45 minutes or longer.
- Offering cutting only services as well as cut and finish.
- Step by step procedures for consultation, shampooing, conditioning and finishing, i.e. identifying who does what at each stage.
- Keeping your costs low by tightly controlling:

  (a) Ratio of support staff to stylists
  (c) Stock wastage
  (c) Stock purchasing
  (d) Laundry costs

- Instituting pay systems which are incentivised to reward volume but not necessarily quality, or at least being realistic about the quality. This means identifying the minimum standards of performance required in terms of money, client numbers, mix of services and quality.

This strategy is effective if the following criteria apply:

- A short term business goal, e.g. you do not wish to remain in the area or the industry for more than three to five years.
- New markets are being penetrated, such as a new area within the locality or if you are setting up a new salon in the area.
- You are setting out to attract price-conscious clients or those whose

circumstances may have changed e.g. young families reduced from two incomes to one.

This approach does not necessarily mean that the average spend per client visit is low but that 'core services' such as cutting are affordable when clients are short of cash. This gives the opportunity to 'trade up' technical services and retailing.

The disadvantage of this strategy can be getting into a price war with other salons, forcing further reductions in prices and therefore profit margins.

(2) Differentiation strategy

This approach means the salon seeks to be *unique within its area or to offer some advantage* that is valued by clients. This 'uniqueness' would usually claim a premium price.

To assess whether this is achievable requires the following action:

Step 1: Compare your strengths and weaknesses with your competitors. Measure the gap. Promote the strengths, then . . .
Step 2: Identify which services are required which are not available in the area, for example:

- Creative colouring
- Long hair services
- Stylists handling the total service from consultation to completed look
- Top to toe advice
- One stop hair and beauty service

Obviously, there is no such thing as a truly 'unique service' *but how it is packaged and promoted can make it appear special compared with what may be available elsewhere.* Select no more than two special features but promote them constantly. Don't keep changing – it confuses the message to the public.

The promotional activities *must be consistent to enhance the difference.* They must not confuse or detract from the message of 'keep it simple, keep it different'. Every time the salon deviates it confuses the marketing message to the public. Examples include:

(a) Discounts on services instead of complimentary services
(b) Window displays or stickers that detract from the visual image (hand-written posters or fluorescent stickers as displayed in butchers' shops and supermarkets)
(c) Customer care that does not justify a premium price

To maintain 'differentiation' means monitoring the competition. A successful strategy is likely to be copied, thereby narrowing the difference to the client. Maintaining 'differentiation' requires a fresh approach every two or three years to reposition your business in the minds of your clientele.

(3) Focus strategy

This approach 'focuses' on a narrow competitive edge of a market segment or group of segments and *meets the particular needs of these people.* The salon may not have a competitive edge over all, however, if there are many salons offering some of the services.

In an area where there are many salons trying to be all things to all people the danger is that the public do not know that the salon caters specially for their needs. The range of market segments could be:

- Children
- Teenage/young market
- Family market
- Business market
- Male market
- Older men and women
- Discerning men and women
- High fashion

The needs of some market segments are compatible whilst others conflict. For example, business people may not like children in the salon; or older discerning men and women may not want the latest music which appeals to the younger market.

The key to achieving this strategy is to:

- Decide which market segments are compatible.
- Identify what proportion of your existing client base falls into the market segments selected. Establish the gap to see what percentage of new clients will be needed. *It is important to build from what you do best and not start from 'scratch'.*
- Ask those clients who fall within the market segment what they need from the salon, e.g. services, prices, hours and facilities.
- Decide on a marketing campaign to 'positively market' to the segment. For example, if you want to attract families offer what they need instead of complaining about the disadvantages of family hairdressing. All market segments have pros and cons.

Focusing on a narrow market segment does not mean that other clients will not be attracted to the salon as some of the services will meet their needs. By clearly focusing the promotions, services, prices and staff, the strategy and its image does not become blurred.

1.10 Putting new life into your services – the demand life cycle

Salons promoting services to attract new clients and/or to generate more business often give up after one advertising splurge or expect an enormous response to the promotion without understanding the 'demand life cycle' (Fig. 1.10).

Every service and product has a natural life cycle *unless something is done to prevent it from burning out*. Some services and products are short term. Others can span 20 years or more. The old saying that 'nothing lasts forever' is not true if a salon actively does something about it. Some things do come back again. Understanding why is the key.

Introducing new ideas

When a new service or product range is introduced it tends to make no profit until a sufficient number of clients want the service and the start up costs have been recovered. It may involve additional purchasing or equipment. It

Fig. 1.10 The service life cycle.

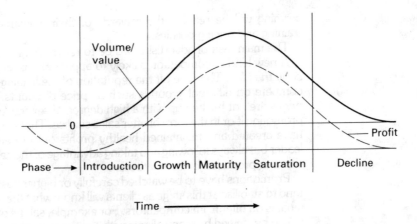

may need to be promoted, incurring advertising, shows, complimentary offers or discounts, which need to be written off against the first influx of sales.

The types of clients who buy new services will be *experimenters and fashion leaders*. How many of your clients were the first to wear hair extensions, wax or gel? This means that a high proportion of your clients will never buy new products or services *until they have been on the market long enough to make them acceptable*.

A promotion at this stage is aimed at creating awareness of the service and introducing it on a trial basis, often free or subsidised. A good example of this is offering complimentary fashion colouring for a limited period, *but the success of the promotion depends upon the volume of repeat business followed through by the stylists when the client returns*.

With a completely new service, competition from other salons will be low, which means the salon has the opportunity to charge a high initial price which can be reduced later when competition forces price reductions.

The growth phase

At this phase the promoted service should show a profit. The 'trendsetters and pacesetters' who have taken time to make up their minds become the buyers now. Demand increases and makes it easier for competition to enter.

Major competition such as large salon groups or salons with a strong foothold in the local market will muscle in on a new idea. Advertising needs to explain more than it may have done originally to create awareness. For example, a new perming look must explain the *benefits* to the client. Price features strongly at this stage, and often one can be undercut by large salon groups who can afford to work to narrower profit margins due to the volume of business.

The maturity stage

The 'followers' will now have moved on the scene. This is the period of real profit and one which most companies would like to prolong. Salons who generate a high proportion of technical services such as colouring and perming will be reaping the rewards of their investment in promotions, training and pricing policies.

The main task of advertising will be to retain clients against competition.

A new kind of competitor is likely to appear at this stage – *imitators who copy the idea.* They live off the reputation of the leading salons and usually compete on different grounds such as price discounts. These discounted prices are not backed up with a high degree of service, either at the time of promoting it or in the form of after sales service. There are many salons who have created and maintained healthy profits out of never being a market leader but always following and taking advantage of the development of other services produced by competitors.

Promotions have to be watched carefully or higher costs will occur. Prices tend to stabilise at this stage as clients will know what the service is worth and what is on offer from competitors. For example, salons offering £5.00 perms would be viewed by many clients with suspicion regarding the service or the quality of the product.

The saturation phase

At this stage all those clients who are likely to use the service, the 'traditionalists', are doing so. Profit can decline rapidly, due to clients being reluctant to accept price increases if a similar service is available elsewhere, unless there is an add on novelty that will encourage them to use your service, for example, 'perms offered inclusive of cutting, conditioning, and after-sales hair care advice'.

The decline phase

'Nostalgics' tend to be the main buyers at this stage – and they tend to get older and more nostalgic as the years go by! Shampoo and set clients fall into this category. They become price conscious due to the frequency of using the service. Many salons continue to humour these clients for quite some time. If the service can be provided *without turning away new business or continues to generate profit* there may be little harm.

Response from promotions falls dramatically during this phase and there is a constant battle to avoid increased costs. The clients will have fallen into a routine and boredom has set in and they often need a sharp jolt to arouse their interest. Give away incentives are frequently used. Remember, the worst type of give away incentive for weekly clients is retail products as these clients very rarely wash their hair at home! Many salons prefer to charge prices that reflect the true cost to fewer clients, assuming that anyone who wants the service badly enough will pay for it.

Re-launching services

(1) Identify each service's position in the *demand life cycle.* (For example perming is at saturation point and shampoo/sets are in decline.)
(2) Which services can be re-launched to appeal to a new market segment?

Children ☐
Teenage/young clients ☐
Families ☐

Older clients ☐
Men ☐
Business community ☐
Discerning clients ☐
High fashion ☐

(3) Re-package the service by its

- Name, e.g. colouring touches/flashes/stars!
- Technique: winding/application/cutting.
- Added value extras – inclusive of ... ?
  – complimentary ... ?
- Benefits to clients not promoted before.

1.11 Applying the theory

So far in this chapter we have mentioned a number of areas where we recommend the collection of information. There are four key areas of information which will help in marketing and promoting the business. These are:

(1) Information on clients
(2) Information on competitors
(3) Information on products
(4) Information on staff

1.11.1 Information on clients

- Name
- Address
- Telephone number
- Birthday (not year)
- Estimated age group:
  Under 22   23–35
  36–50   50–60
  Over 60
- Preferred products/services (from client record card and information from stylist)
- Distance from salon to home
  Up to 1 mile   2–3 miles
  4–6 miles   7–10 miles
  Over 10 miles
- Distance from salon to work
  Up to 1 mile   2–3 miles
  4–6 miles   7–10 miles
  Over 10 miles
- Frequency of visits
  Every week
  2–4 weeks   5–8 weeks
  9–12 weeks   Occasionally
- Occupations
- Children's ages and whether male or female
- Usual colour/hair type

This allows you to know your clients, provides you with a mailing list for promotional purposes and allows you to monitor your ability to retain clients. It helps you to identify your market segment.

1.11.2 Information on competitors

- Location/image/type of salon
- Number of staff employed
- Prices for services/products
- Assessment of strengths and weaknesses versus your own salon
- Estimate of turnover, e.g. how busy/number of chairs/number of staff

1.11.3 Information on products

- Manufacturers' literature on products
- Summary of features and benefits of products
- Detailed instruction on use or limitations
- Price information/costs (not for publication to clients)

This information should be available for every product and service in the salon.

1.11.4 Information on staff

- Training required/received
- Selling/commission record
- Has selling and selling training occurred?
- Have they been coached or counselled on any problems which have occurred?
- How do they compare with other staff?

This kind of information provides the basis for business planning, see Section 7.3 Business planning, and for good decision making in the area of promoting the business.

1.11.5 Promotional ideas

(1) Try one new promotion every month. Monitor the success and repeat successful ones.

(2) Experiment with salon hours. Close during low periods. Train staff/ clean up the salon. Try evening appointments using special pricing if staff are willing.

(3) Advertise within the salon. Use posters and photographs to show what you have to offer. Keep them in line with your image.

(4) Encourage your staff to sell up, i.e. perms and tints and retail products. Pay them a bonus whenever they do.

(5) Research your customers. Analyse results, seek criticism/complaints. Act on it. Retrain staff. Help them, don't criticise them.

(6) Ring up your own salon and make an appointment (or get a friend to do it). Would you go there? No? Improve it now. Train your staff in handling calls from clients.

(7) Send clients (including ex-clients) a birthday or Christmas card.

(8) Introduce credit cards or cashcards or even accounts for key customers. It's a bit tiresome but research shows clients spend more!

(9) Give all new clients a leaflet or letter thanking them for coming and a small gift (or discount voucher for the next time) for coming. They will love it and come back.

(10) Give all existing clients a 'bring a friend' (and they get the service half price) offer (on less busy days). See how many new clients you can get and keep.

(11) Introduce differential pricing. Charge more on busier days, less on quieter days. Offer discounts on quieter days, i.e. charge more for shampoo/sets and shampoo/blow dries on Fridays and Saturdays, less at the beginning of the week.

(12) Introduce self-service retail sales racks with products near the stylists' working area. Train staff to mention retail sales to all clients.

(13) Train staff in client-handling and selling skills. Many manufacturers offer training free-of-charge and the standards can be good.

(14) Keep in close contact with suppliers. Write and thank them when they are good. Write and complain when they are not. You will be amazed by the results! (Even from the biggest companies.)

(15) Use your window space effectively. It should be clean, tidy, professional. Look at yours. Would it attract you into the salon or send you running off home? Remember it's your public image. No grotty handwritten posters advertising models or reduced prices.

(16) Eliminate unused space. Look at the use of posters, photographs, information to enhance areas. Ensure it's in keeping with your image however.

(17) Say 'thank you' to regular clients. A gift, birthday or Christmas card or even a special letter/note/leaflet just to remind them that you care. 'They take me for granted' is the commonest reason for client dropout!

(18) Introduce a staff suggestion scheme. Give a cash prize for the best successful new idea. Staff can often solve your problems, as they see the alternative ways to tackle them.

(19) Try ringing up some ex-clients inviting them to some special offer or promotion. People love a personal approach.

(20) If you are in a city-centre location, do you have a parking area? Or an inexpensive car park nearby? Then offer a 'get your hair done, free parking all day' deal. Many families might come shopping.

(21) Give a free hair colour/condition and advice offer or invite clients in for coffee (on quiet days). You will be amazed at how many will buy.

(22) Try promoting one of your staff each month in your window. Name/age/biography/interests/work samples. People are fascinated.

(23) Give your staff *name* badges. Clients like to deal with *people*.

(24) Put leaflets in schools, hospitals, colleges, hotels offering special offers on special days.

(25) Display some *before* photographs versus *after* material to show your expertise.

(26) Try a client relations group, i.e. a few regular prominent clients who meet to discuss possible improvements to the salon.

(27) Special offers for particular groups, e.g. 60s women, new job/interview, newly marrieds, brides to be, twenty-first birthdays. Don't worry if people cheat.

(28) Give regular clients (and new ones) a booklet and each time they come

stick on a stamp which they can cash in at any time, e.g. 1 stamp = 10% off, 2 stamps = 20% off. It builds loyalty.

(29) If you sell lots of retail products or have a big salon examine your 'own brand'. It might pay off, but the packaging should reflect your image, and the staff must believe in the products.

(30) Introduce the notion of 'standby' or 'apex' haircuts, i.e. low price if you turn up and/or wait for a cancellation. Issue 'ticket' and provide a free 'drink', e.g. wine.

(31) Promote special groups, e.g. twins or working wives, and offer gift/discounts/vouchers, especially if it links in with local events, e.g. all clients who wear a football scarf etc.

(32) Run *joint promotions* with local supermarkets or OAP centre for mums or OAPs.

(33) Run *joint promotions* with discos or record shops or fashion shops especially if you wish to attract trendier youngsters.

(34) Do something 'freaky' occasionally, e.g. have an 'owner and pet' evening or a 'singles' evening and attract an unusual segment.

Chapter Two
Understanding Money

2.1 Raising finance

It does not matter how good the idea, service or hairdressing is likely to be in a new salon or how hard working and skilful the staff – the business will not succeed unless it has sufficient funds. But what constitutes sufficient funds? This depends to a large extent upon what the salon owner wishes to achieve. It depends upon how quickly the salon owner wishes to grow, and on the type of image he or she wishes to project, which will have a direct effect upon the range of equipment and fitments that need to be purchased. It also depends upon another factor which is much more subjective – that is the amount of personal income the salon owner is willing to forgo in order to reap long term financial rewards.

When considering raising finance we have to look at the amount of control over the business the owner is prepared to give up as well as the rate of interest the business will be paying to raise the finance. This factor is much more subjective and emotional in a smaller business than in a larger, well established business. The key sources of funds are:

(1) Shares or share capital (limited companies)
(2) Loans or loan capital
(3) Current liabilities (short term debts)

and we shall see that there are advantages and disadvantages to each.

The risk element

When you are trying to raise finance a potential source of finance will consider not only the proposal itself but also the past record of the salon or the individuals concerned. Different sources of finance will weigh past performance against future prospects in different ways. In a new salon or new venture the risk is automatically assumed to be greater and therefore the cost of borrowing will be higher. Banks and other financial institutions will want to do business with you if they possibly can – after all that is how banks make their money, upon the interest rates they charge. But they have to feel assured that the risk will be secured in some way. Often a condition of financial support from an outside source may be that adequate life assurance should be taken out or that one's home must be set against the loan as security.

Principal sources of finance

In general, the most important source of finance for a small business is the salon owner's! If the owner's capital is insufficient to provide an adequate base it will not normally be possible for the salon to raise outside finance. In other words, we cannot borrow all the money from a financial institution without being prepared to invest our own cash or personal security against a loan. This reassures the lender that the salon owner is serious about the venture and is prepared to risk his or her own finances.

Property

Your most important asset may well be your own home. Most people have a mortgage on their property but if the property value rises and the mortgage is partly paid off, it is possible to borrow against any increase in equity. Building societies are often the cheapest source of mortgage funds, but invariably see their role as providing first mortgages to owner-occupiers. Second mortgages are available from a number of organisations which advertise nationally. If your first mortgage is small, you may be able to raise 70 per cent or more of the value of your house with no restrictions. Professional mortgage brokers do exist but look very carefully, not only at the true rate of interest, but also at the conditions attached to the loan.

Relatives and friends

These are a potential source of finance for one's new business, but money from this quarter can be a mixed blessing. First, can you be sure that the people concerned are really able to afford the loss of their money if things go wrong? Secondly, would the person involved adopt a professional attitude towards his/her investment by striking a balance between interfering in your business and complete indifference to the utilisation of their money? Thirdly, is it likely that the investor would wish to withdraw his or her money from your firm at short notice? If so, could you allow for this and what would be the effect on your business?

A way of minimising these difficulties would be to ask the friend or relative to act as a guarantor of a bank loan rather than put money into the business directly. However, a tangible support of the guarantee would probably be required.

Bank loans

Many well known clearing banks such as the Big Four are major sources of finance for small businesses and will, under certain conditions, help finance a new business. They will insist upon safeguarding the security of their loan by either property or the fixed assets within the firm.

Hire purchase and leasing

It is possible to buy many types of equipment on hire purchase. The procedure is much the same as with domestic hire purchase and the principle is identical. The purchaser pays the deposit or initial payment to the finance company or supplier of goods. The purchaser then takes possession of the goods or equipment once they have signed the hire purchase agreement.

Leasing is similar in that a regular flow of small, equal payments over a fixed period replaces a lump sum purchase, but the goods remain the property of the leasing company at the end of the period. There is no formal agreement that the lease will be renewed or the goods sold to the customer, but either procedure may be followed in return for a nominal sum.

Wella is a manufacturer who can supply fixtures and fittings through its subsidiary 'Welonda Serventi' and may also be able to help with advantageous financial arrangements.

2.2 How is the business doing now?

Understanding the basic documents

To you, your business probably consists of staff and clients, one providing a service to the other in exchange for money which goes to pay bills and hopefully will make you rich and help your business to expand and grow. To a financial expert, your business is a large box which takes in cash and gives out cash.

Cash in	Business	Cash out
from clients		wages
		expenses
		profits

In financial terms we do not talk about *cash* but about sales or turnover and costs and/or overheads.

Profit

To you, the meaning of profit will be clear – it is what is left at the end of paying all the bills as follows:

Sales/Turnover minus All costs equals Profit

but you need to understand not so much how the money comes in, because in a hairdressing business it comes in through the services you offer, but where the money goes. In order to monitor and control the business you need to keep records which will help you to understand how the money comes in and how it is spent. You need to examine the two main published documents of most businesses – the *balance sheet* and the *profit and loss account* (trading and profit and loss account). These tend to be limited in what they tell you but they do give you some insight into your business.

The balance sheet

The balance sheet is best described as a 'snapshot in time' of:

• Where the money in the business has come from (liabilities or sources)
• Where it is currently being used (assets or uses)

The business, in other words, gets its money from the sources and places it in the uses.

Fig. 2.1 Balance sheet of Headlines Ltd.

Balance sheet at 31 January 1994[1]

Capital	£	Fixed assets	£	£
Share capital[2]	10,000	Fixtures and fittings	3,000	
		Motor vehicle	1,500	
				4,500
Loans		Current assets		
Bank loan	5,000	Stock	1,000	
		Debtors	200	
Current liabilities		Cash	800	
Creditors	1,500			
				2,000
	6,500[3]			6,500

[1] Balance sheet is always at a point in time.
[2] Probably put in by *you*.
[3] Notice the balance: Liabilities: Assets, i.e. Sources: Uses.

Sources of funds
The key sources of funds are:

- Shares or share capital
- Loans or loan capital
- Current liabilities, e.g. creditors

Uses of funds are:
Fixed assets – things which are bought to make the business possible such as work tops, backwashes, chairs, driers and property if bought freehold, e.g. fixtures and fittings, premises, motor vehicles.
Current assets – things which are used in the business, e.g. cash, stock, debts.

The balance sheet for a hairdressing business might look like Fig. 2.1.

The profit and loss account

The second document, the profit and loss account (or income statement) gives the recent history of the business and describes how well you have actually done. It also gives you clues as to where you may go in the future. Figure 2.2 shows a sample of a profit and loss account (or income statement).

Cash flow forecast

The third document can be considered as the crystal ball which reflects the *exact timing of payments* and sales/turnover coming into the business and allows you to plan your cash requirements. It must also tally with the bank deposits or overdraft. The objective of completing this form is that you enter income or sales and payments only when you actually receive or pay them. For example, if you receive an electricity bill for the period January to March on 5 April which you pay in May it would not be shown in your cash flow

Fig. 2.2 Profit and loss account.

```
                        Headlines Ltd
        Profit and loss account (income statement)        Period: 1 year

(1) Sales   (Turnover) ex VAT                                    114,000

(2) Cost of sales                £
        Consumables¹          7,000
        Wages/salaries       53,000                              60,000
        (incl. employer's N.I. contributions)   Gross profit    54,000 (47%)

(3) Expenses
        Salon operating                        £          £
            Rent, rates and water           14,000
            Repairs and renewals             1,000
            Light and heat                   1,200
            Insurances                         600     16,800

        Salon administration
            Telephone                        1,500
            Accountancy and audit fees       1,500
            Stationery and postage           1,500
            Advertising/promotion            5,000      9,500

        Motor vehicle costs
            Running expenses                 1,300
            Leasing/hire                       -        1,300

        Financial charges
            Bank interest and charges        1,200      1,200

        Depreciation                         5,000      5,000      33,800

                                         Net profit            20,200 (18%)
```

¹ Consumables are materials used in the salon for hairdressing.

statement until May – in other words when you actually pay it.

The cash flow forecast is particularly useful for showing when you need to have cash available or need to borrow cash and banks expect you to have this kind of document available when they lend money (as it also shows when you plan to pay them back). Figure 2.3 is an example of a cash flow forecast.

These three documents together:

● Balance sheet
● Profit and loss account
● Cash flow forecast

give an overall picture of the money in the business, where it came from, what it was used for or invested in, how the business has been performing over the past trading period and how it is managing its cash now and in the future.

It is these three documents that will tell you how well you are doing now and will give you a clear indication of what the strengths and weaknesses are within your business. They do, however, have limitations and you need to examine other ways of collecting information to tell you how well or badly the business is doing.

Fig. 2.3 Cash
flow forecast.

Item	Jan	Feb	Mar	Apr	May	June
Income						
Cash sales						
Credit sales						
Other income						
Total income						
Expenditure						
Wages/salaries						
Commission						
National insurance						
VAT						
Taxation						
Fees						
Goods (consumables)						
Stock for resale						
Rent/lease						
Rates						
Gas						
Electricity						
Water						
Telephone						
Laundry						
Stationery						
Postage						
Advertising/promotions						
Staff training						
Staff travel						
Motor expenses						
Servicing/repairs						
Leasing						
Bank int/charges						
Total expenditure						
Balance (+/–)						
Cumulative						

There are a number of ways of judging how well the salon is doing such as:

- Am I turning away clients?
- Do I have a healthy bank balance?
- Am I busy?
- Am I expanding/growing?

First of all, you need to understand the *calculation of ratios*. The ratio of two
figures, e.g. wages to sales, can be expressed in a number of different ways.

Suppose your sales turnover is £50000 and our wages are £30000 then you can say any one of the following:

(1) The ratio of wages:sales is 30000:50000 or 3:5.
(2) Wages are 3/5 of sales.
(3) Wages are 60% of sales.

(4) $\dfrac{\text{Wages}}{\text{Sales}} = \dfrac{30\,000}{50\,000} = 0.6$.

(5) $\dfrac{\text{Sales}}{\text{Wages}} = \dfrac{50\,000}{30\,000} = 1.67$.

(6) Each £ of wages has produced £1.67 of sales.

The standard measure of business performance is *return on capital employed* which is the ratio of net profit before tax to capital employed, i.e.

$$\frac{\text{Net profit before tax}}{\text{Total assets}} \times 100$$

Net profit before tax is obtained from the profit and loss account and total assets is found in the balance sheet. For most businesses, returns of 15–30 per cent are considered good. In hairdressing, because there is a lower investment, especially if premises are rented, returns of 30–120 per cent are possible!

In practice, we can look at two other measures related to sales which are our starting points. These are:

$$\frac{\text{Gross profit}}{\text{Sales}} \times 100$$

and/or

$$\frac{\text{Net profit}}{\text{Sales}} \times 100$$

(Note: Sales or turnover excludes VAT.)

Gross profit

This is the difference between sales or turnover (obtained from your profit and loss account) and direct costs, i.e. wages for staff (and you if you cut hair) and consumables, i.e. stock (not retail stock which should be calculated separately), cups of coffee, towels etc. You may need to do some extra calculations to arrive at this figure as most accountants do not present the data clearly in the correct form.

Example

Turnover excluding VAT		£50,000
Wages (including employer's National Insurance contributions)	£26,000	
Consumables (excluding VAT)	£ 2,000	
	£28,000	£28,000
Gross profit		£22,000

Gross profit as a percentage of sales = 44%

(i.e. % = $\dfrac{22\,000}{50\,000} \times 100$).

This figure gives you a measure of how well you are controlling your wages and consumable goods. A good hairdressing business must not exceed 53 per cent as a wage cost (including employer's National Insurance contributions) for productive staff, e.g. trainees, receptionists and stylists. If it is significantly less then one of the following areas could be the problem:

(1) Wages are too low and do not provide an incentive to staff to produce more.
(2) The salon owner works harder than any of the staff to pay the stylists' wages.
(3) The staff are being paid cash-in-hand which is illegal.

A good business should achieve 38–48 per cent gross profit. If it is less then you are spending too much on wages and/or consumables. *Consumables will approximately equal stock used* during the year provided you do not have extensive retail sales. *Retail sales should be itemised as a separate stock figure.*

Net profit

The second measure is the ratio of net profit before tax to sales/turnover and, again, we examine the percentage value.

$$\text{Net profit \%} = \frac{\text{Net profit before tax}}{\text{Sales (ex VAT)}} \times 100$$

We obtain the net profit figure from our accounts but we must ignore depreciation, i.e. add this back into your reported profit figure. We do this because depreciation is not a real expense, i.e. you do not pay out depreciation, you simply set aside the money to replace assets when they wear out or become out of fashion.

The difference between gross profit and net profit is clearly *expenses* and we would expect a hairdressing business to return between 12 and 20 per cent. If it is lower than this then possibly expenses are too high or your business is not big enough to support them.

The question to be asked is, how well should you be doing? How much profit should you make? Well, apart from as much as possible, you should generate enough to pay the income you want, to earn a reasonable return on the money you have invested and to finance expansion if you wish to expand. We have listed at the back of this book sources of further reading to help with this subject or you could attend a course on pricing and profit run by your local Chamber of Commerce or the series of courses ISM designed especially for Wella.

2.3 How to improve performance

In this section we examine some of the theories behind profit generation and some of the myths, and introduce a new concept – contribution – which is very useful in analysing a hairdressing salon's performance. By now you should be in a position to describe your business in financial terms and to be able to identify the main areas of expense and the way that your profit is generated. You should also be able to calculate the percentage wages, the percentage stock figure, gross profit, expenses and net profit. This

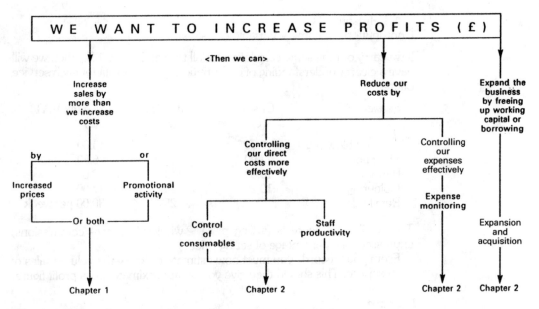

Fig. 2.4 Ways to increase profits.

information will show you whether the costs are excessive or reasonable. Figure 2.4 shows a model of how to increase profits.

2.3.1 Calculating contribution to gross profit

A powerful method for looking at a salon business is to consider the process by which revenue is generated and how costs are incurred and to examine the behaviour of these costs.

Example
A client has cut and blow dry and pays £10. In doing so she 'uses up' certain things needed to carry out the treatment:

- Staff payment
- Stock – shampoos, conditioners, perms, finishing aids
- Hot water
- Towels
- Refreshments

Also, of course, she makes use of other things – the overheads – which must be covered in order for the salon to function, e.g. telephone, heating, receptionist costs.

These costs can be split into two distinct categories: those which can be considered as direct and variable costs, i.e. which relate directly to the number of clients and type of service, and those which can be considered as fixed costs, i.e. they do not vary directly with the number of clients.

Cut and blow dry
   Variable costs:
   - Wages
   - Hot water/products

● Refreshments

Contribution = Income – Variable costs.

If we carry out the same calculation for all the services we offer then we will have a clearer understanding of contribution to gross profit for each service offered:

Services	Costs (£)	Contribution (£)	Price (ex VAT) (£)
Cut and blow dry	6.00	4.00	10.00
Shampoo/finish	3.90	2.60	6.50
Perm	16.80	11.20	28.00
Colouring	10.20	6.80	17.00
Retail sales		25%	30.00 per week

The retail sales figure is (selling price – wholesale cost – commissions) expressed as a percentage of selling price.

From your records you must now estimate or know the volume sales of each service. This should then give you an approximate gross profit figure.

Example

Cut and blow dry	40 per week
Shampoo/finish	30 per week
Perm	8 per week
Colouring	6 per week
Retail sales	£30 per week

} number of clients handled per week

Item	Price/unit (£)	Contribution/ unit (£)	Total sales (units)	Total contribution (£)	Total sales (£)
Cut and blow dry	10.00	4.00	40	160	400
Shampoo/finish	6.50	2.60	30	78	195
Perm	28.00	11.20	8	89.60	224
Colouring	17.00	6.80	6	40.80	102
Retail sales £30 p.w. × 25%				7.50	30
			Totals	375.90	951

You should by now be able to understand where your gross profit is coming from – which type of customers and which type of work generate most revenue. It is this understanding of your business that helps you to improve your profit.

If you estimate the time taken for each service then you can calculate the contribution per hour of staff time. Suppose we estimate:

Cut and blow dry	30 minutes
Shampoo/finish	20 minutes
Perm	1 hour
Colouring	45 minutes
Retail sales	3 minutes per sale (dependent on numbers of clients through the salon per hour)

(The estimates should be based on time staff actually spend on the service, i.e. when they cannot do other work, *not* how long the client is in the salon.)

Then our contribution rate per hour is:

Cut and blow dry $\dfrac{4.00}{30}$ = 13.33p per minute   = £8.00 per hour

Shampoo/finish $\dfrac{2.60}{20}$ = 13p per minute   = £7.80 per hour

Perm $\dfrac{11.20}{60}$ = 18.66p per minute   = £11.20 per hour

Colouring $\dfrac{10.20}{45}$ = 22.66p per minute   = £13.60 per hour

So how do we interpret these results? If staff spend one hour doing each of the above then they would generate:

£13.60 per hour for colouring
£11.20 per hour for perming
£7.80 per hour for shampoo/finishing
£7.80 per hour for cut/blow drying

So how do your staff spend their time? Where should your greatest effort be? We leave you to see the answers – the facts are clear.

2.4 Increasing sales revenue

There are basically two ways of increasing sales revenue – by promotion (including reducing prices) or by raising prices. We will discuss each of these in turn but will concentrate primarily on the second as the first is detailed in section 1.8 Pricing.

Firstly, we must question if there is potential to increase staff productivity. This means calculating how effectively staff use their time. To do this we need to calculate the number of hours worked by staff involved directly in the services to clients, i.e. stylists and trainees.

Suppose we have two full time and two part time staff:

2 full time staff   38 hours each per week × 2 = 76 hours
2 part time staff   10 hours each per week × 2 = 20 hours   } Total 172 hours
2 trainees   38 hours each per week × 2 = 76 hours
(don't forget to take off holidays, sick leave and days off)

Now we need to examine the number of hours actually worked on clients. We calculated previously the average time per client per service and by calculating out the services provided:

Example
40 cut and blow dries × 30 minutes   = 1200 minutes
30 shampoo/sets × 20 minutes   =   600 minutes
8 perms × 60 minutes   =   480 minutes
8 colourings × 45 minutes   =   360 minutes
30 retail sales × 3 minutes   =   90 minutes

Total productive time   = 2,730 minutes or 46 hours

The productive time ratio is

$\dfrac{\text{Productive hours}}{\text{Total hours}} = \dfrac{46}{172} = 27\%$

Thus, this salon could potentially increase turnover if its staff were correctly utilised – and this ratio was increased to nearer 100 per cent. In practice, however, it is difficult to improve much past 70 per cent and typically salons achieve 40–55 per cent utilisation. We must remember that a proportion of the salon staff's time will be spent on cleaning, making and serving refreshments, answering the telephone and booking appointments if there is no receptionist, and training staff.

It does draw attention to the need for careful planning of time and spreading clients throughout the day and the week as a whole. You must also question whether you should be employing what will become a rare commodity of young trainees to clean the salon and serve refreshments, particularly as market forces will require salons to pay trainees much higher salaries and develop them in a shorter space of time.

Raising prices

We have mentioned raising prices and some hairdressers reading this will say it will drive customers away. If they are customers we do not need then that is good. Let us use an example:

Example

Two hairdressers, Michael Idlerich and Tony Graftanbroke, run salons in Anytown. Both have turnovers of £75 000 per annum. Mike runs a Porsche and Tony a Mini. How? Mike's prices are 57 per cent higher than Tony's and Tony has almost twice as many customers (as you would expect) yet their costs are much the same. We show the analysis in Figure. 2.5.

Mike makes four times as much profit as Tony! Yet he only has half as

	Cut/blow dry	Shampoo/set	Perms	Retails	Totals	Notes
Tony Graftanbroke						
Price	11.52	9.00	23.00	3.00		
No. of clients	80	50	5	10	145	Per week
Weekly turnover	922.00	450.00	115.00	30.00	1,517	£75,850*
Direct costs/unit	10.36	6.00	10.00	2.00		As we estimated earlier
Contribution unit	1.16	3.00	13.00	1.00	per unit	
Gross profit/ week	93.00	150.00	65.00	10.00	318.00	£15,900*
Expenses						£8,640
Profit						£7,260 p.a.
Michael Idlerich						
Price	18.72	13.00	35.00	14.00		
No. of clients	50	25	5	5	85	Per week
Weekly turnover	936.00	325.00	175.00	70.00	1,506	£75,300*
Direct costs/unit	10.36	6.00	10.00	9.00		
Contribution/unit	8.36	7.00	25.00	5.00	–	
Gross profit/ week	418.00	175.00	125.00	25.00	743	£37,150*
Expenses						£8,640
Profit						£28,510

* calculated on a 50 week trading year

Fig. 2.5 Comparison of two salons.

Fig. 2.6 Price demand curve.

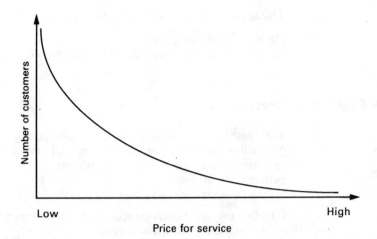

many clients. Mike has realised by analysing contribution that he is better off by having fewer clients paying more per person than dozens paying less. This is the basic law of profit. You allow your prices to drift to the level at which profit is maximised. Figure 2.6 shows you the theory. For any given price there is an associated demand. If the price is very high you will have too few customers. Too low and you will be swamped. If you calculate your contribution versus price curve it will look like Fig. 2.7.

What this analysis shows is that raising prices and losing customers is not necessarily a bad thing. A major problem for the industry is that prices are generally too low and thus competition revolves around price. If you *selectively* raise prices, e.g. on busy days, this will improve staff utilisation by moving some customers to other days and will prevent clients from being turned away; then you have the key to keeping clients at prices that will make your business profitable. This in turn means more time for the salon owner or manager to manage instead of running around in circles. More time on planning, promotions and managing our businesses profitably. The concept of pricing can be used to:

- Raise prices on busy days and times
- Reduce prices on quiet days and times

Fig. 2.7 Contribution versus price curve.

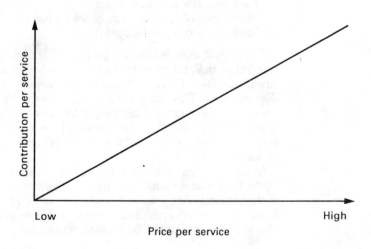

This achieves both of our goals which are to:

(1) Raise total contribution
(2) Increase staff productivity by increasing throughput

2.5 Controlling direct costs

In the previous section we aimed to increase your gross profit by improving productivity and raising or reducing prices. In this section we examine how to monitor and control your direct costs and try to improve your performance of them.

First of all you need to ask yourselves the following questions:

(1) Have my direct costs gone up, down or remained the same over the last six months, year or two years?
(2) How do my costs compare with the competition?
(3) Do I pay my staff more, the same, or less for the equivalent work than my competitors?
(4) Do I manage my stock properly?

The answers to these questions lie at the heart of effective gross profit management.

Let us first of all examine *consumables*. From your records let us look at the value of your stock. You need to separate out the stock for retail sales and the stocks of products used in producing the service.

Carrying excess stock is a serious problem for hairdressers. Imagine you cannot buy more products at all: how long would your stock last? One week, month, year? Ideally, you should carry as little as possible, i.e. one week–one month at the most. Yet we have found hairdressers carrying over a year's stock – usually because they wish to go on an overseas seminar provided by a manufacturer! So why is too much stock bad news? Here are some reasons:

(1) Stock is money tied up (this is particularly important if your business runs on a bank loan).
(2) Excessive stock causes waste because staff use more and throw away more.
(3) Excessive stock gets damaged.
(4) Stock goes off and becomes obsolete, especially colours.
(5) Excessive stock gets stolen.

The second aspect of stock is getting it at the right price. If you buy in large catering or bulk packs and wish to avoid waste ensure you issue stock in small quantities to avoid unnecessary waste, such as using shampoo dispensers etc. This way you can get the benefit of bulk. A stock room or at least a lockable cupboard can keep it safe when not needed. Put a member of staff in charge of noting when things get low and reminding you to re-order and ensure that you have a staff purchase record book to control staff usage at home.

Stock, however, is likely to be a relatively small cost compared to staff costs. These can account for anything between 50 and 80 per cent of all costs of the business. Are your staff productive and do you use them effectively? If you have done the calculations in the previous section you will have some idea as to how well you utilise the staff. As we have mentioned in the previous sections, we do not believe in back-door payment methods or underpaying staff. A payment system should ensure that staff get a reasonable level of pay for a given level of work and should also motivate them to work efficiently without lowering standards. This is important if you are to retain staff in the business and to keep costs under reasonable control.

An analysis that is helpful in this area is the turnover–contribution–wages analysis. Many systems of pay are straight commission, e.g. 50 per cent, and these have disadvantages in that they understate the contribution made to the business. The problem with straight commission schemes is that as the productivity rises the wage costs rise in proportion to productivity. This creates 'a bottoming-out effect' as stylists can only generate so many clients and so much work per day *unless they concentrate their energies on selling more services that generate a higher contribution to gross profit, e.g. colours and retail sales.* This is where technical skills training, speed training and your pricing strategy are essential in increasing productivity and reducing wage costs.

Let us examine these approaches in more detail. Salons could weight the prices of certain services more heavily so as to encourage staff to work harder to sell certain types of product.

Another low cost way of increasing staff salaries and reducing wage percentages is by encouraging retail sales. We are amazed that the enormous retail market for hair care and beauty products is so small in the hairdressing industry. Recent market research shows that 1.25 per cent is the national average for retail sales in hairdressing salons yet the market is worth £488 million. We believe the key to retail selling is as follows:

- Retail sales training of staff
- A good display area
- Products displayed at styling positions
- Incentive schemes to generate sales
- Staff understanding *why* retail sales are part of the service to be offered to a client

A further analysis is to examine how much work each member of staff brings in – preferably work on contribution not turnover – and examine which staff are low and why. Salons frequently have poor appointment procedures which leave some stylists exhausted and others bored. It is better to encourage clients to change stylists within the salon than to lose them. Why is it that often older stylists receive all the shampoo/blow dries or shampoo and sets which are traditionally priced at a lower rate than cuts and finishes? By the pay scheme and price structure that are traditionally in force in the industry we are penalising older stylists for taking older clients who, traditionally, have blow dries and shampoo and sets at a lower price. It is not surprising, therefore, that they become bored and demotivated. An interesting exercise to adopt in a salon would be to ask staff the following question:

Imagine you had to pay all staff £200 per week including trainees and you could not sack anybody. How would you do things differently?

Another approach, which some salon owners find profitable, is the use of good part-time staff, especially married women or women returners. These will be people who may not necessarily wish to work long hours or every day but if the hours and pay were right would willingly work. In fact, these are often mobile or home hairdressers who work on the side but who, if properly channelled, could produce good work for you rather than against you.

In conclusion, you need to carefully analyse your staff costs, productivity and the payment system to ensure that they meet the criteria we set earlier. You must:

- Control your costs effectively
- Motivate staff
- Guarantee reasonable income levels for all
- Utilise a system that is easy to understand and administer
- Utilise a system that is credible to staff
- Be competitive in your locality to avoid losing your best staff to competition

2.6 Controlling expenses

In previous sections we have looked at increasing productivity and controlling direct costs. In this section we examine the nature of expenses and ways of systematically reducing them. It should not need to be emphasised that every pound saved is a pound extra profit. The same principles apply as to all other items:

- Where exactly is the expense?
- Is it necessary?
- Can we get the item cheaper?
- Are we spending more than last year?
- Are we spending more than competition?

Bear in mind the following commonly used quotes:

'Every business overspends and does not control costs.'
'The man who thinks he is efficient is on the way to insolvency.'

2.6.1 General guidelines

(1) Whenever purchasing any item over £50 always get three quotes and choose the middle one.
(2) Avoid credit if you have cash.
(3) Always ask for discounts – even solicitors' and accountants' fees are negotiable.
(4) If you feel over-charged, pay what you think the job is worth and invite them to sue for the rest.
(5) Keep your eyes open for ways of saving money. Have a staff suggestion scheme and give prizes for ideas.

2.6.2 Salon operating expenses

Rent

(1) See if it is negotiable.
(2) Have you spare space? Can you let it without interfering with your business?
(3) Can you get a discount for payment in advance?

Rates

(1) Are there any grounds for a rate reduction (leaflets from your local council)?
(2) Is there any discount for paying in advance? Probably not, so pay by instalments if there is no penalty.

Water

(1) As Rates above.

Repairs/renewals

(1) Can you do any yourself? Or can the staff?
(2) Any OAPs/handymen locally (cheaper than builders)?
(3) Are you buying fittings etc. at trade discounts? Find a customer whose husband is in the trade.

Light and heat

(1) Is your lighting efficient and adequately planned? Is it timed properly, e.g. time switches? Use halogen bulbs and get rid of spotlight bulbs.
(2) Bulbs etc. Can you buy them at trade prices?
(3) Is your heat insulation adequate?
(4) Is your equipment modern and efficient?
(5) Do you use off-peak electricity?
(6) Avoid leaving heaters on.
(7) Install a double-door to reduce heat losses.

Insurances

(1) Have you shopped around (not just a 'friend of the family'!)?
(2) Have you insured for exactly what you want?
(3) Consider different companies for different things.
(4) Can you get discounts?

Cleaning

(1) As in Repairs/renewals.
(2) Consider possible investment in equipment.

2.6.3 Salon administration

Telephone

(1) Have you a call-box for staff?
(2) Monitor for yourself (or buy a kit to do it).
(3) Look at other systems such as Mercury which can be cheaper.
(4) Don't wait – get them to ring you back.
(5) If it's non-urgent, use a letter!

(6) Avoid long distances/overseas calls.
(7) Fax messages after 6 pm.

Accountancy/audit

(1) Shop around carefully.
(2) Ask for a breakdown of costs.
(3) Keep books properly yourself and reduce work.
(4) Computerise your accounts – it will save you time, lower administration wage costs and keep your accountant's bill down.
(5) Use him effectively – he should save you his fee. Fire him if he can't!

Stationery/postage

(1) Use second class always.
(2) Use scrap paper – both sides.
(3) Shop around for printing.
(4) Use two qualities – image/non-image.
(5) Re-use envelopes – non-image.
(6) Ask for cheapest methods at the Post Office (parcels and mail shots).

Advertising/promotion

This is a hard area on which to give definite rules but Chapter 1 Marketing and promotions gives some special low cost methods of promotion. The general guidelines are:

(1) Shop around
(2) Measure cost-effectiveness
(3) Use manufacturers' specialist resources – they want your business, e.g. to buy their products, and in return it is often better to negotiate a lower discount but with specialised promotional, technical and management training support instead.

This is the area which can bankrupt you. Manufacturers' resources can be a low cost method.

2.6.4 Motor vehicle costs

Running expenses

(1) Shop around for insurance.
(2) Use small local garages not *main dealers*!
(3) Avoid obscure cars.
(4) Buy parts trade.
(5) Do it yourself.
(6) Buy oil from discount stores.

Leasing/hire cost

(1) Is it worth leasing? (Ask your accountant.)
(2) Use cash or HP at 0% finance.
(3) Ask for discount.

2.6.5 *Financial costs*

(1) Use as few accounts as possible.
(2) Do not keep money in deposit or current accounts except to avoid bank charges.
(3) Use a building society.
(4) Read *Money Which*.
(5) Change banks to the best one for you (it depends on savings or borrowings).
(6) If possible, increase your mortgage rather than a get a bank loan to finance your business.
(7) Avoid bank charges – ask about 'trigger' accounts.
(8) Use your financial adviser for advice!

If you review the above points regularly about your business you will be surprised at how much you can save.

2.7 Acquiring or selling a business

There are a number of considerations involved in buying or selling a business, both financial and non-financial, and in this section we examine the methods available for putting a value on the business in purely financial terms. The other factors are outside the scope of this book but we have detailed some further reading on this subject. An alternative approach to acquiring a business would be franchising – a growth business within the UK and Europe which we predict will continue to grow during the remainder of this decade. In Chapter 10 The Future of the Industry I give my thoughts and views on franchising.

In this section we will look at the valuation of business in the purely financial sense. When any business is purchased you purchase two aspects:

(1) The assets of the business less any liabilities or outstanding debts
(2) The ability to earn future profits or future earnings – sometimes called the 'goodwill' of the business

(Note: Goodwill in accounting terms is measured as the difference between the price paid for the business and the above two items)

In the worst case we consider buying an unsuccessful business or one where there is considerable doubt as to future profits. In this case you should pay only the market value of the assets, i.e. what they would realise if sold separately, such as equipment or styling chairs. Whether we value these at crisis sale (sale at gunpoint!) or sale without duress is open to question. The starting point would still be the balance sheet.

Balance sheet of Graftanbroke

Assets	£
Property (at cost)	15,000
Fixtures/fittings	5,000
Stock	1,200
Cash	500
Assets	21,700
Creditors	700
Net valuation	21,000

Unfortunately, balance sheets tend to show historical figures and some assets, especially property, may need to be valued upwards, whereas other items, especially if sold under duress, may go down sharply, especially stock and fixtures. Therefore, revaluation in the light of market conditions may be:

	£
Assets	
Property (current value)	17,000
Fixtures (market value)	2,000
Stock (market value)	500
Cash	500
Assets	20,000
Creditors	700
	19,300

Under these conditions, £19300 would be a better price to pay.

In practice, we normally buy a business as a going concern, i.e. with a history and a future of profits. In this case we may have a number of methods available to us.

Hairsense

Balance sheet	(revalued as before)
Assets	£
Buildings	20,000
Vehicles	2,000
Fixtures/fittings	2,500
Stock	1,000
Assets	25,500
Creditors	500
	25,000

Profits 1989–1993

1989	£ 9,000
1990	£10,000
1991	£12,000
1992	£13,000
1993	£15,000

We value this company in two stages. Firstly, if we assume a reasonable rate of return for this type of business is 15 per cent, then a reasonable profit would be 15 per cent of £25000, i.e. £3750. Thus the excess profits (called super profits) were:

1989	£ 5,000
1990	£ 6,000
1991	£ 8,000
1992	£ 9,000
1993	£11,000

It is for these superprofits that we will pay goodwill and two methods of valuation are common:

(1) Purchase × years, e.g. last 3 years, i.e. £28000 or 3 × last year, i.e. £33000. This would value the business at either £25000 + £28000 = £53000, or £58000.

(2) Capitalise profits at higher rate, say 25 per cent (because they are riskier), thus take the average figure for the last 3 years, i.e. £9000 and multiply by 4 = £36 000. On this basis the valuation is £25 000 + £36 000 = £61 000

Note: capitalisation

Rate	Factor
10%	10
15%	7
20%	5
25%	4
33%	3
50%	2

i.e. $\text{Factor} = \dfrac{100\%}{\text{Capital rate (\%)}}$

So we see that this valuation offers a range of £53 000 – £61 000. It is in this area that we would negotiate.

Another method sometimes used is to choose a suitable capitalisation rate and capitalise all profits.

Example
If we decided a rate of 20 per cent here then we would value the business at 5 × recent profits:

$$5 \times 11\,000 = £55\,000$$

Notice all methods give a similar result.

The choice of capitalisation rate is dependent upon:

- Rates of interest available for money
- Plus risk allowance (the riskier the business the higher the rate): 20–30 per cent seem appropriate rates at the present time for hairdressing businesses

In conclusion, there are more complex issues involved. Buying into a share of a business, a partnership or public quoted company is outside the scope of this book but the principles are similar. In this section we have argued that the business must be seen as a financial vehicle taking in cash and producing cash and that we must examine ways of increasing profit by:

(1) Increasing revenue
(2) Reducing direct costs (increasing gross profit)
(3) Decreasing expenses

We have emphasised the need for monitoring performance and keeping records to analyse potential areas for profit improvement by the use of contribution analysis. We examined this concept in relationship to staff productivity and pricing and showed its effects on staff motivation by relating it to wage costs. We also looked at methods of reducing expenses and examined briefly how to value a business for sale or purchasing purposes.

Chapter Three
Finding Staff and Keeping Them

3.1 Introduction

Recruitment and selection begin with the notification by a member of staff that they are leaving, or the opening of a new salon, or the decision to employ additional members of staff. They end with the arrival of the new staff member, his/her induction and, where used, the satisfactory completion of a probationary period.

One of the things which untrained people are surprised at is how much work there is before the interview. It is not simply a case of advertise – pull them in – pick them (and sack them if they are no good!). In selection one needs to adopt the role of a detective, collecting facts, sifting evidence, coming to logical conclusions and learning by experience. These are the key skills involved in recruiting and selecting staff effectively.

If we adopt an analytical approach to these procedures of selection and make the integration of that new staff member as smoothly and quickly as possible into our salons then we will have much greater success in keeping that new staff member employed for a number of years.

In the hairdressing industry the turnover of new trainees is at its highest within the first three months of employing them. Why is this? Is it because we do not take time to select staff correctly? Is it that we see selection of staff as a one way process – the salon decides who they will employ? In reality the selection of staff for a new job is always a two-way process. This may surprise you. The salon must make the job as attractive as possible but must also point out the pitfalls. The salon must also select the correct person for the job by comparing facts about the potential candidates as opposed to selecting staff on gut-feeling, instinct or the 'I can pick them as soon as they walk through the door' approach. The potential new staff member selects whether they wish to work for your salon depending upon how it is packaged.

Many of you, as you read this chapter, will have begun to realise the shortage of school leavers and the potential problems this will have for the hairdressing industry. In fact, the shortage of school leavers will continue to blight the industry until the end of the century. But we can turn this apparent problem to one of advantage by seriously looking at the way in which we select staff, the way in which we train and develop them, the type of employment package we offer to staff to attract them and the various incentives that can be used to ensure that they continue to stay with us.

Later on in this chapter I have detailed potential ways in which we could rethink the whole way we approach employing apprentices and young people within the hairdressing industry.

3.2 Analysing the job

We can distinguish between recruitment and selection in that *recruitment* is concerned with producing a field of potential candidates and *selection* is the choice process between them. Many activities are clearly common and we will label these as both recruitment and selection.

Whenever and wherever vacancies occur, this should be an opportunity to rethink staffing issues:

- Are we over/under-staffed?
- Do we lack certain skills that we need?
- Do we need an exact copy of the person who left or not?

These are the sort of questions that need to be considered before making any further move towards recruiting more staff. This clearly requires consideration of the current workload and the current staff levels and their skills in order to identify exactly what is needed.

The two key questions to ask are:

(1) Why has the vacancy occurred?
(2) What skills are needed to fill the vacancy?

Why has the vacancy occurred?

Check the following list:

(1) Member of staff leaving due to:

- Another job
- Moving from the area
- Pregnancy

(2) Promotion
(3) Ill health
(4) New skills required, e.g. tinting, long hair work, training skills, photographic skills
(5) Salon expansion

Asking the above question helps us to identify if there is a pattern in our business as to why staff may be leaving, which may affect our future approach to recruiting staff.

If you have, however, decided to go ahead and recruit, then consider recruitment as consisting of a number of stages:

(1) Job description – defining the job, its responsibilities and levels of authority
(2) Person specification – defining the person and skills required to fill the job
(3) Attracting a field of candidates
(4) Selecting the staff
(5) Incorporating the staff into the organisation

If we look at the flow chart shown in Fig. 3.1 we will see a very clear stage by stage process which is necessary in the recruitment/selection process.

Now complete Exercise 3.1. This will give you a measure of how much work needs to be put into practice in order to make recruitment/selection an effective process.

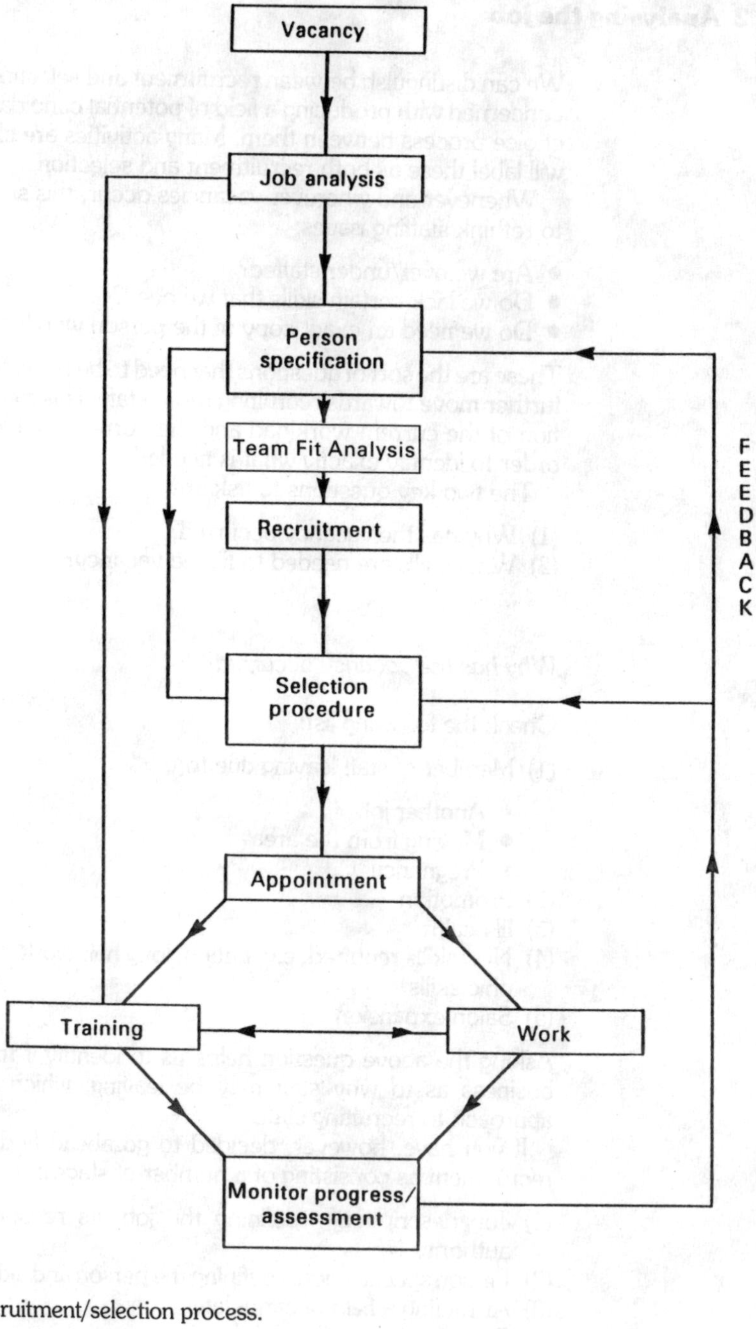

```
                    ┌─────────────┐
                    │   Vacancy   │
                    └─────────────┘
                           │
                           ▼
                    ┌─────────────┐
                    │Job analysis │
                    └─────────────┘
                           │
                           ▼
                    ┌─────────────┐
                    │   Person    │
                    │specification│
                    └─────────────┘
                           │
                           ▼
                    ┌─────────────┐
                    │Team Fit Analysis│
                    └─────────────┘
                           │
                           ▼
                    ┌─────────────┐
                    │ Recruitment │
                    └─────────────┘
                           │
                           ▼
                    ┌─────────────┐
                    │  Selection  │
                    │  procedure  │
                    └─────────────┘
                           │
                           ▼
                    ┌─────────────┐
                    │ Appointment │
                    └─────────────┘

   ┌─────────────┐                 ┌─────────────┐
   │  Training   │◄──────────────►│    Work     │
   └─────────────┘                 └─────────────┘

                    ┌─────────────┐
                    │Monitor progress/│
                    │ assessment  │
                    └─────────────┘
```

F
E
E
D
B
A
C
K

Fig. 3.1 A model of recruitment/selection process.

Exercise 3.1 Recruitment/selection
Answer TRUE or FALSE to each statement.

(1) All my staff have written job descriptions. _____

(2) I use job descriptions when I interview new staff. _____

(3) I prepare person specifications for each interview. _____

(4) I interview in a quiet room free from interruptions. _____

(5) I always take up basic references for staff. _____

(6) I always prepare an interview plan before I interview
for new staff. _____

(7) I have never picked a bad member of staff. _____

(8) I always tell staff about the bad parts of the job as well
as the good. _____

(9) I always get my receptionist or senior stylist or
another stylist to 'look after' a new member of staff. _____

(10) I always sit down and talk to a new staff member a
short time after they've joined to discuss progress and
problems. _____

Scoring
Score 1 for all TRUE answers except for (7) score –2 (everybody makes mistakes). Score 0 for all FALSE answers.

Score interpretation
Less than 2   You are either lucky or unsuccessful in the way you select staff.
2–5   You have still a lot to learn about successful staff selection.
More than 7   Excellent. You are well on the way to success.

3.3 The job description

A job description is a statement of the overall purpose of the job and the main tasks to be carried out. A good job description is essential to effective selection but it is also relevant to all the other processes by which we manage our staff. It is a vital document which notes what the staff are actually doing.

Purposes of a job description:

- Motivation of staff
- Staff appraisal/monitoring their progress
- Disciplining staff and handling staff problems
- Training staff
- Man-power planning
- Part of their contract of employment

A good job description should contain the following items:

(1) Location of job
(2) Job title

(3) Job title of immediate superior/supervisor
(4) Job grade (if relevant)
(5) Job titles of any staff for whom the job holder is responsible (numbers)
(6) Brief description of overall purpose of the job
(7) The main tasks to be carried out by the job holder listed preferably in order of importance
(8) The standards required from the job holder
(9) Details of any special requirements, e.g. supplying of equipment, travelling or outside visiting etc.
(10) Special circumstances of job, e.g. hours, overtime (evening) or weekend working, unpleasant conditions etc.

Sample job descriptions for a stylist and salon manager are shown. These are examples and not intended as perfect specimens. The needs of each salon are different and general job descriptions are of little use – they must reflect the actual job as it is required to be done.

Job description

Job title: Stylist

Location:

Main purpose of job: To ensure that the standards of the Company are reached and maintained under the following key categories:

- Financial/productivity standards
- Hairdressing standards
- Service standards
- Image/appearance standards
- Behaviour standards
- Salon procedures.

Responsible to: The Salon Manager and, in the absence of the Manager, the Assistant Manager.

Responsibilities:

Financial/productivity standards

(1) To achieve a realistic pre-set target of takings.
(2) To ensure that daily/weekly worksheets balance with the takings.
(3) To ensure that retail sales figures are recorded accurately and balance.
(4) To ensure maximum use is gained from the appointments system.
(5) To ensure all services provided are charged for at the correct current price list.

Hairdressing standards

(1) To achieve and maintain hairdressing standards and techniques in keeping with the clients' wishes and current fashion trends.
(2) To take fullest advantage and use of all training available within the Company.
(3) To assist in the training and to encourage all trainees in the practical application of hairdressing skills and service standards.

Service standards

(1) To advise clients of all services and products available and, in particular, those for retail purchase in order that they keep their hair in good condition.

(2) To ensure clients are offered and are aware of all non-hairdressing services available, e.g. coffee/tea, magazines etc., in order to ensure client comfort.

(3) To maintain and update client record cards for the following reasons:

- Technical
- Client complaints

Image/appearance standards

(1) To ensure your personal appearance is in keeping with the standards set by Management with regard to staff dress, hairstyles, make-up and personal hygiene as set out in the Company's Rules and Regulations.

(2) To ensure that salon cleanliness and hygiene is maintained and in keeping with the Company's policy in services.

(3) To work with the Manager in promoting the Company's image through all media, e.g. advertising, shows (trade and public) and local publicity to increase the Company's reputation and client count.

Behaviour standards

(1) To adhere to the Company's policy on staff behaviour as set out in the Company's Rules and Regulations, e.g. hours of work etc.

(2) To be loyal to other members of staff and management at all times.

(3) To ensure a friendly and approachable attitude towards clients is maintained at all times.

(4) To be aware of the grievance procedure and to ensure it is carried out as laid down in the individual's Contract of Employment.

Salon procedures

(1) To carry out all reasonable duties and tasks which may be requested of you.

Job description

Job title: Salon Manager

Location:

Main purpose of job: Responsibility for the efficient running and profitability of the salon by ensuring that the standards of the Company are reached and maintained under the following key categories:

- Financial/productivity standards
- Hairdressing standards
- Service standards
- Staff management standards
- Image/appearance standards
- Salon procedures

Responsible to: General Manager with a close direct working relationship with Training Manager

Responsibilities:

Financial/productivity standards

(1) To adhere to the financial guidelines as follows:

- To achieve quarterly financial/service mix targets for the salon.
- To ensure staff offer a full range of services that the salon has available.
- To ensure the smooth running of reception area, in particular with overall responsibility for cash and paperwork procedures.

- To ensure all services provided are charged for at the correct current price.
- To ensure daily takings and float balance with work carried out.
- To ensure correct information is recorded by staff on daily/weekly worksheets

(2) To achieve a realistic pre-set target of promotional activities as and when they occur.
(3) To ensure the ordering and maintaining of stock levels are carried out according to the guidelines set by the General Manager and that paperwork procedures are completed accurately.
(4) To ensure that reception and bill procedures are completed accurately according to the Company policy currently in force.

Hairdressing standards

(1) In conjunction with the Training Manager to organise and put into action a full training programme for junior staff to ensure that the required standard of proficiency is reached within the required time.
(2) To work with the Training Manager in maintaining hairdressing standards and techniques in keeping with clients' wishes and current fashion trends.

Service standards

(1) To maintain and constantly review client service standards.
(2) To advise clients of all services and products available and, in particular, those for retail purchase in order that they keep their hair in good condition.
(3) To ensure that staff update and maintain client record cards for the following reasons:

- Technical
- Client complaints

(4) To ensure the salon has sufficient stock in order that sales and services are not inhibited.

Staff management

(1) To motivate and guide all members of staff to create a happy working atmosphere for the benefit of both staff and clients, e.g. working hours are adhered to etc.
(2) To encourage and motivate all staff to maximum potential, both technically and professionally, for their individual benefit and the future growth of the Company.
(3) To communicate through all staff levels, i.e. stylists, trainees, receptionist, the following information:

- Company policies and procedures
- Staff changes
- The Company's future plans
- Management satisfaction and dissatisfaction
- Feed-back through correct channels on staff criticisms, ensuring that these are given a satisfactory answer

(4) To ensure that grievance procedures are carried out as laid down in the individual's Contract of Employment.
(5) Together with the General Manager to plan future staff requirements to maintain staff levels with fluctuations in trade throughout the year.
(6) To plan a holiday rota for staff ensuring that only one stylist is absent at any one time and to take into account the salon's needs regarding busy periods.

(7) To carry out first interviews to find suitable candidates before final selection is made by the General Manager and/or Training Manager (dependant upon the level of the job).

Image/appearance standards
(1) To ensure that staff's appearance is in keeping with the standards set by management with regard to staff dress, hairstyles, make-up and personal hygiene as set out in the Company's Rules and Regulations.
(2) To ensure salon cleanliness and maintenance is in keeping with the Company's policy on services.
(3) To ensure that there are suitable merchandising displays for both salon services and retail products.
(4) To work closely with the General Manager in promoting the Company's image through all media, i.e. advertising, shows (trade and public) and local publicity to increase the Company's reputation and client count.

Salon procedures
(1) To ensure the salon is secure at all times and, in particular, with regard to cash/financial procedures.
(2) To ensure that the systems and procedures which may be in force at any time are adhered to.
(3) To carry out all reasonable duties and tasks which may be requested.

So how do you go about writing a job description? There are a number of options:

(1) Sit down and write up the job as you see it.
(2) Ask the person doing the job to produce a synopsis as they see it.
(3) Interview the job holder about what he/she actually does.
(4) Get him/her to keep a detailed log or record (diary) of his/her activities.
(5) Get a consultant to do it for you.
(6) Any combination of the above or *all* if you wish.

The important thing to bear in mind is that the aim of the exercise is to produce the best possible job description available in the time.

Standards

What must be included in a job description is the approach to the standards required. There are five main standards within the hairdressing industry:

(1) Standards of hairdressing
(2) Standards of appearance
(3) Standards of productivity
(4) Standards of service
(5) Standards of behaviour

Figures 3.2–3.6 show flow charts of the areas in which, in our opinion, standards should be measured within the hairdressing industry. Without standards how is it possible to have any level of professionalism? These standards must be:

- Definable
- Measurable
- Achievable

Fig. 3.2 Setting standards of hairdressing.

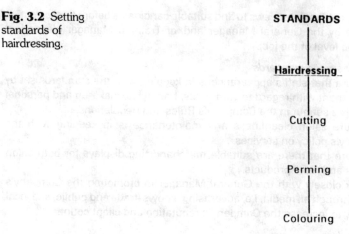

STANDARDS

Hairdressing

Cutting

Perming

Colouring

Fig. 3.3 Setting standards of appearance.

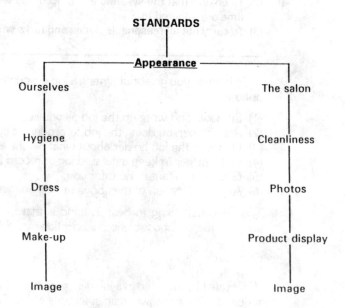

STANDARDS

Appearance

Ourselves	The salon
Hygiene	Cleanliness
Dress	Photos
Make-up	Product display
Image	Image

Fig. 3.4 Setting standards of productivity.

STANDARDS

Productivity

Targets　　Time　　Wastage　　Prices

Fig. 3.5 Setting standards of service.

STANDARDS

Service

Clients
not kept waiting

Coffee/magazines

Hair happy

Hair care advice

Fig. 3.6 Setting standards of behaviour.

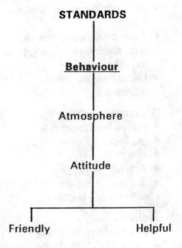

STANDARDS

Behaviour

Atmosphere

Attitude

Friendly   Helpful

Each salon will have different standards, for example, of hairdressing and service depending upon their client mix, the area in which the salon is situated and all the other factors discussed in Chapter 1 Marketing and promotions.

Finally, if you already have a job description with all the things detailed as previously discussed, it is important to revise it:

- Regularly
- Whenever it changes

Fig. 3.7 Person specification form.

Characteristics	Minimum requirement	Desirable requirement
(1) Physique, health and appearance • Height and build • Hearing and eyesight • Looks, grooming, dress/clothes • Voice and personal manner • General health/fitness		
(2) Education and previous experience • Education level – GCSE grades, etc. • Specific training, apprenticeship, professional training • Job training • Experience required, number of years/type required		
(3) Intelligence level		
(4) Special talents • Does the job involve practical things? • Skill with writing reports and communicating with clients/staff • Skill with figures or handling money • Artistic flair/ability e.g. dressing hair, stagework, photographic experience • Using tools or special equipment		
(5) Personal interests • Active or outdoor • Intellectual/logical • Practical • Artistic • Social – persuading, managing, entertaining people		
(6) Temperament • Acceptability to others • Leadership/influencing • Stability/steadiness • Self-reliance (working alone and accepting responsibility) • Ability to handle stress		
(7) Personal circumstances • Married/single • Dependents • Age preference • Travel requirements		

A vacancy gives you a natural opportunity to check out whether the current job description is still valid, and if not, to correct it.

3.4 Identifying the right person

Now that a description of the exact nature of the job has been produced, the next stage is to analyse the qualities of the person required to fill the job. This is the stage which requires human judgement and there is no real alternative. There are a number of check lists which help you to achieve this and we will use Alec Rodger's *Seven Point Plan* which identifies seven aspects of the individual which are:

- Physique
- Attainment
- General intelligence
- Special aptitudes
- Interests
- Disposition
- Circumstances

Figure 3.7 shows a person specification form which has been designed for use in the hairdressing business. Try to complete it for a job of your choice. In doing this bear in mind two questions:

(1) What is absolutely *essential* for reasonable performance of the job?
(2) What is *desirable* or *preferable* in a candidate if you have a choice?

These are recorded in the 'minimum' and 'desirable' requirement columns of the person specification and must be quantified wherever possible and written in a way which indicates how they will be measured. Figure 3.8 indicates some of the key aspects we would include in a person specification for a stylist.

Points to remember

(1) The person specification should not be simply a copy of the last job holder but should be considered in relation to the current job.
(2) Beware of asking too much – remember if you over-specify or your standards are too high, you will find it difficult to recruit anyone at all.
(3) Be as clear as possible – imagine you had to give this form to someone else to do the interview for you.

Fig. 3.8 Key qualities of a stylist.

(1) Attractive appearance
(2) Fashionable clothes
(3) Outgoing personality – 'bubbly'
(4) Artistic flair
(5) Proper professional training
(6) Ability to relate to clients
(7) Social skills
(8) Energy and stamina

(4) Try to be objective and avoid your own prejudices/biases. Try to match each feature back to the job requirements.

(5) Try to note which requirements could be achieved by training and which cannot be changed in the potential candidate. For example, selling skills may be desirable but not essential; people can be trained in selling! People can be trained in advanced colouring techniques.

(6) Aim to produce a clear mental picture of the person you want to fill the job. This framework can be used for shortlisting and selection.

3.5 Analysing the person

The following points can be considered under the various headings:

(1) Physique, health and appearance

- Standard of health/fitness required
- Importance of first impressions (appearance, speech etc.)
- Social skills and experience
- Clothes sense

(2) Education and previous experience
What knowledge and/or experience does the person need

- General education – GCSEs, etc.
- Specific training, apprenticeships (was it a traditional apprenticeship; through a college of FE; or a private school), professional qualifications, job training
- Experience required. Number of years/type required

(3) Special talents

- Does the job involve practical things (working with the hands)?
- Does it involve writing reports or communication with clients/staff?
- Does it involve calculating, figurework or handling money?
- How much artistic flair/ability is needed? For example dressing hair, stagework, photographic experience
- Does it involve using tools or special equipment?

(4) Intelligence
Most difficult to estimate – above or below or about average?

(5) Personal interests
Interests are often a guide to a person's personality and preferences. Beware of people with too many interests! What interests does the job appeal to?

- Active or outdoor interests
- Intellectual or logical
- Practical
- Artistic
- Social – persuading, managing, entertaining people

(6) Temperament
What sort of person is required to do the job?

- Acceptability to others
- Leadership or influencing

- Stability and steadiness
- Self reliance (working alone and accepting responsibility)
- Ability to handle stress

(7) Personal circumstances
Any personal circumstances relevant to job, e.g. married/single, dependents, age preference, travel requirements etc.

Now using the person specification form shown in Fig. 3.7 prepare a person specification for the job of a stylist or trainee. Once you have done this a clearer picture can be formed as to the type of person required to fill the position.

3.6 'Will they fit into the team?'

How many times have you been in the situation of selecting someone based upon their background, experience, qualifications only to find they do not fit into the team or the job. The experience can prove not only disappointing but can also have disastrous results. Staff will often say of someone who does not fit in that he or she 'was absolutely brilliant at hairdressing but did not fit in with the way we operate'.

Team Role Theory was developed by Dr Meredith Belbin and is widely used throughout the management world as an effective way of explaining why some teams perform better than others – some succeed, others fail.

Team Role Theory shows how the answer lies in the two concepts of *eligibility* and *suitability*.

Eligibility is defined as 'Does the candidate have the qualifications and special experience to do the job?'

Suitability is defined as 'Does the candidate fit in with the team, the job shape and the boss?' (See Fig. 3.9.)

3.6.1 Eligibility

Eligibility involves measuring *past achievement*:

- Qualifications
- Relevant experience and track record
- References from previous employers
- Acceptability of performance at interview

It is usual to give most weight to the eligibility of the candidate because it is probably easier to measure. The kind of questions asked when someone is eligible would be:

- Can you do the job?
- Have you done it before?
- Where did you go to school/college and which exam passes did you get?
- Have you got a driving licence?

Eligibility is important in accepting a person's credibility. This is why stylists promoted to managers from within the salon often do not have the credibility of someone who is moved from another branch or when they are given temporary manager status have difficulty getting staff to perform. Sometimes a better way of looking at a job is to draw up a list of 'semi-eligibles' by which is meant those who are partly eligible but can learn.

Fig. 3.9 Eligibility compared with suitability.

Entry criteria (for Eligibility)	Performance criteria (for Suitability)
(1) Qualifications	(1) Talent/capacity to do the job
(2) Relevant experience	(2) Versatility
(3) References	(3) Assessments – tests/monitoring
(4) Acceptability at interview	(4) Role fit to those already doing the job

Dangers of high eligibility

There is nothing wrong with appointing highly eligible people but it is not a guarantee that they are going to be right for the job or the team. They may look and dress right, enjoy all the same things as you do and have lots of things in common but none of these things will tell you whether they will fit as members of the team.

Highly eligible people can often be over-rated. The skills needed in most jobs are normally not so very difficult to learn. Frequently these skills can be acquired by training. Highly eligible people can often be very inflexible as they have a higher view of what they are worth in terms of their experience in the job or their expectations of pay. So salon owners can end up paying more for less benefit.

3.6.2 Suitability

Does the candidate fit in with the team, the job and the boss?

To assess a candidate's *suitability* we need to look for indicators of *future performance* such as:

- General ability
- Versatility
- Flexibility
- Self-assessment by the candidate and the opinions of those they work with
- How well the person will fit with the rest of the team

When appointing people, the main concern should always be *future performance* rather than *past achievement*. It is a true saying that you only find out what people are really like once you have got to know them. That is not so easy when dealing with external candidates.

People within the company have inside knowledge but outsiders seldom show their real selves at interview. This is why identifying *team role types* is important because it will help us to shape what exactly we are looking for and to decide how we think the candidates will fit in with the team.

3.7 Team role types

There are nine team roles. Every team role type has a strength and an allowable weakness. To understand why some teams will always perform better than others, we need to appreciate the difference between a person's functional role – that is the job they are actually paid to do such as salon manager, stylist, receptionist etc. – and their *team role.*

Functional role: The functional role is the job we are hired to do. We are often selected largely because of our ability, experience and skill.

Team role: We also fill a *team role* which becomes important whenever we form part of a group of people. The team role is our tendency to behave, contribute and inter-relate in certain ways and *is likely to be shaped more by our personality and learned behaviour than by technical skills and the knowledge we possess.*

Whenever we are part of a staff meeting, a sports club, a social gathering, our team role is likely to reveal itself in certain predictable ways.

The teams that are likely to perform the best are the ones that have the best blend of team roles to play off and balance against each other. It is not necessary to have nine people in a team, but ideally in every team each role should be present. For example, in a smaller team each of the team roles may be represented by fewer people because it would be unusual for us not to have more than one strong team type.

The benefits of having a perfectly constructed team include:

(1) Fewer clashes between individuals competing for the same team role;
(2) More mutual appreciation and recognition of each other's ability;
(3) A greater contribution from the whole team instead of from just one or two team members;
(4) Insurance against the mistakes that can arise when an individual carries too much of the responsibility. A good example of this is when one person is responsible for putting together a show and, because of his or her team types, misses out on certain aspects of the planning, such as the detail for the costings or meeting deadlines.

The nine team roles are:

Plant:	Creative, imaginative, unorthodox – solves difficult problems.
Resource investigator:	Extrovert, enthusiastic, communicative. Explores opportunities, develops contacts.
Co-ordinator:	Mature, confident and trusting. A good chairperson. Clarifies goals, promotes decision making.
Shaper:	Dynamic, outgoing and highly strung. Challenges, pressurises, seeks ways around obstacles.
Monitor/evaluator:	Sober, strategic and discerning. Sees all the options. Judges accurately.
Team worker:	Sociable, mild and perceptive and accommodating. Listens and builds on ideas. Tries to avoid friction.
Implementer:	Disciplined, reliable, conservative and efficient. Turns ideas into practical actions and solutions.
Completer/finisher:	Painstaking, conscientious and anxious. Searches out errors and omissions. Delivers on time.

Specialist: Single minded, self-starting and dedicated.
                                     Provides knowledge or technical skills.

Avoiding confusion between similar types

Since there are nine separate team roles each of us may fill both primary and
secondary roles. Sometimes people feel that the types overlap. These are the
most common areas:

- *Plant or resource investigator*
  These two roles tend to be confused because they are seen as 'creative'.
  In practice, the distinction between the two is important. Plants are more
  creative when left alone and kept free from disturbance, whereas resource
  investigators need the stimulus of others to build ideas. They think under
  different conditions. Plants need a sympathetic and appreciative boss, a
  relaxed and unstructured or loosely structured environment with few
  rules and regulations. Resource operators, on the other hand, operate
  well under pressure and in coping with sudden or unexpected crises.
- *Plant or monitor/evaluator*
  These are both 'thinking' roles but they think in different ways. Plants
  operate through inspiration and creative intuition. Monitor/evaluators are
  better at diagnosing problems, assessing situations, choosing best options
  and planning ahead. Simply put, plants look at the 'bits of a situation – not
  necessarily in a logical fashion and come to conclusions' whilst monitor/
  evaluators analyse through a step by step, logical process to identify the
  issues.
- *Resource investigator or co-ordinator*
  Both of these are good at liaising, but operate in different ways. Resource
  investigators seek adventure and thrive on the discovery of new contacts.
  Co-ordinators prefer the process of pulling together all the resources and
  making sure they work in harmony to reach the goals.
- *Co-ordinator or shaper*
  These two are both strong at leadership roles but they tend to adopt
  different styles. Co-ordinators are skilled at getting the best out of people
  and using other people's talents to the full. Shapers expect to be followed
  and drive those who work for them to the limit. Co-ordinators and shapers
  tend to clash when they work alongside each other at the same status
  level.
- *Teamworker or co-ordinator*
  Both seek and enjoy harmony but teamworkers tend to avoid friction
  through building one to one relationships (networks!). Co-ordinators are
  better at handling groups and instilling the sense of a common purpose.
  Teamworkers are often skilled at *working* for very difficult people,
  whereas co-ordinators are good at *managing* difficult people.
- *Implementer or completer*
  These are regarded as 'action roles' but their approaches are different.
  Implementers are good at building up systems and taking practical steps
  to make things happen. Completers are more concerned with the
  thoroughness of any action. They see the method as less important than
  achieving the end results.
     Completers are self-motivated and usually do not need incentives to
  spur them on.

- *Completer or specialist*
  Both of these aim to achieve the highest quality standards in their work. For a specialist, his or her specialism generates its own standards against which everything else is measured. Specialists become ill at ease when subject to close supervision from non-professionals or 'outsiders'.

  Completers, however, are ready to accept a wider range of bosses and they carry out all their responsibilities with the same level of urgency and thoroughness.

3.7.1 Analysing your own team

A team which is out of balance will under-perform. For example, there may be too many people of the same or similar team types such as shapers and finishers. A vital team role may not be covered, which can undermine the efficiency of the team. If you carry out a *team role audit* it will be possible to:

(1) Identify the gaps in the team that will need attention;
(2) Improve the awareness of team roles for the team members;
(3) Heighten their understanding of each team member's team role;
(4) Help colleagues to agree how to divide work between themselves, based upon the strengths and abilities of the team.

How to rebuild the team

(1) Select new team members either from:

    (a) other departments or branches, or
    (b) exchange team members from one group to another, e.g. a creative group who may have a team member moved to a training group or vice versa.

(2) Adopt a management style that suits the particular characteristics of the team, e.g. consultative, participative or autocratic, to give tasks and responsibilities to team members that suit their strongest team role.
(3) Encourage team members to draw on the strengths of each other.
(4) Coach each member of the team on how to develop a secondary set of team roles in order to increase their versatility.
(5) Suggest where there is repetition of primary roles for members to rely on their secondary roles instead. Thus where there are too many shapers a suitable secondary role may be as a monitor/evaluator.

3.7.2 Team fits and misfits

(1) The ideal fit

The ideal fit is both eligible and suitable but the problem is that they often turn out to be short stayers because they cease to find a challenge in the job. They may devote a lot of their time and energy in the job towards building up their experience and eligibility for a bigger and better job. The result is that ideal fits who have often been recruited at great expense in terms of advertising and training use the job as a stepping stone to higher things.

(2) The surprise fit

This is where surprise fits score. People who are very suitable but barely eligible, e.g. may not have the appropriate qualifications or background experience, are a very interesting category. Surprise fits feel happy that they have been able to obtain the job and feel it is a constant challenge. Being ineligible by lack of experience or qualifications for other senior jobs outside the company means they are less inclined to look for greener grass on the other side of the fence.

These people often get into the job in the first place because they are filling the post temporarily and then surprise everyone by performing really well. They often turn out to be long stayers as well as being good at the job.

They fit comfortably into a team, they are stimulated by new challenges and they are often given the time and opportunity to develop, unlike ideal fits who are expected to perform immediately.

(3) The poor fit

Someone who is entirely eligible but not very suitable is usually a poor fit. This results from placing too much emphasis on experience and qualifications, and not enough on how well the individual will fit in with the rest of the team and the actual job to be done.

Such appointments usually cause the most problems. For the person in the job, failure is seen as a personal slight and he or she will probably reject what is being said to them. Where team roles are not used in companies, it may be difficult to explain why a person who is well qualified for a job is unsuitable. The attempt to shift a person who is eligible but unsuitable is likely to result in a great deal of unpleasantness all round.

Because the problem of moving unsuitable people who may be very eligible can be difficult the common response from management is to allow sleeping dogs to lie! A situation may then come about where almost everyone recognises the mistaken appointment but no-one is prepared to do anything about it. The team then has a major weakness.

(4) The total misfit

To be ineligible and unsuitable seems an unlikely situation. Total misfits do not tend to present a major problem since they usually leave quite quickly.

Total misfits often come about as temporary appointments, sometimes to fill in following a crisis, e.g. when many people leave an organisation all at the same time. When they do not work out, few tears are lost. There is seldom any hassle and life starts afresh with no bad feelings on either side.

3.7.3 *Selecting the perfect team*

Applying eligibility versus suitability in practice

(1) Internal appointments are less risky
Recruiting from outside the company should be the last resort rather than the first. The more you can develop people from within the

organisation, the more you can use your existing knowledge and information to maximise their talents and minimise your mistakes.

Placing 'outsiders' into key positions is a risky business. If they are to be introduced, it should be because their experience is very special and cannot be repeated by someone in the firm or because they possess abilities superior to those within the company.

(2) *Internal appointments develop talent*

There are often staff within companies whose special abilities have not been recognised. By identifying the plus points of employees, they can be placed in jobs where their abilities can blossom.

Employees whose performance is no more than satisfactory in one job may prove themselves in another where a different set of demands are made. Knowing where people perform best can help in identifying where they would best be positioned, such as moving to other jobs more suitable to their talents.

A major pay-off of training and developing suitable people is that they feel more involved and committed to the company and have a greater sense of belonging. They do not regard the company as simply a stepping stone to their personal career path.

(3) *The fast track can lead nowhere*

Those whose promise has been identified are more likely to succeed than newcomers who have been placed into the 'fast track' because of their academic or previous experience. A good example of this is trainees who have performed well on their college training course or at a private hairdressing school covering three years' hairdressing training in six to nine months. All salons really need is an entry stream of able people who come from various backgrounds into basic jobs and then they can be developed within the organisation.

(4) *Train what is trainable – not what is not*

Eligibility is about those already trained or experienced. But what is more important is whether people are trainable. Provided people's capabilities are good they can be trained to become more eligible, e.g. gain qualifications or further experience.

Team role weaknesses of people are seldom corrected by having them pointed out or 'remedied by training'. It is much harder to try to train people to be suitable. That is like taking a square peg and making it oval in the unlikely event it will fit in a round hole.

(5) *Experience is not everything*

When 'experience' is needed to fill a job, it is important to distinguish between familiarity with techniques, technical terms, clients' names and so on, and in-depth experience which entails a considerable passage of time. Employees with talent and capability can rapidly develop skills.

(6) *The more views the merrier*

In assessing an employee, do not rely upon the views of one person. The most accurate observations are made by colleagues rather than bosses or subordinates. When people agree independently on a particular characteristic, it is usually a pretty fair indication that it exists.

When external candidates are being considered, there is considerable advantage in introducing them to the people with whom they would work. Their views should be considered. New staff seldom work out if they cannot get on with those with whom they have to work.

3.8 Finding suitable people

Now you have done your homework on the person you are looking for you can decide from where to recruit them. There are a large number of places to recruit staff from and Fig. 3.10 lists them, notes the advantages and disadvantages of each and suggests what they might be useful for. Notice that some of the methods are free or at least inexpensive. Most hairdressers fail to use all the options open to them.

(1) How can we find suitable people to fill the gaps not only in the job but within the team? Asking all the people with whom they will be working as to the qualities needed to fill the job will give you a clearer idea of what to look for.

Fig. 3.10 Methods of attracting applicants.

Method	Advantages	Disadvantages	Use for
Previous staff	You know them. Low cost.	Does not introduce new ideas.	Any.
Previous applicants	Low cost.	May not be interested.	Any.
Personal recommendations (Clients/staff/friends)	Low cost. Can get good information.	May not be reliable information. Difficulties if unsuitable	Any.
Schools (Careers Office)	Low cost. Can get good choice of students.	Takes time.	Trainees.
Hairdressing colleges	Trained. Low cost.	Training standards vary.	Trainees.
Job centre	Low cost. Quick response.	Quality unpredictable unless good rapport with Job Centre.	Any. Junior stylists and trainees.
Local papers	Quick response. Usually effective.	Can be expensive. Attractive ad crucial.	Any.
National press	Attracts non-locals.	Very expensive. Requires professional copy.	Any. High fliers for top jobs.
Local radio/TV	As national press, also attracts locals.	Very expensive – needs recording.	Any (top jobs best).
Specialist journals	Select audience. Good response usually.	Copy deadlines. Expensive. Attractive ad crucial.	Stylists and higher.
Show window adverts	Cheap, quick. Attracts locals.	Must be tastefully done.	Any.

(2) You could ask people generally within the salon to put forward nominations of people they think are capable of doing the job even though they may not be eligible (may not have the experience or qualifications). This can be a good way of generating a short list which can be worked upon.

(3) You could ask open, general questions on application forms, such as:

'What do you enjoy most about working?'
'Why would you like to work within our salon?'

(4) You could stage an event with a large number of candidates who may have been shortlisted from their eligibility details on the application form. You could:

(a) Show them around the salon. This is particularly effective in recruiting trainees or receptionists.

(b) Introduce them to the rest of the team they will be working with.

(c) Give the candidates name badges so that everyone knows who they are and tell your own people ahead of time to make notes on who asks questions and what they ask.

(d) Ask the candidates after the visit what they saw and compare notes with the rest of the team.

These approaches involving the team give greater insight than the one-to-one interview and interviews can be conducted as a second step once you have pre-selected those most suitable from the group meeting.

(5) You could conduct a personality test known as *Cattell's 16 Personality Factors Test*. This needs to be scored and interpreted by a trained professional but it is a particularly useful approach when recruiting managers.

The points to remember about eligibility – i.e. entry criteria versus performance criteria – are:

(a) People may compensate for lack of talent or ability to do the job by seeking recognised qualifications. Talent usually wins through in the long run.

(b) Previous job experience where staff have concentrated a lot of their energy can sometimes channel their behaviour down a particular path. Thus the fastest hairdresser may be very productive but may not make the best manager.

(c) References often distort the ability of candidates and should only be used as a yardstick to measure attendance, honesty and accuracy regarding the length of employment.

(d) Applicants who give good impressions at interview are not necessarily the easiest people to work with.

3.8.1 A guide to writing job adverts

If you use a method which requires an advert then you will need to design it in an effective way. This section sets out suitable guidelines but you must be careful to avoid infringing the Sex Discrimination Act (1975). Figure 9.1 in Chapter 9 summarises the main points as they apply to hairdressers. The Equal Opportunities Commission provide a booklet (see further sources at the back of the book) which is worth acquiring.

The points in these guidelines apply to all advertisements.
The aims of recruitment advertising are:

(1) *Reach* the target audience.

(2) *Attract* and *retain* attention.

(3) Produce a *compact* field of acceptable candidates who are:

- Capable/equipped to do the job
- Motivated to apply for it
- Motivated to actually *do* the job if successful

It is a fallacy that a large number of applicants means a good advert.

(4) The contents of the advert should be:

- *Concise*
- *Factual*
- *Relevant* to the job, the applicant and method of recruitment
- *Unambiguous*

(5) Ideally the advert should contain:

- The *job title*, or an easily understood phrase to help convey the job
- The *rewards* (salary and relevant fringe benefits)
- The *location(s)*
- Brief *description* of the *job*, its position in the organisation and relationships with other jobs
- Brief *description* of the *business* (where relevant)
- The ways in which the job makes any special demands or differs from a normal person's expectations, e.g. hours, travel, prospects, responsibility, safety, etc.
- The *minimum* requirements in terms of the seven-point plan demanded. Physical requirements are as important as qualifications/age/experience etc. *Be careful of Sex/Race Discrimination provisions*
- Instructions as to how a candidate, if interested, should proceed further. A number of options are available:

  write or telephone
  send in a letter or complete an application form
  visit for discussion

In general use simple language and sentence structure ('*Daily Mirror* language') and aim to give candidates enough information to decide if they are interested and if they are suitable.

An additional objective of advertising is to build up a public image of the business through the advertising effort over a long period. It is this type of argument that often makes the use of house style/logo/agency particularly attractive.

Seven-point checklist for advertisements

(1) *Headline*
The immediate identification of your potential candidate by a meaningful job title or the work subject.

(2) *Refining features*
One or two words, or a short phrase, to amplify the above or unique interest factors which may cover industry, location or incentive.

(3) *The business*
This should provide a brief understanding of your business to help build up interest and promote your advertisement against a competitor's who may have an identical post.

- What it does
- Size
- Achievements
- Growth in future
- Future projects or development
- Interest factors
- Special features

(4) *The job*
Brief details clarifying job, main duties and special features.

- Reason for appointment
- To whom responsible
- Duties/tasks
- Opportunities for personal development
- Support (management and/or subordinates)
- Interest factors

(5) *The requirements*
Candidate requirements summarised, but when possible, emphasising absolute essentials as opposed to preferences.

- Age
- Education and training
- Qualifications
- Experience (necessary years and particular methods worked or understood)
- Management techniques (if required)
- Specialities

(6) *Incentives*
- Pay
- Benefits, inducements, (commission, bonus, car, pension, holidays, removal assistance)
- Job satisfaction/interest
- Working conditions/equipment
- Prospects/development
- Location and travel prospects

(7) *Action*
This should be created with the candidate's habits in mind unless anonymity is required. Tell the candidate what to do.

- Telephone
- Call in/visit
- Write in for information/application form

JUNIOR STYLISTS & STYLISTS   CONFIDENTIAL

APPLICATION FOR EMPLOYMENT

SURNAME AND
MAIDEN NAME IF APPLICABLE: OTHER NAMES:

HOME ADDRESS:

Telephone No.:   Next of Kin:

               Address:

Date of Birth	Place of Birth	Nationality	Married/Single	Children

POSITION APPLIED FOR:

SOURCE OF APPLICATION: Newspaper/Agency/Friend please state:

DETAILS OF EDUCATION FROM AGE 11, include University Course and Part-time study

Date started	Date left	Name & address of Schools, Colleges, University	Exams taken, subjects passed	Quals. & Grades

Other training such as Evening classes:

APPRENTICESHIP:

Date started	Date left	Name of Company	Salary	Reason for leaving

LANGUAGES: Bilingual/Fluent/Useable

HOBBIES & INTERESTS (names of Societies/Institutions of which you are a member

MEDICAL HISTORY
Have you ever had or do you suffer from:-

Any serious illness . . . . Major operation . . . .

Epileptic fits . . . . Asthma . . . .

Bronchial disorders . . . . Skin complaint . . . .

Are you willing to have a medical examination? . . . .

3.9 Initial selection

If you have carried out all the previous stages correctly in a real situation you will have drafted an advert and may have placed your advert. So people are either ringing up, or writing, or calling in. Now you need to begin collecting your information in a systematic way and for that we use an application form.

JOB HISTORY (start with most recent Company)

Employer's name and address	From	To	Position held	Salary	Reason for leaving

Notice of termination required by present employer? . . . .

When could you start? . . . .   Do you have any holidays already arranged?
. . . .

Have you ever been asked to resign or been dismissed? . . . .

Give a brief reason why you wish to work for our Company? . . . .

. . . .

. . . .

The Company may approach any of the Employers listed to provide a reference on your behalf.

Names and address of TWO people, not relatives, from whom personal references may be obtained:—

1.   2.

DECLARATION:

The above particulars are correct and I understand that all appointments are subject to:—

    a)   satisfactory references

    b)   the entries on this form being accurate, and

    c)   may be subject to a medical report

Signed . . . .   Date . . . .

FOR OFFICE USE ONLY

Starting date . . . .   Position . . . .

Salary . . . .   Full-time / part-time

Salon / Branch . . . .

References applied for: Received:

Interview Notes:

Fig. 3.11 Sample application for employment form.

The application form serves as a quick and easy way of collecting much of the information we need about our possible new staff member. Experience has shown that very few people in the hairdressing industry have used application forms yet this is one of the quickest forms of:

- Collecting information
- Screening-out those people unsuitable for the job

Figure 3.11 shows an application form specially designed for the hairdressing industry. All applicants should complete this as it forms the first key part in the selection process. Application forms of this kind are useful for a number of reasons:

(1) It collects the same information on every applicant.
(2) It is a valuable aid to the interviewer. It gives basic information and highlights areas to question.
(3) If the person is selected it can form the basis of his/her personnel (and personal) record.
(4) It will tell you the kind of people who saw your advert and who want to come and work for you.

Remember, too, to be observant if the applicant comes into the salon or rings up or even writes a letter in to you:

- What did they look like?
- How did they speak? Confidently? Brightly?
- What was their handwriting/spelling/English like?

You must adopt the detective role, always looking for new clues.

Many salons, when candidates apply, send not only an application form but also further information/details on the job, salon etc. This can be useful as it saves explanation in the interview and allows the time to be more profitably used.

Now let us assume you have a number of returned completed application forms. Now you can use your 'seven-point plan' person specification to sift through the candidates and to identify which one(s) you wish to interview. Sort them into three piles – *possibles*, *doubtfuls* and *rejects* – according to whether they meet the criteria you have used, e.g. suppose you had three applicants – the data might be:

		Copied from forms		
Item	Required	Person A	Person B	Person C
Age	21–30	35	24	21
Experience	2–3 years	7	3	2
Health	excellent	poor	very good	?

This would make A a reject, B a possible and C a doubtful. Would you agree?

Now interview only the possibles unless there are only one or two, in which case look very carefully at the doubtfuls to see if they might be worth a chance. Notice how this analysis will help you interview by identifying areas of uncertainty, e.g. you would ask C about their health.

So now you have decided which of the potential candidates to interview you need to write or telephone and invite them. Include details of how to get to you and be sure they are clear as to time and place and tell them how long it will take. If you need other staff to be present then make sure they will be there. Let candidates know if you are not going to interview them and thank them for applying. Be polite and don't hurt feelings.

So we come to the day of the interview. Make sure you read each applicant's form before you interview them, and identify the areas which you particularly wish to question them on. Make sure you have all your papers with you:

- Job description
- Person specification

- Application form
- Notes/questions

Make the necessary arrangements to see their work if this is going to be necessary. You may like to prepare *questions in advance*. Many professional interviewers do this.

The five basic rules of interviewing are:

(1) Preparation before interview.
(2) Establish rapport with the candidates.
(3) Structure the content of the interview in order to get the information *you* want.
(4) Control the interview in an unobtrusive way so that it appears logical.
(5) Give the candidates the information *they* want to make a decision.

We discuss interviewing skills and techniques in more detail in the next section.

3.10 The interview

What is the secret of good interviewing? Many books have been written on this subject but we indicate the guidelines we feel you need to bear in mind when interviewing. The key points are to:

(1) Establish rapport and ensure that the candidate will talk freely with you
(2) Structure content to obtain the information that you require
(3) Control structure to keep on track and collect relevant information

3.10.1 Opening the interview

(1) It is vital here to establish rapport. Introduce yourself. Welcome the candidate. Offer coffee/tea etc. Make a small amount of small talk, e.g. how did they get here, what do they think of the salon?
(2) Next explain to the candidate exactly what will happen to him/her, i.e. practical test and when he/she will know if they are successful.
(3) Beware of immediate impressions. They are usually false.
(4) Mention you intend to take notes if you intend to.

3.10.2 Running the interview

(1) The aims are to get the person to talk freely and openly about relevant areas and to check out specific information.
(2) Remember you also need to complete the information on all the candidates as per your person specification.
(3) One of the common sequences used in interviews is:

- What they are doing now – skills etc.
- What they have done in the past – skills etc.
- What they want for the future – development/ambition
- Why they have applied for the job
- What about leisure activities/interests
- Their family background and personal circumstances
- Check facts collected

- Allow candidate to ask questions or to offer any additional items about him/herself
- Close interview – see later

The first two items are relative 'safe' areas and candidates can relax and discuss themselves freely before you move onto more searching areas.

We discuss questions and questioning techniques in the following section.

Questions and questioning techniques

Interviewers distinguish between a number of types of questions – namely:

- Open
- Closed
- Probing
- Multiple
- Leading
- Ambiguous
- Linking

Some of these are to be avoided, but others have different levels of usefulness. We discuss the main types below.

Open questions are particularly useful in that the candidate has to give information and by acting on this the interviewer can follow on and investigate points.
e.g. 'What do you enjoy doing in your spare time?' or 'Tell me about your present job?'

Closed questions are questions with yes/no answers and are useful for checking points but bad interviewers use too many and they make the interviewer do all the work.
e.g. 'You left XYZ in April?' (Answer: Yes or No)

Probing questions follow on and investigate areas of interest in more depth. They get to the real issues.
e.g. 'Tell me why you left . . .'.
A useful trick is to remember the sequence:

- Open
- Close
- Probe.

e.g.
'Tell me about your last job.'   (open)
'It was awful, well pretty bad.'
'So you didn't like it much.'   (closed)
'No.'
'Why exactly was that?'   (probe)

This is a powerful technique.

Multiple questions are to be avoided and are where the interviewer asks more than one question at the same time.
e.g. 'Did you want to go into hairdressing or did you prefer beauty therapy, or perhaps you wanted to stay on at school, or was it your preference to get married?'

Fig. 3.12 Sample interviewing questions.

'Tell me about ....?'

'Please go on ....?'

'That is interesting. Tell me more ....?'

'What exactly do you mean by ....?'

'What do you like best about ....?'

'What do you like least about ....?'

'What did you enjoy most ....?'

'How did you feel about ....?'

'Why did you ....?'

'What did you ....?'

'Who did you ....?'

'Where did you ....?'

'When did you ....?'

'What exactly happened ....?'

Leading questions are also to be avoided and are questions which contain the answer, i.e. the interviewee knows what you want?
e.g. 'You wouldn't want to move in the next year . . .?'
'Is your health good?'
You will tend to get the answer you want rather than the truth with leading questions.

Ambiguous questions are also to be avoided as are unclear questions, i.e. where people can misunderstand the question.
e.g. 'Do you chat to clients?' could mean:

● Do you talk to them, i.e. friendly
● Do you talk to them all the time, i.e. 'chatter on'

So when the person answers – which do they mean? Using simple, clear and precise language bearing in mind the needs of your interviewee is the secret.

Linking questions are useful whenever you wish to move onto a new topic or develop logic – they are often reflective.
e.g. 'So you left school . . . then . . . so what do you wish to do next?' They link the various sections of the interview together.

Some interviewers learn questions and we have recorded some generally useful ones in Fig. 3.12. You might like to look at these and categorise them to help you at the interviewing stage.

3.10.3 Ending the interview

(1) The candidate may well decide he or she isn't interested in which case thank them and close the interview.
(2) If you are unhappy with the candidate thank them for coming and say you will get in touch (indicate *when*).
(3) If you think the candidate is a strong one then check vital details, e.g. availability/salary etc. You may want to arrange a second interview.

In any case make sure you thank them for coming and *do* contact them. Courtesy costs little and does a lot for your reputation.

3.10.4 Immediately after the interview

(1) Write up your notes immediately and check your findings against the specification.
(2) Draw a conclusion about whether the candidate is *strong, medium* or *weak* in terms of what you wish and note particularly the *good* and *bad* features.
(3) Review your own interviewing technique. Was it fair? Did I get all the information I needed?

Self review is the key to interview success!
   You may have the interview within a framework which involves the use of other kinds of tests/measures, e.g.:

- Written tests
- Trade tests/practicals
- References, etc.

In the next section we show you other methods and look at their usefulness as a means of improving selection.

3.10.5 Basic interviewing checklist

(1) Decide in advance the purpose of the interview and the key areas you wish to examine in it.
(2) Collect in advance as many relevant facts as possible (e.g. a job specification and completed application form and the person specification).
(3) Think in advance about the interview:

- Study the information available against the criteria you have set.
- Consider the context of the interview and the known characteristics and expectations of the interviewee and decide what behaviour would be most appropriate.
- Decide on the main points you need to cover in terms of *both giving* and *obtaining* information.
- Consider the type of question\which will encourage unbiased response.

- Plan a (flexible) scheme.
- Decide on roles for each member of the panel (if appropriate).

(4) Inform the person to be interviewed in a way which does not arouse anxiety or hostility (e.g. by an informal letter; by keeping to appointment times so that he or she does not wait and wonder).

(5) Open the interview in a way which puts the interviewee at ease. Avoid rushing to the most significant or complex topic before the person is fully at ease.

(6) Interview in comfortable surroundings. Consider the impact that the location and its layout will have upon the interviewee. The aim is to make the candidate feel at ease.

(7) Avoid interruptions, e.g. try to have telephone calls transferred. Try to put other pressing matters out of your mind.

(8) Interview alone wherever possible. When you must interview with another interviewer, give careful consideration to your respective roles and the effects of your interactions on the interviewee.

(9) Preserve an atmosphere of calm. Never show that you have other things to do. Do not argue with the interviewee.

(10) Talk as little as you possibly can. Aim for the candidate to give you as much as possible.

(11) Do not interrupt; do not criticise; do not make moral judgements about opinions expressed (even favourable ones); do not express your own opinions (even by leading questions).

(12) Listen to what the interviewee says; listen for things that are not or cannot be said; and show that you are listening. Be interested in the candidate and what he/she has to say.

(13) Look for underlying feelings and attitudes.

(14) Summarise from time to time. It helps the person being interviewed to realise your interest and to see problems more clearly. It also checks out that you have understood the replies.

(15) Ask questions

- Which need more than yes or no for an answer
- Which do not suggest how they should be answered
- Which require specific replies
- Which help to reveal feelings
- Which are unambiguous
- Which are clear and comprehensible

(16) Time your questions. Follow the interviewee's lead whenever possible. Keep difficult questions until confidence is established. Keep the interview relevant. Be sensitive to the interviewee.

(17) Recognise your own biases/prejudices/stereotypes:

- Personal prejudices and associations, e.g. He looks like the last person (awful!). Crooked stockings mean an untidy mind. A dead fish handshake means a flabby personality.
- Too much reliance on outstanding merits and demerits (halo effect).

(18) Do not try to achieve too much in one interview. Set a realistic finishing time and handle what cannot be achieved by that time on another occasion.

(19) Agree on future action with the interviewee and inform the interviewee of what is to happen.

(20) Leave the person being interviewed with the feeling that he or she has had a satisfactory hearing. Give an opportunity to ask questions and give reasonable answers if you can.

After the interview

- Aim for a balanced judgement.
- Take notes while impressions are still fresh (to counteract halo effect).
- Collect collaborative evidence, references, test results, etc. where appropriate.
- Take any necessary action promptly.
- Compare candidates against the criteria developed in the employee specification.
- Decide whether you have a poor/average/good candidate and note specific strengths and weaknesses.
- Question yourself: 'Did I give a fair interview?'

3.11 Other methods of selection

The evidence on interviews is that they are not particularly valid as a means of selection and it is a common observation that mistakes can in fact occur. This is no justification for poor interviewing however as this will simply

Fig. 3.13
Sources of information about candidates.

Area of interest	Method(s) available
(1) Physical appearance, health etc.	Interview/observation Medical examination References
(2) Attainments or achievements	School records/certificates Work experience/references Interview Trade tests Demonstration/practical
(3) Intelligence	Interview Tests
(4) Special talents or abilities e.g. numeracy	Interview Tests
(5) Personal interests or leisure activities	Interview Checklists Tests
(6) Disposition or personality factors	Interview/references School records/personality tests
(7) Personal circumstances	Interview
(8) Motivation to work	Interview/references Tests

worsen the situation further. Perhaps an analogy would be to try to cut grass with scissors – not particularly suitable but sharp scissors would certainly be better than blunt ones.

However, remembering that the aim of the selection interview is to gain information then there are other ways we can obtain information about candidates. Figure 3.13 shows areas of interest and the selection techniques available to us. Notice that the interview is the best single way and all the other methods supplement and check it.

These alternative methods can support the interview however and the evidence is that they will make it more realistic and hence more valid. The problem is that in some cases these alternatives may be unreliable and we have to cross-check the information. Also some of these techniques require expert use and interpretation and are not for the amateur interviewer. The methods discussed below are:

(1) References
(2) Medical examination
(3) Use of school reports/records/certificates
(4) Demonstration/practicals
(5) Tests and checklists
(6) Use of outside consultants or selection agencies
(7) Probation period

3.11.1 *References*

References should be used to check *factual data only* in most cases, e.g.:

- Date of joining
- Date of leaving
- Job/duties
- Salary
- Days absent etc.

Under these questions most people will give honest and truthful answers.

If you know the *referee* personally then it may be worth asking for other information if you know that person to be genuinely honest and truthful. Otherwise the information may be suspect. The telephone is the quickest method to obtain such references. Ask the candidate for permission to do so *beforehand* though.

3.11.2 *Medical examinations*

These are essential for senior positions especially if you have extensive pension or sick pay schemes.

Many hairdressers ask *all* new staff for a doctor's report (at employer's expense) as a means of checking they are not ill, do not have infectious diseases etc. (Doctors will only send this information to you if the candidate permits.)

Our view would be to obtain a doctor's report for people in senior positions who have extensive pension or sick pay schemes or if you have any concern that the candidate's health may be suspect.

3.11.3 *Use of school reports/records/certificates*

School certificates etc. are useful evidence that qualifications have been obtained and that training has been undergone. It is not uncommon for candidates to pretend to have done things they have not.

School reports are often illuminating insights into the candidate's personality and for young school-leavers possibly the only evidence of what they are actually like. Use these carefully however and take the overall view – sometimes teachers don't get on with students and so on. Use them as a check against your own findings.

3.11.4 *Use of demonstrations/practicals*

This is clearly a most powerful method of finding out what candidates can do. Note that although many hairdressers use it to see how technically competent candidates are, you could also use it to see how candidates deal with clients and their selling skills – two difficult areas to measure. You could do this by *role play* i.e. get one of the staff to 'play' a customer and the candidate to 'play' the stylist and look at how they perform.

These methods could also be used to look at the manner in which receptionists answer the phone or managers talk to staff etc. In the US many interviewers use long periods of such methods to try to see how people will actually perform 'on the job' before taking them on to do that job.

3.11.5 *Use of tests*

There are probably no selection methods more misunderstood, misinterpreted or abused than tests. For our purposes we consider tests of four types:

(1) 'Trade tests'
(2) Simple skills tests
(3) Aptitude tests
(4) Personality tests

In all cases the user of the test *must be properly trained to administer it and use it*. This means in the case of (4) a psychologist or trained tester. Also only use tests which have been properly designed, tested and validated for the purpose for which you intend to use them. Improperly used tests are:

- Immoral and possibly illegal
- A waste of time as they give no useful information
- Likely to cause loss of faith in test procedures

We have been appalled at the abuses we have seen and by no means only in the hairdressing industry.

Trade tests are special tests designed to test knowledge of facts/skills needed to do the job. They have been designed specially for the trade and are a measure of how much the person knows about the job. Sometimes they are written (pen/pencil), sometimes they are practical, sometimes a mixture of the two. They are useful for testing areas of professional competence.

e.g. How many towels should you use for shampooing? . . . Why?

ISM can provide specially designed tests of this type if required.

Simple skills tests test additional abilities and skills and might for example:

- Ask candidate to 'cash up'
- Ask candidate to add up figures and calculate wages
- Test client handling or selling skills

These are useful as a way of checking the impression at interview against factual data.

Aptitude tests test not a skill but ability and hence potential for achieving certain skills, e.g.:

- Numerical aptitudes (numbers)
- Verbal aptitude (words)
- Reasoning and intelligence and so on

These are useful for young people who have not yet had the opportunity to acquire skills. You need to know if they have the potential to do so.

Personality tests try to assess a person's personality, or creativity or attitudes or interests (depending on the exact test). These are among the most controversial tests and are usually best used (if required) by trained people (psychologists or teachers) but they can be used to check one's own impression from the interview.

Psychometric tests can be used, particularly for management positions, to assess the personal qualities or capabilities of candidates, but properly trained professionals should be used to ensure the test is validated. Cattell's 16 Personality Factors Test is considered to be the most universally reliable but it must be interpreted by a person trained to this.

Hairdressing tests – working in the salon for a day – can all give a clearer picture of the candidate's ability to 'fit'.

3.11.6 Use of outside consultants/agencies

Consultants can help in a number of areas:

- Improving your selection procedure and documentation
- Interviewing skills training for you and your staff
- Selecting appropriate tests
- Interviewing senior staff with you

They are not cheap but you will get a good level of service, expertise and value for money if you are careful.

Employment agencies will for a fee help you to recruit staff. This can be particularly useful for special staff, e.g. receptionists and managers.

3.11.7 Probation period

We say more about this in Section 3.13 Integration of new staff, but you should remember that this is in one sense part of your selection process as it is an ideal time to correct any errors that may occur during the initial employment period.

3.12 Terms and conditions of employment

Now you have decided the person you wish to employ, you should do a number of other things:

(1) Check he/she wants to come and when etc.
(2) Write to all unsuccessful candidates.
(3) Send new recruit contract of employment and joining information.
(4) Inform other staff of new person's arrival.
(5) Make arrangements for induction.

A Contract of Employment or written particulars of an employee's terms and conditions of employment is important for all employees and Fig. 3.14 shows what should go into a Contract of Employment. This shows the new recruit all the relevant parts of his/her employment relationship and helps him/her to understand exactly what is involved.

Radius clauses

Many salons often ask about radius clauses and it is perfectly possible to incorporate one of these into a Contract of Employment. The key things to remember about radius clauses are:

- They act as a deterrent but can be difficult to enforce unless they are reasonable
- They must have a distance element
- They must have a time element, e.g. one mile restriction for six months

If the salon trades in a busy town then it is much more likely that a radius restriction clause of half a mile and six months would be reasonable and in a city a quarter of a mile for three months.

3.13 Integration of new staff

Informing staff of the new appointment is important if they are to welcome them and give them the initial help and support required during their

Fig. 3.14 What should go into a Contract of Employment.

- Names and addresses of parties
- Date of commencement
- Scale or rate of pay or method of calculation of pay
- How/When paid
- Hours of work
- Holiday entitlements
- Sickness absence arrangements and sick pay scheme details
- Pension scheme details
- Maternity leave provision
- Job title
- Notice period required by both sides before termination
- Disciplinary procedure (including rules)
- Grievance procedure
- Union membership details
- Health and safety provision
- Details of any probation period

These are not always spelt out in detail but one can refer to other documents, e.g. job description/rules etc. These must be available (e.g. on a noticeboard or in a staff manual) for scrutiny.

introductory period. Many salons do not concentrate enough time and thought into this aspect of their business and it is for this reason that staff take longer to integrate into their new environment. In fact, research shows that many people leave salons within the first three months of their employment due to lack of thought in this area. In the next section we concentrate on induction training and training requirements.

Induction

Some (larger) salons have a formal induction period to familiarise staff with everything. Others produce a Company Handbook but whatever it is called it needs to tell the new recruit about the items covered by the contract as shown in Fig. 3.14. In addition, the following areas should be included:

- A brief description of the company and its history
- Promotion and training opportunities
- Medical and first aid facilities
- Restaurant/canteen arrangements
- Social/welfare arrangements
- Telephone calls and letters
- Travelling/subsistence

This may be a booklet or just a typed document.

The induction process is designed to:

- Familiarise new employees and put them at ease
- Interest them (motivate) in the new job
- Provide basic information about the new job/company
- Indicate standards and behaviour expected from them
- Show them prospects of development in the company
- Provide product knowledge training, e.g. if a stylist is familiar with one major manufacturer's products and your salon uses another product range then it is essential that product knowledge training is given at this stage if the salon wishes to ensure productivity is reached within a short space of time
- Provide training in the new skills that the new employee does not possess, starting as soon as possible after employment

The aim is to encourage and to motivate staff to stay. Remember perfect jobs for perfect people do not exist! We must, when employing staff, identify the gaps in their skills and ensure that the new skills or re-training skills required are introduced at this stage. It is lack of training, not just in procedures but in skill knowledge, that is one of the greatest reasons why staff do not integrate quickly into a new environment.

Trial period

A trial period can be used to see if both sides are suited. Although this can be useful, salon owners should beware of using it as a substitute for good selection as you should only not renew contracts for extreme reasons, usually discipline/behaviour, and not incompetence. 'Hire and fire' policies demotivate *all* staff and should be avoided if at all possible.

You have now learnt the whole process of:

- Analysing the job

- Deciding the person you are looking for
- Recruiting them
- Selecting them
- Taking them on and inducting them

If you implement what we have suggested then you have the key to successful salons – good staff!

Good staff, as many salon owners are aware, do not just happen, they are created by the amount of time, energy and training that is invested in them. In our opinion, training is the answer to all of the ills of the hairdressing industry and those salons that have recognised this element and use it effectively are the ones that will have successful salons.

3.13.1 Induction training

In the previous section, we stressed how important it was to integrate new staff so they became effective in the shortest possible time. The hairdressing industry lacks a minimum standard of skills required to be able to do the job of hairdresser, hairdressing manager or salon owner so that when we recruit new staff they bring with them methods and ways of working which we may not like. It is the salon owner or manager's responsibility to ensure that staff are able to work within their framework unless they want to adopt the new employee's methods of work.

We have already mentioned that there will never be perfect people for perfect jobs – we must make square pegs fit into round holes by *training*.

Training can be categorised into the following areas:

- Trainee/apprenticeship training
- Technical training, e.g. perming and colouring, hairdressing
- Communication skills training
- Service skills training
- Administrative/systems training
- Management training

Trainees/apprentices

Traditionally, the industry has trained apprentices and trainees by the 'sitting watching Nelly' or 'watch what I do then have a go yourself' approach. Some salons train staff by the watching and practising approach but use colleges or manufacturers to help them with the technical and theoretical side of hairdressing.

Most salons, however, train staff in the evenings on the pretext that working on models affects the service to clients. But why do we employ trainees anyway? Are they cleaners and coffee makers or do we wish to develop staff at the optimum pace in order to employ them as stylists in the shortest possible time? If we want cleaners and coffee makers why don't we employ assistants to do these menial tasks?

Anyone who has ever gone to adult evening classes or had to study a new subject will tell you how tired they are at the end of the day. Our ability to absorb new information when we are tired is limited, which is why it takes so long to learn! Add to the tiredness factor the fact that most trainees are also trying to acclimatise themselves to working long hours and standing all day after many years of school hours and it is not surprising that an apprentice, on this basis, takes two to three years to learn hairdressing skills. In fact, most trainees receive three hours training per week, 44 weeks a year (deducting seasonally busy times and holidays) which means they receive 49 days of training or 396 hours to become a hairdresser!

If we trained trainees one full day a week we would complete their training in 12 to 18 months and still during that time give them ample opportunity to practise.

Decline of school leavers

Due to the drop in school leavers available for employment, the industry is now competing for the same people as other sectors of industry. This has been caused by:

- Reduction in the birth rate during the 1970s which continued until 1984
- Parents encouraging children to obtain qualifications and higher education
- Parents/children wanting high pay upon leaving school

Banks, insurance companies, the armed forces, the police force, hotels, catering and retailing are all competing for school leavers. The question we must ask within the hairdressing industry is why should young people want to work in hairdressing? What does it have to offer?

At the moment it has the image of offering:

- Low pay
- Poor quality training
- Bad conditions of employment
- Fragmented career opportunities

We must make the industry more attractive in the future by the following approach:

- Formalised, systematic training held during the day in the company's time
- Recognised qualifications
- Shorter training period, e.g. 12–18 months
- Realistic pay
- Terms and conditions of employment comparable to other industries, e.g. holidays, sick pay
- Promote career opportunities
- Offer on-going training

Technical training

The most profitable area of a hairdressing business is the technical services we offer clients – if we get our prices right, train staff to work at speed and to sell the services with confidence.

Many staff do not sell technical services because they do not feel confident about this side of their work. There are salons who train their staff in perming and colouring techniques, ensuring they understand the theory and have product knowledge and continue to receive on-going creative training in technical work. *The majority, however, do not.*

That is why salons are frequently looking for staff knowledgeable in colouring and perming and is one of the reasons why manufacturers offer courses on technical work to ensure stylists become competent and confident at technical work.

We must ensure staff are thoroughly trained in this area otherwise they will not sell technical services. Promoting these services becomes a waste of money if the staff lack confidence to carry out the work. In fact, colouring is one of the most profitable areas of hairdressing yet, along with retailing, is the greatest weakness within the industry. Recent manufacturers' surveys show that the entire industry generates just 7 per cent of hairdressing services from colouring. A sad state of affairs. No wonder the chemists and supermarkets are laughing all the way to the bank!

Communications skills training

If staff were asked to write down how much of their day is spent communicating they would find that 80 per cent of their time is occupied in giving information and listening. Analyse the job of a stylist and we find that 40 per cent of the work of the hairdresser is practical skills such as hairdressing, paperwork and cleaning and 60 per cent communication skills.

To be able to communicate is not a talent – it is a *skill*. We can all learn to communicate effectively if we want to and, more importantly, if we realise how important it is so that our working day runs smoothly. Yet many stylists have spent a number of years learning how to cut, colour and perm hair but have never been trained in how to talk and listen to clients. We have all heard of brilliant hairdressers who are creative and produce fabulous haircuts but they do not talk to their clients. The client begins to think that she has upset the stylist.

If we look at the cycle of communication in a salon, we will see that from when a client first contacts us to when she leaves communication is vital. We must communicate effectively at the consultation stage because it is *this stage where misunderstandings begin*. The client is trying to express what she wants, the stylist fails to understand what she requires, so she leaves the salon unhappy or dissatisfied with the service or style she has received.

At the backwash, we can begin to reinforce what was said at the consultation stage or to sow the seed of the products which we will be using on her hair. How many times have you heard at the backwash a trainee asking a client 'do you want a conditioner' or 'I don't really use the products myself'?

When the client reaches the styling position, how many times does the stylist listen *actively* to what the client is saying or recognise the signals which indicate an interest in additional services? We are often too busy being concerned about what else is going on in the salon to notice.

When the client goes to the reception area to pay her bill how often do we check that she is happy with her hair and the service she has received? The correct questioning techniques at this stage will help us to identify how she feels. It is also the key time to ensure she rebooks for a future appointment.

Finally, how often do we place emphasis upon the client departing and thanking her for her custom so that she leaves with a good impression?

Communication skills training must cover how to give and receive information and the part our body language plays in communicating. We must learn that it is not what we say but the way that we say it that generates a positive response. We need to learn questioning techniques to extract information from clients and to learn to actively listen. We need to be aware

Fig. 3.15 The cycle of communication.

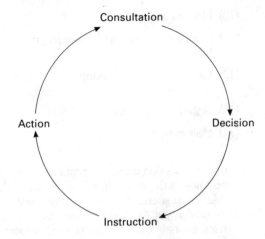

of the physical and emotional barriers that prevent us from listening so that we can overcome them. All of these skills are crucial if we wish to be successful hairdressers.

Service skills training

We have already mentioned that the industry places too little emphasis upon communication skills but another area of neglect is that of service training. Many hairdressers believe that their job is to produce high quality work whereas in fact it is just as important if not more so to make the client happy to part with her money.

Market research shows that clients visit a particular salon for a variety of reasons (see Fig. 1.1). Very few of them are to do with hairdressing. It is service, personality and atmosphere which make clients return regularly.

How much training is given within the salon on offering *a consistent standard of service* because the salon has not clearly identified how each client should be treated? Look at the following areas and tick which ones are clearly defined within the salon:

	Clear procedure	No procedure
(1) Telephone technique	————	————
(2) Welcome procedure	————	————
(3) Collecting client information	————	————
(4) Coat/gowning-up procedure on arrival	————	————
(5) Consultation	————	————
(6) Home care advice	————	————
(7) Backwash procedure	————	————
(8) Refreshments	————	————
(9) Styling position procedure	————	————

(10) Home care advice by stylist

(11) Check-out procedure – settling the
bill

(12) Coat/gowning procedure on
departure

(13) Booking appointments

(14) Hair care advice

If you are a salon owner or manager reading this book ask your staff what
they think is the procedure in each area. The answers may surprise you.

Market research also shows that clients want more information on home
care advice yet we seem reticent at providing it. Why is this? Professional
advice on hair care products from supermarkets and chemists does not
happen so we must use our knowledge to ensure the client feels confident
about our services – *otherwise why should the client visit our salon instead
of our competitor?*

Administrative/systems training

Hairdressers often hate paperwork and systems of any kind but without
them salons cannot function. The more a salon group expands, the more
systems and procedures are required. Without them the salon is chaos and
projects a disorganised image to the client as well as making it more stressful
for the staff to function on a daily basis.

Training must be given in salons to ensure the systems are understood and
continue to function. The following areas need systems to make the salon
function smoothly:

- Appointment system
- Bill procedure
- Client record cards
- Technical records
- Cashing-up procedure
- Recording client service information
- Holiday records
- Absentee procedure
- Time keeping
- Stock control

Management training

Many staff promoted into management or supervisory positions do not
receive any kind of management training. Out of 165 000 people employed in
hairdressing, only 4000 have ever been on any kind of management training
course or seminar. The UK invests less money in training, particularly
management training, than any other country in Europe. If we wish to
overcome the skills shortage at management level first and foremost we must

train people, by developing our staff to set standards of professionalism within the industry.

At present, the process of developing management tends to be 'sink or swim'. Unfortunately, many people drown this way or lose their confidence so that they never want to try again. We must have recognised qualifications within the industry. This would set a standard of the way we run our businesses in the future. In many European countries at the present time hairdressers are unable to open hairdressing salons unless they have passed a Master's Certificate or employ someone within their organisation who has passed this certificate.

The Management Charter Initiative has pioneered two levels of recognised management qualifications to set minimum standards of good management practice that are recognised throughout the UK. The first is MCI I Certificate Level which is NVQ Level 4, and MCI II Diploma Level which is NVQ Level 5. The scheme helps managers to gain recognised qualifications by building up a portfolio of work-related evidence such as the Systems, Procedures and Practices that are already used within many professionally run hairdressing salons. The MCI have licensed Crediting Competence Centres and there are a number of awarding bodies who can award the Certificates and Diplomas to candidates who have successfully reached the standards. Further information regarding this is available from the Management Charter Initiative – see further details under 'Useful Addresses' at the back of the book.

Few managers are given job descriptions which clearly define their responsibilities and their levels of authority (see Section 3.3). For example how much authority does a manager have to recruit or terminate staff?

Many managers often feel their job is dealing with problems and aggravation from both sides – staff and salon owners – without any clearly defined areas of responsibility and authority. An impossible situation in which to function effectively, which is one of the reasons why managers become demotivated, opt out of making decisions or pass the buck up or down the hierarchy.

Having a clearly defined job description is no use whatsoever if the person responsible for doing the job does not *know how to do it*. Staff must be trained in the principles of managing and how to develop their skills to accept the responsibilities of the job. Without training a job description is a useless document.

Those salon managers or owners who have been managing for several years need to recognise that they continually need to be effective and ahead of their competitors. They must learn how to train the staff that they have and how to manage the most valuable asset in their business – people. Without the people, salon owners and managers might just as well rent a chair in a salon or become a home hairdresser. Staff who have a good education and receive training and development, however, will question and challenge decisions made by managers and salon owners. We can overcome this by involving staff in the way we run our businesses and by consulting them. We must reward the staff that work for our businesses, not just financially but by recognition, by praising them and, certainly at management level, by giving them a profit share of the business. It is better to give part of the profit back to the staff as opposed to spending years training and developing them only to find that because they are not rewarded accordingly or consulted they open up their own businesses in direct competition.

This approach may sound totally alien to some salon owners but we do not live in the days of the lord of the manor and the serfs and we cannot run our businesses in this way if we wish staff to continue to work for us and to be committed and motivated. We must involve them, share our successes with them and develop them wherever possible.

Chapter Four
Managing People

4.1 What is managing?

It is not our intention in this chapter to re-write all the management theories which can be obtained from the local library, but we have listed in the Appendix some recommended books for those readers who wish to pursue this subject in greater depth.

Ask a salon owner what is meant by 'managing' and the answer will be many different things. The role of the manager, however, can be split into fourteen key functions covering five major categories. These are:

(1) The relationship roles
(2) The information role
(3) The decision making role
(4) Trainer
(5) Worker

Fig. 4.1 The five management roles. (1) The relationship role. (2) The information role. (3) The decision making role. (4) The manager as trainer. (5) The manager as worker.

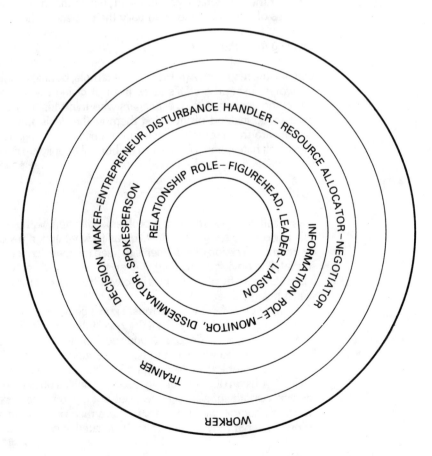

4.1.1 *The relationship roles*

These fall into three key categories – figurehead, leader and liaison with others.

(1) Figurehead

As head of a salon the manager has to behave as a figurehead when carrying out his or her function. Whether this is awarding promotional prizes, inter-salon trainee awards or long service awards, the building of these relationships is important not only within the organisation but externally with the consumer and the trade.

(2) Leader

The manager or owner must act as a leader – either directly using formal authority or indirectly using other methods of influencing people. He or she has to direct and motivate staff to achieve goals, to help them to see that they can satisfy their personal needs by working on agreed tasks. The manager is exposed in this role – the success of the salon depends very much on developing and practising the necessary influencing skills and making good use of his or her authority.

We must all lead by example. In other words, we cannot have one set of rules for the staff which, as the leader, we continually break. This will result in a loss of credibility and eventually the respect of the staff.

Leading from the front

Leading the team from the front – for example, by always using our own ideas or, worse, using the staff's ideas but not giving them proper credit – has unwanted consequences. Managers who think for their staff and tell them what to do instead of involving them in the decision-making process will demotivate them, create a lack of commitment and generate resentment. Most staff hate being told what to do but will happily carry out an instruction if the reasons are explained.

Leading from behind or the Centre

Many staff, if presented with a problem, will often, with some guidelines, be able to come to a logical conclusion as to what action needs to be taken to overcome it. The job of manager is to keep the team focused on the problems so that, like driving a car, they stay on the road and get to their destination. It is much more fun if the team is involved in arriving at the destination instead of just being passengers.

As the leader of a team, you must expect people to come to you for advice. In fact, you should be worried if they don't. It may not always be convenient or easy but it is an obligation of your position as well as an act of friendship. Being prepared to listen and to act as a sounding board will often help staff to put their problems into perspective. Your staff will come to value your advice if you can offer useful suggestions, such as putting them in touch with the appropriate support services, but not if you make unrealistic promises which are not followed up or try to solve their personal problems for them. Above all, what they tell you must be treated in confidence – they may talk about it to others but will not expect you to do so. The following action should be taken:

(a) Take a personal interest in all your staff. Don't say 'don't bring your problems to work; pull yourself together'. Be available for advice and help.
(b) Be a good listener and try to offer helpful suggestions.
(c) Take the initiative in introducing staff to support services which may be helpful to them.
(d) When asked for advice concentrate on the facts, not the emotions.
(e) Keep your counselling confidential.

(3) Liaison with others

The manager needs to establish and maintain relationships with others outside the normal chain of command. For example, in a large salon group he or she needs to maintain contact with his peers and people outside his own salon. He or she also needs to spend time with his or her boss! Time needs to be spent building relationships to increase the manager's own personal information network and to make it possible to acquire informally the information needed to do the job.

4.1.2 *The information role*

Managers spend about 40 per cent of their time handling and processing information. This may well be spoken, written, formal or informal. Information can be power, but it can only be used as a basis for decision making. The manager has three information roles:

(1) Monitor

As monitor he or she collects information from his or her network (information network). This may not always be factual – it could be gossip or other third-hand information – but may because of the way in which much of it is gathered consist of inferences and assumptions which he or she has to sift and filter into some relevant form.

(2) Disseminator

As a 'sifter' of information the manager passes on any necessary information to the staff. Anyone who leads a team needs to communicate with them. Communication is a two-way process – we must give information and keep the team informed but, just as importantly, we must take time to listen.
Make sure the team knows what they have to do and why
This means explaining the goals and objectives to the team, and the particular task that has been set. Explain why it is important and tell or show them how to achieve it.
Listen to the team's views
Have regular meetings even if you work with them on the salon floor every day. Set time aside for regular, if brief, meetings with your staff, not only to pass on information but to invite comments and listen to suggestions.
Tell superiors what is happening and pass on the staff's views
There is no point in consulting your staff unless you pass on the findings or any queries that they raise to higher management. This does not mean

discussing all the detail with your boss but he or she should know what is going on and what people are thinking so that they are not faced suddenly with an unexpected crisis.

(3) Spokesperson

As spokesperson the manager passes some information to people outside his or her salon or branch. For example, he or she keeps other salons or departments and key people in the company informed of his or her performance and the performance of the salon. (He or she must take responsibility for this function and not expect senior people within the organisation always to ask for information.)

4.1.3 The decision-making role

An important factor in the performance of the manager is the quality of his/ her decision making. Generally, the higher in the hierarchy the position, the greater the time span of decision making. (Directors make strategic decisions – managers make day-to-day operational ones.) But no matter what the time span may be, eventually the effectiveness of decisions can be and is measured. Managers perform in four decisional roles:

(1) Entrepreneur

The manager looks for changes or potential changes in the environment and tries to modify and adapt his salon to cope with these. Customers, for example, may expect the stylist to handle the hairdressing service through-out the total visit; they expect inclusive pricing and dislike extras on the bill.

(2) Disturbance handler

This is the role which occupies most of the time of many salon managers – reacting or responding to pressures and unexpected events. Short-term decisions have to be made to deal with staff shortages or running out of stock. The culture of many salons is that the owners expect managers to produce short-term results but at the cost of putting off planning and thinking long term.

Disturbance handling means often acting as a referee or umpire and being seen to be fair. This sometimes means not being the most popular person, but if you fail to enforce the company's regulations when someone breaks the rules and fail to assert your authority either from fear, lack of confidence or indifference, you are being unfair to the rest of the team as well as to the management of the salon.

There are times when a manager has not only to interpret the company's rules and procedures but to enforce them as well. People at work are fulfilling a contract with their employers which gives both sides privileges and obligations. These are worked out as a set of rules of behaviour which may be partly written, partly verbal. It is essential that you, as the manager, know these rules for you will have to act as an umpire or referee to see that they are observed. This does not mean that you have to be heavy-handed and constantly pointing the finger or taking disciplinary action. Indeed, you will soon be in trouble both with senior managers and staff and demotivate people if you do. If a breach of discipline is serious, or is an open challenge to your authority, then you have no alternative but to act firmly. If the problem or issue is outside your experience or competence you will need to refer it upwards to your immediate superior. On every occasion it is important for you to be seen to be fair and impartial. The chances are that the rest of the team will then support you. The following action should be taken:

- Make sure that every member of the team pulls his or her weight
- If there is a breach of discipline do not reprimand staff in front of others, but do it privately
- Try to find out the reason for what has gone wrong, avoid speculation, and give fair warning of any steps you intend to take
- Refer upwards any difficulty if it is beyond your competence or experience
- Be seen to be fair and impartial

(3) Resource allocator

The manager decides how resources of both stock and people are to be used. He or she decides who gets which clients and when, how much of his or her own time is to be spent on various aspects of the job. Perhaps the most valuable resource is his or her own time – this is where good time management is the measurement of a successful manager.

(4) Negotiator

The manager has to spend considerable time negotiating not only with his boss but also his staff and with colleagues. Negotiating and influencing skills are essential to be an effective manager – not telling people but influencing the way they think.

4.1.4 The manager as a trainer

As head of the team the staff will rely upon you to teach them the 'tricks of the trade'. You will already be skilled in many of their tasks. Part of the job is to pass on your knowledge in a way and at a speed that is suitable for them (see Section 4.2: Communication and Chapter 6: Training).

There may be some tasks with which you are not familiar, either because you have never had to do them or because it is some time since you last did them. It is impossible to be able to carry out every aspect of your staff's job as capably as they can. Acknowledging that you can learn from them too will help them feel they have a genuine working partnership instead of a know-it-all, seen-it-all, done-it-all manager. We must, therefore, ensure that we:

- Understand fully the job of each member of staff;
- Ensure that each team member understands the job and can do the job;
- Are not afraid to learn even from subordinates.

4.1.5 The manager as worker

On the one hand it is important that you should be seen to be doing a reasonable portion of productive work, and that your standards should be as high as the staff's to set an example, e.g. quality haircuts, offering good service, treating clients civilly (even if they have been coming to you for twenty years), dressing the part, selling profitable services and generally setting an example. On the other hand, it is just as important to share out the key work, particularly the new clients, so that everyone has some incentive to get on with their part of the job.

4.1.6   Conclusions

There is a balance between being prepared to shoulder responsibility for the whole team of which you are a working member and ensuring that you delegate sufficient work so that you do not put yourself in the position of doing everything yourself while the staff sit and drink coffee in the staff room. Delegating always involves some risk but that does not mean to say that we should not give staff responsibility. Being allowed to practise and make mistakes is one way to learn. The role of the manager is to ensure through training and good communication skills that the staff are allowed to develop at the pace that is right for them. The following action should be taken:

- Learn to delegate while doing a fair share of the work yourself.
- See that your standards set an example to the team.
- Give credit where it is due.
- Remember, you are responsible for your whole team's efforts.

As a manager there is a lot to think about. Watching your team grow and develop so that they take responsibility for achieving goals and help to identify the problems as well as work out the solutions is one of the most rewarding aspects of managing people. We must therefore remember the following points:

- Set and maintain standards for the team by giving them clearly defined job descriptions and levels of authority.
- Train them to carry out their duties effectively at the speed and pace that is right for them.
- Be loyal to management and staff.
- Make sure everyone knows what is happening within the company and why.
- Listen to the team's views.
- Face problems before they get out of hand.
- Be firm but fair and try to understand the other person's point of view.
- Be responsible for the team's performance.

4.2 Communication

Communication, whether we are giving or receiving information, is the most fundamental skill that we must learn if we wish to be successful as a trainee, stylist or manager. Everyone plays a role in communication from the most junior member of staff to the manager or salon owner, making the salon function smoothly, efficiently and professionally. The process begins every time we have contact with a client or potential client, whether it is by telephone or in person.

Communication – what is it? The word 'communication' means to impart, transmit or share information. That means to give or to make known to people what it is they need to know. It also means to transmit information by the best possible method which will be explained later in this chapter.

4.2.1 *Why is communication important?*

Communication, if used positively, can help us to:

- Communicate with staff
- Communicate with superiors
- Communicate with clients
- Resolve conflict with staff and clients

Negative communication can easily take control if we become emotional in a situation. This in turn creates misunderstanding so that the relationship between staff, superiors and clients breaks down. Nothing is ever achieved from argument because the situation gets out of control. When we are emotional we do not hear what is being said and often our minds are already made up about the situation or the people. For example, if we do not like someone, then we are much harder on them or we look for the bad points in that particular person. Negative communication means that we will fail to understand our client's needs which, in turn, means that we will fail to offer the services of our salon. This has a direct effect upon everything within the salon. It can affect the amount of commission we earn or whether a client returns. It can prevent the business from growing and prospering. It can affect our image so that people feel we do not care about them, usually because we are too wrapped up in our thoughts or problems of the day.

Positive communication will therefore help us to reduce the day to day stress and pressure of working in the salon because we understand clearly what people want from us, or what we want from them.

Information, ideas, attitudes and knowledge must be freely interchanged within any salon if we want everyone to achieve their goals and for the salon to operate efficiently. The reasons for communication are:

(1) To share information with employees whether they are trainees, stylists, receptionists or managers.
(2) To issue instructions to ensure co-operation and motivation so that staff know what is going on.
(3) To establish positive behaviour in an informal working atmosphere.
(4) To promote training and education – if we cannot communicate how can we train our staff?
(5) To ensure that problems within the salon are identified and dealt with swiftly.

Effective communication is important to ensure that the manager or salon owner gives instructions which are:

- Relevant to the situation
- Communicated in a clear manner
- Understood by the receiver
- Acted upon

This involves the manager or salon owner satisfying the following conditions:

- Be clear as to what you wish to communicate.

- Consider the person to whom you are communicating.
- Use the most effective means of communication to fit the person and the situation.
- Transmit the information at the most appropriate time.
- Try to ensure that your communication has been understood and that the necessary action will be taken.

This means being sensitive to the ability of the person to take in the amount of information you give them. Watch for the following points:

(1) *The amount of information* – information is more effective in small doses, in a logical order rather than large quantities so that it can be readily absorbed.
(2) *Speed of assimilation* – this will vary according to the nature of the information and the receiver. Just because we are in a rush does not mean to say that by passing the information on quickly the receiver will absorb it.
(3) *New information* – this is only meaningful if the brain is also able to associate it with existing knowledge and experience. For example, young people have different life experiences than those of forty plus.
(4) *Interest* – people do not readily absorb information if they are not interested. Where possible, the method of communication should appeal to more than one sense.
(5) *Memory* – communicate the information in such a way that it will be remembered. Use examples and illustrations that will conjure up mental pictures or funny sayings in people's minds, e.g. if we build our people, our people will build our business.

4.2.2 *The process of communication*

When we communicate we go through a number of processes in giving information and receiving it (see Fig. 4.2). During this process we often create different barriers on different occasions or in different situations but once we are aware of what they are, then we can decide what we must do to communicate effectively all the time.

Message

When communicating we must first of all ask ourselves what we wish to achieve – in other words, what is the goal?

If our thoughts are jumbled then the message will be jumbled. There is no computerised sorting system between the brain and the mouth that will put it into a logical sequence. Many hairdressers often say 'I know what I feel but I have difficulty in expressing myself!' An effective way of describing the message is to jot down on a piece of paper what it is we are trying to achieve. When we see all the information written down it often helps us to clarify what we are trying to say and the order in which we say it. It is essential that we give people information in a logical sequence, otherwise we will leave people more confused than when we started.

Method

Once we have decided upon the message we must then decide upon the best

Fig. 4.2 The process of communication.

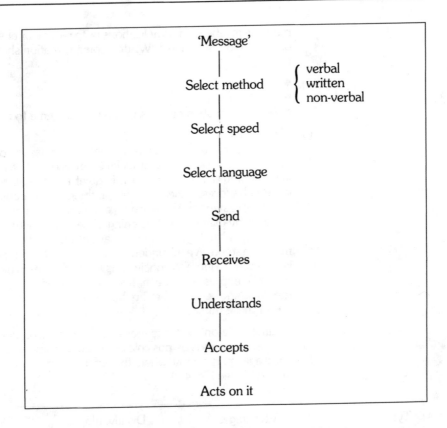

'Message'
|
Select method   { verbal
written
non-verbal
|
Select speed
|
Select language
|
Send
|
Receives
|
Understands
|
Accepts
|
Acts on it

possible medium to use to communicate the message. There are three methods or channels of communication:

(1) *Verbal*

Verbal communication means to speak. The advantage of verbal communication is that it is quick and personalised. When we speak to people on a one-to-one basis face to face we can watch for the reaction to the message showing whether it has been received, accepted and understood.

The disadvantage of the spoken word is that we tend to forget some of the information that has been given. Most people take in approximately 40 per cent of the information particularly when the message is complicated, is new information or they are inexperienced in the area or subject of the message.

The other disadvantage of verbal communication is that there is no action replay. We cannot press a button and remind ourselves of what has just been said.

(2) *Written*

The written word as a method of communication has a number of advantages and disadvantages. We can use sketches, drawings, diagrams and photographs as a method to reinforce the message. We can absorb the information at our own pace and go back over what might have been forgotten, to reinforce the message.

The disadvantage of written communication is that it is often impersonal. There is usually no opportunity to question what the message means and its implications or to receive or observe the reaction of the person receiving it. Written communication should be used if the message is:

- Important
- Complicated
- New information or ideas which will take time to absorb

(3) *Non-verbal*

Non-verbal communication is the method we use to convey information through either our bodily or facial expressions. The advantage of non-verbal communication is that it is quiet and visual. Many people who work in hairdressing learn by visual things, by watching as opposed to reading or listening. The advantage of non-verbal communication is that we learn by example, by watching or seeing something demonstrated.

The disadvantage of non-verbal communication is that it is often misunderstood. We misunderstand others and they misunderstand us. It is very easy to jump to conclusions as to what we think someone's facial or bodily expressions mean. If we see someone laughing at a party are they laughing because they are happy, nervous, or drunk? It could mean any of these things.

To summarise on the three methods of communication we recommend that as many methods as possible are used to communicate and reinforce the message, particularly when the information is new, complicated or controversial (see Fig. 4.3).

Type	Advantages	Disadvantages	Other comments
(1) *Verbal* Talking, meetings etc.	Quick and straight-forward. Cheap. Feedback immediately possible. No distortion if direct.	Requires speaker to be skilful in how to communicate. Choice of language, style etc.	Practice two-way communication *especially* listening skills.
(2) *Written* Noticeboards, letters, memos, handbooks etc.	More permanent record. Can be proven to have been sent. Usually more explicit and needs to be kept simple.	Slow – takes time. Expensive. May not be seen/ received.	Use to support verbal communication as a permanent record etc.
(3) *Non-verbal* Signals	Secretive. Visual and can be done where there is much noise. Difficult to falsify.	Easily misunderstood. Ambiguous.	Use to check for effectiveness of verbal communication and to verify response.

Fig. 4.3 Advantages and disadvantages of different forms of communication.

Speed

By this we mean the speed at which people can take in new information or how quickly we tend to talk. The speed must vary according to the kind of information and the person who will be receiving it.

We also need to remember the size of the audience. One-to-one conversations mean that we can speak at the speed that the other person can take in the information. Ten people – we must speak at the speed everyone can understand. One hundred people – we must speak as if there is a pause between every word. Finally, we must vary the light and shade in the voice – speaking in a monotone makes it very difficult for people to concentrate and receive the message.

Language

This area is of particular importance because hairdressers and manufacturers are very good at talking in a language and jargon that clients do not understand. The term 'acid balanced perm' has quite a different meaning to a hairdresser than it does to a client. This is just as bad as the man in the shop selling us a camera who talks about shutter speeds or a car salesman who talks about front wheel drive. We must always remember the person receiving the message and pitch our language and terminology at the level that the receiver of the message can understand.

Send

Once we have mastered these five areas of communication when giving information to people then we must check that the message has been understood.

Receiving information

We can check that information has been received by the receiver's body language, facial expressions and the questions they ask. For example, nodding the head, smiling, leaning forward in the chair and eye contact all indicate that the message is being received.

Understanding the message

Receiving the message clearly is not the same as understanding what the message means. We must explore this area with the right questioning techniques. Do not take at face value nods, smiles and eye contact as meaning the message has been understood. Use open and probing questions to ensure that it has (see Section 3.10.2 on Questioning techniques).

Accepted

Understanding the message does not mean that we have agreed with it! Listen carefully to the way in which people respond. Does the 'yes' mean 'no' and the 'no' mean 'yes'? Sometimes the receiver may say 'yes' they understand and agree but there are tell-tale signs which show us that they do not. This is where our listening skills must come into play in terms of asking open questions and listening carefully to the replies.

We must *look* for signs of disagreement in the staff's facial expressions or body language. *Listen* to the way in which they reply and if we are in doubt we should *explore* further by asking open and probing questions.

There are other reasons why the receiver may not accept what we have to say. They could be:

- They do not like us or the position we hold
- They may have a grudge towards us over an event in the past
- They may have problems not connected with the salon
- They lack experience and knowledge

If any of the above happen we cannot off-load responsibility but we must try harder to get the receiver to accept what we have been saying.

Act upon it

Once the message has been received, understood and accepted there is still no guarantee at this stage that the receiver will put the request into action or operation. There could be a number of reasons for this:

(1) We may not have explained how important it is to do it now.
(2) We may have given them several other instructions all at the same time.
(3) The receiver's priority may not be ours unless we have clearly identified the order in which we would like them carried out.

4.2.3 Listening

There are also a number of barriers to listening effectively and once we identify them, we can look at methods of improving our ability to listen more carefully.

Self-consciousness

If we are too concerned about the way we look or how we may appear particularly if we are in a new job and want to impress someone, we often fail to hear what is being said. We can overcome this by admitting that we feel self-conscious or concerned about the impression we might make. This often helps to change the atmosphere.

The long speech

Some people seem to take forever to make their point. The trouble with long speeches is that the listener tends to lose parts of what is being said – particularly the middle parts. Overcome this by interrupting the speaker if you feel you have lost the thread. Summarise what you think you may have heard and check it out with the sender of the message.

Repetition

There are some people who switch into the same groove of the record with certain people or situations so that the receiver of the message switches off. If we do this we must ensure that we 're-package' the message on different occasions so that people start to listen.

Dislike

If we dislike the message or the person this may arouse anger or hostility. We need to be aware of our feelings and, if appropriate, share them with the other person. Concentrate on what is being said and do not take the message personally.

Noise

Noise may prevent the message from being heard, either by drowning the message or causing concentration or attention to be shifted elsewhere. Remove obvious distractions such as telephones and interruptions.

Assumptions

We may be familiar with the task or information we wish to communicate and often assume that the person receiving the information has the same level of knowledge and experience as us. We tend to miss out vital clues and links and jump from A to Z and assume the person receiving the message understands all the connecting bits in between. Remember the age, knowledge and experience of the person to whom you are talking – particularly in young people.

Tiredness

Tiredness tends to make people switch off or become easily distracted when listening. We can avoid this by ensuring that important messages or conversations are restricted to times or periods of the day when they are less tired, stressed or pressurised. The result of tiredness is often emotion which creeps in and creates a barrier in communicating or listening to information.

In conclusion, there is more to giving and receiving information than meets the eye. If we identify at each stage or step where communication may break down then we can take the appropriate action to improve communications within our salon.

4.3 Motivation

There has been more research and interest in motivation than in any other area of managing people because, clearly, motivation holds the key to successful salon management. Motivated staff work hard, attract and keep clients, give good service, and are loyal. On the other hand, demotivated staff create a bad image and can be lazy which in turn can affect other staff. Motivation for the owner or manager is vital to get the business forging ahead and to keep it there.

When we discuss motivation we are usually seeking the answers to two questions:

(1) Why do people work?
(2) Why do some people work harder than others?

It is the experience of all of us that two almost identical people will be differently motivated – one requiring constant pushing to achieve, the other almost having to be held back.

What does motivating staff mean? In the next section we will look at the theories of motivation and apply them to salon management. An interesting point to look at is what demotivates staff. What makes them continually switch off at work? In Fig. 4.4 we have listed ten guaranteed ways to demotivate your staff. After looking at this list can you say in all honesty that you have never done any of these things? If you have, they are the first things to cut out if you wish to improve motivation. Exercise 4.1 is a motivation questionnaire to look at your beliefs. What does it show you about yourself? After completing this think about what motivates you and secondly, what motivates your staff. What you think motivates them and what they think motivates them will probably be quite different.

Fig. 4.4 Ten guaranteed ways to demotivate your staff.

(1) Never praise them or thank them for their efforts. After all, they get paid.
(2) Tell them as little as possible about the business, its problems and the future. After all, it's none of their business and they are not interested.
(3) If they are a few minutes late occasionally or even just on time, make a point of checking or telling them. You can't trust staff.
(4) Always tell them off in public, especially in front of colleagues or customers. It puts them in their place.
(5) If they are female, keep chatting them up, offering to take them out, and fondling them. After all they really like it and they are your employees.
(6) If they do something well or special, make sure you get the credit and not them. You're more important than they are.
(7) If they come to you with personal problems, do your best not to listen. If you have to listen, say helpful things like:

- Don't bring your personal problems to work.
- Pull yourself together, woman.
- Grow up!

You must never show any sympathy or understanding – life is tough!
(8) Keep changing the rules, i.e. what you expect them to do, but don't tell them. It keeps them on their toes.
(9) Always assume they are wrong without finding out the facts. After all, you are too busy to play detective and they'll only cover for one another.
(10) Pay your favourites more than the rest of them and treat them well – after all they are the best and most reliable staff.

Exercise 4.1 Motivation questionnaire

If you feel the following statement is generally true mark T, if you feel it is generally false mark F and if you think it is neither or you cannot answer mark N.

(1) It would help if people showed more interest in their jobs.   _____

(2) I can offer no real incentives if people improve so I don't really bother.   _____

(3) I find I need to punish more than praise or reward staff.   _____

(4) Staff feel they do not get enough reward already for the effort they put in.   _____

(5) I don't review staff performance, i.e. tell them how they are doing, very often because I am too busy.   _____

(6) I am not able to support the staff as much as I would like as I have a heavy workload myself.   _____

(7) People have to work a lot of hours and hard to earn a proper wage.   _____

(8) People wouldn't welcome more challenge in their jobs.   _____

(9) The business pays less than competition and some staff are unhappy about that.   _____

(10) I don't believe staff are committed either to the job or to the salon.   _____

(11) There is not a very happy atmosphere in the salon.   _____

(12) There seem to be lots of niggling small arguments going on here.   _____

(13) We find it hard to attract and keep good staff in the salon.   _____

(14) Staff often seem to play up and cause disagreements over very minor issues.   _____

(15) I don't feel staff really understand or sympathise with my problems as an owner/manager.   _____

Add up the total number of Ts
Add ½ point for each   N
Score 0 for   F
Then total your score

Minimum = 0   Maximum = 15

Scoring
More than 10   You have serious problems and a lot of hard work to do if you are to change things.

7–10	There are certainly a number of areas in which you can improve.
Less than 6	You seem to have a well-run business unless you have not noticed the problems.

4.3.1 *The theory of motivation*

There has been more written about human motivation than probably any other area of management – literally hundreds of articles. We have prepared here a brief summary on the main theories of motivation but sources of further information are listed in the Appendix. We have summarised the theories into the following three areas:

(1) Basic ideas and conclusions of motivational theory.
(2) Application to the hairdressing industry.
(3) Implications for action.

Early motivational theory

The early motivational theory developed by Taylor and Mayo is detailed below. Understanding where the early motivational theory comes from and how it is still used in the way we manage and develop people is crucial and should not be rejected when understanding more modern theories and who they inter-relate.

Taylor (Principles of scientific management)

Taylor described a number of factors which influenced successful performance:

(1) Choose the best man for the job (selection).
(2) Show him the best method for doing the job (training).
(3) Give him the proper tools for the job.
(4) Relate his pay to his performance or productivity directly. Assuming (1) to (3) are observed, then by relating an individual's pay *directly* to his performance, e.g. commission or bonus, this will produce the necessary motivation.

Thus, Taylor's ideas were the founding ones of many bonus systems still existing today and see staff as motivated primarily by money or economic factors.

The implications for hairdressing are that if you are using a *bonus system* then money (pay) must be within the control of the staff, i.e. they must be able to affect their own earnings. In many salons this is just not true, since clientele are fixed and some days are slack. We explain later how payment systems can be designed to get around this.

Mayo (Hawthorne studies)

Mayo was examining the effects of a large number of factors on work output, e.g. rest pauses, lighting, supervision, etc.

What was found was that staff's individual motivations were modified or affected by the work-group or team in a given situation and that this force could be positive or negative from management's point of view, depending on circumstances.

This is clearly relevant in managing a salon as there is clearly a *team* because:

(1) Staff are physically close together;
(2) They have common goals and objectives;
(3) They are interdependent;
(4) They form (working) relationships and interact together continuously.

The implications of this are that we must consider the effects of changes on salon staff *both* as individuals and as a group and that efforts to improve the image of that group and enhance its status, etc. are likely to be useful. On the other hand, things which damage the harmony or image of the group, e.g. inconsistency and unfairness, may well lead to demotivation and poor output.

It is useful to draw a distinction between theories of motivation that concentrate on the *content* and those that deal mainly with the *process of motivation.*

Content theories describe and categorise the needs, drives or instincts that are believed to underlie all behaviour and suggest that it will be directed towards the satisfaction of these needs. This means they are to do with what people are working towards. Generally, they do not provide much guidance on how a choice might be made between two different ways of satisfying the same need or drive.

A content theory might identify hunger as a basic need and suggest that if a person is hungry he will be motivated towards reducing the strengths of that need by eating. This does not tell us whether he will choose a sandwich or fish and chips, either of which would make him feel less hungry.

Process motivation concentrates on conscious choices about behaviour rather than instinctive or underlying causes. This second group of theories is often called 'systems theory' whereby mechanical methods are used to help to motivate people such as job descriptions, goal setting, pay or reward systems, and appraisals. These can be broken down further into three key categories:

- Need theories
- Incentive theories
- Expectancy theories

Need theories

What are the needs of individuals? If an individual's motivation level is determined by his or her needs then we must seek to understand what needs individuals have. At least three important theories have described the needs individuals have. They are Maslow, McClelland, and more recently Alderfer.

Maslow (a theory of human motivation)

Maslow wrote from the view of a development psychologist and was interested in the fundamental needs which people had. He saw those needs

Fig. 4.5
Maslow's
hierarchy of
needs.

(1) Physiological (Basic needs)	Food Sleep	Water Sex	Oxygen Warmth
(2) Security (Need to feel secure and safe)	Safety Security Continuity		Predictability Comfort
(3) Social (Need to belong and have friends)	Love Friends Affiliation		Affection Belonging
(4) Esteem (Need for respect and to be respected)	Self respect Respect from others Recognition		Pride Status Achievement
(5) Self-actualisation (Ultimate realisation of all your potential as a person)	Being Development Personal fulfilment 100% +	Growth	

as development and hierarchical, i.e. some basic and others high-level which emerged when the lower-level needs were satisfied. Figure 4.5 illustrates the principle.

Maslow's view was that once lower-level needs had been satisfied, then higher-level needs could emerge. Thus for Maslow:

(1) Behaviour attempts to satisfy needs.
(2) Satisfied needs do not motivate.

The implications of all this are to know for all our staff which of their needs are fulfilled and to note that when certain problems arise – marital or relationship break-up or redundancy – we may 'slip down the hierarchy' and safety/security and social needs become important. Youngsters are likely to be satisfying social or ego needs whereas older people may well be concentrating on higher-level needs. Finally, if lower-levels become problematical, e.g. low income or financial difficulties, then these may (temporarily) halt the seeking of the higher-level needs until these lower-level ones are met.

McClelland (achievement motivation)

McClelland notes that some people are highly motivated by a need to achieve, to be successful – he calls it 'NACH'. Not everyone has it and different cultures have it more than others. Achievement-motivated individuals want:

- Improvement
- Performance
- Challenge, etc.

They set their personal targets for accomplishment high and strive to achieve them. They constantly want to receive feedback, and to know how well they are doing. McClelland also notices that this can be learned by using four points:

(1) Teaching people to think, talk and act achievement.
(2) Stimulating people to set well planned targets or goals.
(3) Helping people to become more aware of themselves.
(4) Creating a team spirit for sharing hopes, fears, successes and failures.
   The evidence in many areas was 'it works'.

The implications here are exciting. You can build success. You can change motivation in staff by building (1) to (4) above into your staff training. It takes time, it is hard work but it is worth it! Thus we have to work at building a real functioning team.

Alderfer

Alderfer has recently developed a three factor theory of needs called 'ERG' – Existence, Relatedness and Growth. The theory relates closely to Maslow's hierarchy of needs in that he believes that basic needs need to be satisfied before the higher level needs. Alderfer makes three important points:

(1) The less the need is satisfied, the more important it becomes.
(2) The more a lower level need is satisfied, the greater the importance of the next higher level need.
(3) *The less the higher level need is satisfied, the greater the importance the lower need assumes.*

This last point about frustration is particularly important. If individuals cannot get what they want in a job, then they just demand more of what they can get. Employees may become disruptive at work, demanding more money, when what they really want is a more challenging job. It is important to recognise this behaviour if staff motivational problems are to be solved.

Incentive theories

Whilst *need theories* answer the question 'what causes an individual's behaviour?', incentive theories approach motivation from the other direction. What external factors influence human behaviour? Managers have considerable influence in this area. It is important to select staff with needs that can be satisfied within your salon or company. This is rather like employing a high flyer who is very ambitious and being unable to meet his or her needs within the short to medium term. Incentive theories were developed by Herzberg.

Herzberg (motivator – hygiene theory)

Herzberg researched engineers/scientists to find out what turned them on at work and what turned them off.

He identified two kinds of factors operating at work: those which cause satisfaction at work and hence (says Herzberg) motivate people, called *motivators* or *satisfiers*, and a second group called *hygiene factors* or *dissatisfiers* which cause dissatisfaction and demotivate staff. The other point he made was that by removing the dissatisfiers you do not get motivation, only the motivators can do that. Conversely, the motivation effects can be modified if the hygiene factors go wrong. Figure 4.6 shows the two sets of factors.

Fig. 4.6
Herzberg's
motivator –
hygiene theory.

Motivators
(1)   Achievement
(2)   Recognition
(3)* Work itself (interesting or stimulating)
(4)* Responsibility
(5)* Advancement
* Important for long-term effect

Hygiene factors
(1) Company policy and rules
(2) Supervision
(3) Salary
(4) Interpersonal relations
(5) Working conditions

We must explain the place of salary. Herzberg argues that pay *does not in itself motivate* but rather if people feel underpaid it *certainly does demotivate*. An interesting result Herzberg also noted was that increases in pay have a short-term effect which falls off as we adjust to the new income level.

The implications for hairdressing then are that we should try to get the hygiene factors 'right', i.e. remove the demotivating factors, then attempt to build into jobs as many of the motivators as possible. This process is called *job enrichment*.

Vroom (expectancy theory)

Expectancy theory is sometimes known as *instrumentality theory*, and deals with the question of the individual's process of *decision making*. This work was mainly developed by Vroom. Expectancy theory sees motivation as a logical choice among alternatives. Thus people consider what will be the result and is it worth it (see Fig. 4.7). Suppose you are asked to work hard in exchange for a bonus. Whether you will or not depends upon:

- How much you want the bonus;
- Whether you believe the extra work will bring the return.

Notice that the expectancy and preference are individual things based on personal views and experience. Thus, if your experience is that you never get the return for hard work, even if you still want it your motivation will go down.

This is particularly useful when designing payment systems. If you want pay (or anything else, for that matter) to motivate you must meet four conditions:

(1) Employees must expect effort to be worthwhile.
(2) They must believe results will bring the reward.
(3) They must want the reward.
(4) They must want it badly enough to make the effort worthwhile.

Goldthorpe (affluent worker in the class structure)

This last approach is not a theory of motivation as such but simply notes that

Fig. 4.7
Expectancy
theory.

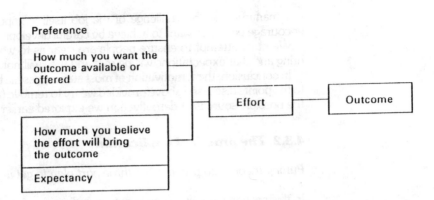

for many people work is not important in itself but is simply a means to an end, e.g. money. Thus, for some people work is only important in that it allows them to earn the money to do what they really want to do – whatever that is, e.g. bring up a family, go out with friends.

This is called the 'instrumental approach' – it is important in that people with this kind of orientation are not motivated by job enrichment and this has serious implications for such programmes if significant numbers of people are instrumental in orientation. They will be more interested in time off, etc. However, they can be motivated by exchanging say 'time off' for hard work or something of that kind. One example often quoted in the hairdressing area is the single parent who, in exchange for being able to take odd days off and work school hours, will be a very 'motivated' worker and 'produce the goods'.

Summary

The various theories of motivation have in common the view that people *do* things in attempting to satisfy personal goals and objectives (whatever these are) and that motivation is about trying to allow people to achieve these through the work that they do in your business.

People's needs are very different and recent research has looked at the way that even for the same person they change over time from young single to married to married with children to retired etc. Money is clearly not the only motivator although it does play an important role; some of the other motivators (see Herzberg's list) can be built into jobs by the process of job enrichment.

People's experiences affect the extent to which various rewards motivate them, and these change as they gather new experiences, and rewards achieve new levels of importance to them.

Thus in order to motivate staff we need to:

(1) Know as much about what 'makes them tick' as possible and hence their needs and orientation to work
(2) Examine the extent to which we can help them achieve at least some of these in the work place
(3) Try to remove the obstacles for motivation (hygiene factors) to ensure maximum benefits
(4) Keep in mind the importance of group motivation as well as individual motivation.

For many people the challenge of the job itself is important and we can encourage people to want to achieve by careful development and nurturing.

We must attempt to ensure people are clear as to what their efforts will bring and that expectations will be met and they will not feel hard done by.

In conclusion, then, motivation of most staff is possible by paying attention to the points discussed above provided we try to remove (and do not add to!) the possible sources of demotivation we explored earlier.

4.3.2 *The practical application*

Putting theory into practice – a three-part plan to get it right

In this section we need to examine an outline plan for effective motivation which will be achieved by the following three approaches:

(1) Managing staff properly and getting communications and relationships right.
(2) Creating an environment in which staff can develop and grow and achieve their own needs.
(3) Designing an effective payment system to motivate staff and to ensure a fair return for their efforts.

We maintain that these three areas, if correctly organised, will create a climate in which there is motivation of staff and a successful business for you, one in which the staff get a fair and just return for their efforts. It is often said that you get the kind of staff you deserve and the staff problems you deserve. Salon owners and managers who are fair and honest and treat staff and clients well generally do well. Those who are greedy, dishonest and manipulative may do well for a time but eventually things will catch up with them and they will experience real problems.

There is no simple magic formula for success. Managing staff requires people skills, an empathy and willingness to see their problems as people and a desire to help them achieve. This must not be at the expense of a successful and profitable business. The two can work together so that everyone, staff, management and clients, can benefit.

In order to examine the question of whether you and your staff have motivational problems we have designed a questionnaire to test whether there is room for improvement or not (Exercise 4.2). Check if your staff have the right attitudes to each other, to you and to your clients. The signs of poor morale and motivation are complex and the methods to improve them follow in the next section.

Managing by motivation

So how do we effectively manage staff? The key is to action the following areas:

(1) The staff must know exactly what is expected of them – the standards required and the rules and procedures of the Company.
(2) They must be involved in the setting of those standards or at least have the opportunity of discussing them with you.
(3) They must understand the goals and objectives of the business – where it is going, why and how they fit into it and what they must do in order to help achieve the objectives.

(4) They need to feel a part of that business and to feel comfortable so that they can raise problems as they see them without fear of criticism or aggravation. They need to know that they will be consulted and informed when changes take place that directly affect them.

(5) They need to know that as a result of keeping their part of the bargain you will keep yours and that they will receive a fair return for their efforts; that they will be treated fairly and equally as human beings not hair cutting machines, so that they can give a proper service to clients and earn respect and self esteem for themselves.

Figure 4.8 details a checklist for effective management in hairdressing.

Setting standards

We cannot stress how important it is to ensure that there are proper job

Fig. 4.8 A checklist for effective management.

(1) (With the person involved) *Develop a simple outline of the job and key tasks to be performed.* This can apply to an individual job or to a complete salon. It should include a simple statement of what people are to do, what authority they have in doing it, and what their relationships with other people are.

(2) (With the person involved) *Develop a simple statement of the results that will be considered satisfactory.* There are many activities for which, at first, it seems impossible to develop standards of performance. However, discussion of them in a sincere attempt to develop standards will often produce definite and acceptable objectives.

(3) (With the person involved) *At regular intervals, check actual performance against the standards that have been set.* If the supervisor is to plan his activities, he must know how big a gap there is between what is being done and what should be done. This should be checked in terms of individual and group attainment.

(4) (With the person involved) *Make a list of corrective actions necessary to improve performance where needed.* An individual cannot develop into a better worker unless he is continuously increasing his skill, gaining knowledge, changing his habits and assuming constructive attitudes. A manager should know where improvement is needed.

(5) (With the person involved) *Select the best sources from which he can obtain help and information.* Sources can be divided into four categories: the immediate manager, the other individuals in the organisation, people outside the organisation who could be brought in, and outside sources of help to which the individual concerned could be referred. These sources should be considered in that order and the one which is most advantageous selected.

(6) (With the person involved) *A time should be set aside in advance for supplying the help and information that is needed.* If we do not plan in advance, the time can be made available only through disrupting the work of the salon. It is of little use to go to all the trouble of deciding what should be done, analysing what has been done, and determining what action is needed, if no action is taken.

descriptions and written staff rules and regulations with clearly defined standards for all. These standards must be encouraged. Every time you make an exception or ask the staff to drop their standards you erode them. Every time you fail to 'pull up' staff who break the rules, you erode the rules. *Consistency is vital.* We have detailed this in greater depth in Section 3.3 on job descriptions but need to add that the standard of performance must be the same for each person who carries out this job. Each stylist must have the same standard of performance in terms of the number of clients they are expected to cover each week if they have had the same amount of experience. A standard is not the same as a goal. A standard is the acceptable minimum requirement to be successful at doing the job. Goals or targets are the level towards which they are expected to work. The goal or target will be dependent upon their experience, the type of clients and the range of services offered to clients.

The standards must take account of:

- The level of training or experience of staff
- The volume of business being done (as this is often dependent upon promotional activity of the salon)
- A reasonable day's work taking into account client cancellations
- The incentive or method of payment

The standards should be reviewed regularly and changed if necessary.

Staff need to have copies or at least access to this information because, if they do not know what is expected of them they cannot meet the requirements. Staff should have regular reviews or appraisals and these should be a basis for discussions and improvement, not simply criticism.

Staff need to feel they know what is going on, to feel part of the business. In particular, they need to know the opportunties for promotion or advancement, any future training or new experience they will have or even any additional responsibilities that they may get in the future.

They also need to feel that they too can make a contribution to improvement and that they can make suggestions about improvements. Have you ever asked them for their views? Do you really listen to their problems? Do you really care about what they think or feel? If you do not, then you cannot really blame them for not being sympathetic to your problems or difficulties.

Communication is a vital part of this process. Staff need to know what is going on, especially when it affects them.

Creating the right environment

It is very difficult to pin-point exactly what is the right environment for staff but certainly we should aim for the following:

(1) An atmosphere of openness and trust
(2) Minimal conflict
(3) Clear objectives, goals and standards
(4) Clear lines of responsibility and authority
(5) Staff who are keen to take on responsibility
(6) A feeling of support, comfort and teamwork
(7) Opportunities for responsibility for staff
(8) Loyalty to the company, staff, products and services
(9) Adequate communication of key issues

(10) Friendliness between staff
(11) Low staff turnover (staff leaving)
(12) High staff productivity and morale
(13) A sense of competition with other salons

In our experience, it is often the management's style or lack of expertise which gives rise to problems of motivation. Exercise 4.2 is a questionnaire upon the climate or environment of the salon. Ask the staff to complete this questionnaire anonymously. The answers may surprise you.

Exercise 4.2 Climate analysis
Answer the following statements about this salon by marking each question according to your answer. If statement is:

Always true	mark	T
Quite often true	mark	O
Sometimes true	mark	S
Very seldom true	mark	V
Never true	mark	N

(1) There are good working relationships between the senior and junior staff here. _____

(2) This salon feels nice to work in. _____

(3) You don't feel you will get chewed up if you make the odd mistake. _____

(4) You daren't argue with the manager/owner's decisions. _____

(5) You get fairly rewarded for what you do here. _____

(6) Everyone is clear what is required of them here. _____

(7) The place is full of rules and regulations – you don't know which way to turn. _____

(8) You are encouraged to show initiative and make decisions yourself here. _____

(9) I feel loyal to this salon and never say bad things about it. _____

(10) I think I would leave this salon if I could get more money elsewhere. _____

Scoring
For questions 1, 2, 3, 5, 6, 7, 8, 9 score:
    5 for T
    4 for O
    3 for S
    2 for V
    1 for N

For questions 4, 10 score:
    1 for T
    2 for V
    3 for S
    4 for V
    5 for N

Minimum score = 10   Maximum score = 50
Add up to get total score.

Interpretations
Under 25   You have serious problems and you should examine them carefully. Look at what your staff are telling you.
25–35   Things are not too bad but there is room for improvement. Start on the worst areas.
Over 35   You have got a good environment. Look at the areas which still need improvement and work on them.

Now you have an indication of the staff's feelings about the climate or atmosphere in the salon – check your own management expertise by considering the questions below:

(1) Am I clear about my own responsibility and level of authority?
(2) Am I clear about the objectives of my salon and the group as a whole?
(3) Have I worked out a plan of action for reaching these goals/objectives?
(4) Can the jobs of the staff be re-constructed to get better results?
(5) Are the physical working conditions, layout, equipment and lighting right for the job?
(6) Does everyone know exactly what their job is? Has each member of staff clearly defined targets and performance standards agreed with them? Have I the same with my boss?
(7) Does everyone know to whom they should report?
(8) Has anyone too many people reporting to them which makes them manage inefficiently? If so, can this responsibility be shared with another?
(9) Is the line of authority clear for each member of staff?
(10) Are there any gaps in the abilities of the staff? If so, am I taking steps to fill them by training, by additional staff or the use of specialists?
(11) Am I aware of how I and my staff spend our time? Is it the best way? Are our priorities right?
(12) Have I achieved the tasks set 12 months ago? If not, why not?
(13) Does my own work and behaviour set the best possible example to the group?

If the answer to any of the above questions is no then you clearly have areas for improvement.

Guidelines for self-improvement

We offer some guidelines on how to improve yourself as a manager or salon owner in three key areas:

(1) New ideas
(2) Personal conduct
(3) Self-development

New ideas
- Look around at your salon internally and externally.
- Look at competitors' activities.
- Read magazines, books and newspapers for ideas.
- Don't jump to conclusions about staff (see Communication section on non-verbal behaviour).
- Listen to staff's and clients' needs even when you are harassed or tired.

Personal conduct
- A manager or salon owner cannot forget his or her position – be friendly but not over familiar.
- Do not invite gossip by your lifestyle because you will not get the respect you would like. This is particularly so if you are emotionally involved with members of your staff.
- Be discreet in your working environment and personal life.
- Do not talk over your personal problems with the staff.
- Do not have favourites within the salon.
- Do not have special friendships with superiors.
- Do not be over familiar at social gatherings and only go to them occasionally, not every Friday night tap-dancing on the pub bar!
- We all like to be liked but our staff expect a code of conduct from us.
- Respect does not necessarily come from our status – we have to earn it.

Self-development
- Mixing with people from a similar environment is good as it stops us from being insular.
- Develop yourself by cultivating other interests outside hairdressing. All work and no play makes for very boring people!
- Try and identify your faults always and work to eliminate them.

4.3.3 Designing an effective payment system

There is probably no area of management activity that causes more difficulty than the determination of pay. In our research and experience in hairdressing it was the single most common cause of annoyance, demotivation and staff leaving the industry.

The range of payment methods is incredible from straight salary, to bonus payments and a wide range of commission schemes from the simple to the complex. We have found many fair, honest and legal pay schemes and some which were blatantly unfair, immoral and illegal in operation.

In order to develop and maintain an effective payment system it is necessary to:

- Understand the basic principles
- Appreciate the range of options available
- Select the best system for your salon
- Introduce changes carefully after planning
- Monitor the effectiveness of the system

There are two basic approaches to wage systems within the hairdressing industry. The first is payment based on the time worked, such as by the hour, week, month or year. The second is payment based on output or productivity. Both approaches can be used satisfactorily, depending upon the job in question. In practice, pay may be made up of both approaches. Look at the following list of factors regarding payment on the basis of time or output.

Output/time factors

(1) Individual output is distinct and clearly measurable.
(2) Concern with quality is less important than concern with quantity.
(3) Quantity is important.
(4) The work is standardised and delays are few.
(5) Supervision is spread amongst a number of staff.
(6) Supervisors know what constitutes a fair day's work.
(7) There is a sizeable relationship between effort and quantity of output.
(8) There are many interferences with work that are outside the control of the employee.
(9) There is little or no relationship between effort and output.
(10) Output is clearly under the control of the employee.

Ouput factors: numbers 3, 4, 7, 10.
Time factors: numbers 1, 2, 5, 6, 8, 9.

Most of the factors concerned with output are not true. In the strict sense, the stylist cannot control how hard he/she works without reducing standards and does not have the ability to generate new clients except in a limited way by personal reference from existing clients and looking after the ones already visiting the salon so that they return again. Salons have quiet days when clearly even if stylists tried to work hard they could not. This would suggest that a pure bonus system or commission scheme is incorrect and that a wage or guaranteed basic wage would be more appropriate.

There are, however, a number of areas where the stylist's expertise contributes to volume of clients:

(1) Client loyalty – new clients returning as regulars
(2) Selling retail products
(3) Selling technical services such as colours and perms

It is for this reason that we feel that some form of bonus system is required and would propose a system of part salary and part bonus as discussed later in this chapter.

Two further complications affect the calculations:

(1) Staff help each other, e.g. trainees wash hair for stylists
(2) The salon needs to be kept clean and tidy and staff need to be trained in all jobs which conventionally do not earn bonus or commission

What, therefore, should be the principles of a good scheme? We feel the following points must be taken into account for a scheme to work well:

(1) Pay must consistently relate to performance whether in terms of productivity or standards.
(2) The system must keep labour costs within reasonable limits – a maximum wage cost of 'productive staff' to turnover excluding VAT of 53 per cent including employer's National Insurance contributions.
(3) The system must be easily understood by staff.
(4) The system must not penalise trainees or inexperienced staff but must create sufficient differentials between them and experienced stylists.
(5) The system must ensure that there are no anomalies, e.g. inexperienced staff earning more than experienced stylists.
(6) The pay scheme should generate a salary roughly in line with competition.

(7) The system should have an in-built flexibility and the option of regular reviews.

(8) It should reward achievement as quickly as possible after results (e.g. not a bonus paid just on an annual basis).

(9) The pay scheme should be instrumental in:

- attracting staff
- keeping staff

(10) The system should be easily administered and not require excessive records or large amounts of paperwork.

Which pay scheme?

We suggest four approaches as the most useful to consider:

(1) A straight commission scheme (a percentage of turnover net of VAT) or a minimum wage whichever is the greater

(2) Group bonus scheme based on total turnover and proportioned by status and/or experience or volume

(3) A bonus system based on points of the individual or the salon group

(4) Straight salaries

Straight commission scheme

We have found this system to be the commonest method used for stylists with juniors/trainees paid a straight wage. It is problematical with many of the commission schemes currently running in the hairdressing industry, in that it is still possible to work very hard on some days yet get no bonus.

Some salons work the commission scheme on a daily basis but this can increase the wage costs although it does motivate staff. Many salons have complete sliding scales and different rates for new or regular clients which no one except the wages clerk understands.

A number of salons have pay schemes which do not have an added incentive to generate extra income as they are only paid the additional commission rate on the difference between the lower scale of earnings and the higher scale not the total amount.

Group bonus scheme

Another basic and simple system is to pay everyone a basic rate and calculate the bonus or commission as follows:

- Calculate the normal wages for staff based on the agreed wage.
- Calculate the percentage of turnover using average past takings less VAT.
- The total bonus is the difference between the figures.
- It is then shared out proportionally so that the manager, stylists, receptionists and juniors all have a share in the bonus scheme depending upon their status.

This system emphasises team effort and status of each staff member. It requires:

- An agreed basic rate not a minimum wage
- An agreed group bonus system

- An agreement as to what happens if they do not meet the bonus on a regular basis – this means that either management bears the cost and staff get basic pay or the shortfall is carried forward and deducted next time
- Historical wage data

The group bonus scheme is an effective and motivating system and has a number of benefits:

(1) It forces management to promote the business.
(2) It generates team effort.
(3) The most junior and inexperienced staff share in the success of the salon, e.g. trainees and receptionists.
(4) It eliminates prima donnas.
(5) It ensures management and receptionists fairly distribute new clients.
(6) It does not penalise long-standing stylists who tend to have a larger clientele of shampoo and sets or shampoo and blow dries and who have difficulty in increasing their maximum takings due to the lower price charged for these services.
(7) It is easy to administer.

Points bonus system

There are a wide range of methods and we outline only a few possibilities. Basically, for every client handled in any way points are awarded as follows:

- 1 point for reception
- 2 points for washing
- 3 points for cut and blow dry
- 1 point for retail sales

This can be extended to non-client activities, e.g.

- 5 points for washing the floor
- 8 points for training and so on

At the end of a given time period (weekly or monthly) the total points for all staff are calculated.

Points are valued at, say, 5p or whatever sum of money the salon can afford and wishes to place upon the work. This is to ascertain the bonus element. The difference between basic pay and the points system is the 'commission'.

Each member of staff would then get paid according to the points as follows:

Staff member A	1000 points
Staff member B	600 points
Staff member C	800 points
Staff member D	600 points
	3000 points

Money available for bonus, say £150, therefore each point is worth 5p, therefore:

Staff member A receives £50
Staff member C receives £40
Staff members B and D receive £30 each

The staff receive this bonus as a monthly sum or in four weekly instalments over the next four weeks.

This scheme can be enhanced by introducing deductions for rule breaking or introducing extra points for extra things, e.g. promoting perms for one month would buy extra points. It does require openness and honesty in its administration and no favourites.

Straight salary

In this system we would recommend paying the straight salary every week or month regardless of turnover. This is a common method of payment in

Fig. 4.9 Fringe benefits for hairdressers.

Option	Net cost
(1) Products at cost or discount	Nil (reduces pilferage)
(2) Reduced prices for friends/ relatives	Small (may bring in new clients)
(3) Free overalls/uniforms	Nominal if rental firm used
(4) Motor car	£3500 pa – becoming common practice in larger salon groups at management level
(5) Bus fares/travel expenses	Variable
(6) Dryers/combs etc. *free*	Can be expensive – better to sell at wholesale
(7) Subsidised pension schemes, particularly for managers	Unattractive to the young
(8) Luncheon vouchers	£10 pw per staff – staff from other industries like this a lot but very rarely used in the hairdressing industry
(9) Extra holidays with service	Nominal
(10) Own hair done free	Small
(11) Mortgages at attractive rates	Small if already negotiating with own financial suppliers
(12) Low cost rent or tied property over salons	Variable – depends on area and whether property could be used for other purposes
(13) Reduced rate package holidays	Variable depending upon local travel agent and personal connections
(14) Private medical insurance	Small – dependent upon size of company

industry but it is difficult to change the motivation of staff with this method and we do not particularly recommend it for the hairdressing industry unless straight salaries are paid at senior management level.

An alternative to the straight salary could be to pay 90 per cent of salary each week and keep a monthly 10 per cent available as a discretionary bonus element which might then act as an incentive system.

Conclusions

We have tried to illustrate briefly in this section the kinds of payment systems that can be used within your business. They are by no means the only ones – there are over 250 different types of pay schemes available.

We would recommend that this is one area where professional advice from management consultants is essential. It is such an important area that mistakes can be extremely costly and very difficult to put right after the event.

Hairdressers are often loathe to use fringe benefits but, in fact, they are amongst the most attractive ways of recruiting and keeping staff. In Fig. 4.9 we suggest some benefits that may be appropriate for the hairdressing industry. Evidence shows that fringe benefits are good for attracting staff and offer a disincentive to leave.

The complexity of payment systems is immense but it is a motivational tool available to you and you should make as much use of it as possible to ensure that your business flourishes and grows.

4.3.4 Conclusions on motivation

We have seen motivating staff as involving a large number of elements which include:

- Staff must know what is expected of them and the implications of performance or non-performance.
- The owner or manager must understand what individually motivates their staff and try as far as possible to meet this where practical in the workplace.
- Regular meetings, systems and procedures for keeping staff involved and informed must be employed. This is to ensure that staff feel they have a role and purpose in working within their salon and that they can see where it is heading and their part in helping to achieve the goals.
- The wage payment system must reward staff adequately for their needs in basic living terms and must be responsive to their efforts, performance and motivation and be seen as fair and equally applied to all.
- Not everyone is motivated by money and it has a short term effect. Pay schemes can be motivating but *also demotivating*, particularly if the pay scheme expects high output factors such as productivity but also quality hairdressing too or *the pay structure demotivates those who work the hardest because there is a limit as to how much stylists can generate without taking into account quality, team work and factors outside their control such as who is responsible for getting the clients through the door.*
- Systems such as job descriptions, minimum standards of performance, goals and objectives, need to be clearly defined, discussed and agreed if they are to be successful.

- Fairness must be applied to everything whether it is a pay scheme, methods of promotion, selection for training course, because if staff perceive it is unfair then they will be demotivated.
- Informal competition can be motivating but formal competition generates a 'selfish' environment.
- People need feedback on their performance so that they know how they are progressing. They need feedback on what you promised to do or instigate. Otherwise, they will stop making suggestions and contributing at staff meetings.

The above items are the building blocks for effective staff motivation; research, theory and practice will give us pointers to achieve these objectives within our own business.

4.4 Behaviour

Managing problem people

In the previous sections on Communication and Motivation we gave some clues as to how to handle people. Most managers are brought up to believe that the answer to managing problem people is to do something to motivate them. The assumption is that people have to be prodded into action because, left to their own devices, they would do little or nothing. *Problem people rarely do nothing.* The problem usually arises because they are busy doing something other than what is required! The key to motivating people is to change the things that are preventing them from behaving as we would wish, rather than dream up all sorts of extra motivators. It is not that problem people are always demotivated – more probably, they are being motivated to do the wrong things.

There are two different approaches when it comes to managing people. One focuses on identifying and meeting people's needs and the other on managing people's behaviour.

The behaviour approach assumes that no behaviour occurs in a vacuum. Something always happens before it and something always happens after it. The surrounding events are crucial because they explain why the person is behaving as they are and give us ideas or clues as to how we can solve the problem. Things that happen before the behaviour in question are called 'triggers'. Things that happen after the behaviour are called 'reinforcers'.

While triggers and reinforcers remain intact and linked to the behaviour, it is predictable that the problem will continue. If either triggers or reinforcers, or both, are changed then it is inevitable that the behaviour will also change. The way to solve problems caused by other people's behaviour is therefore as follows:

Step one	Be clear and specific about the problem behaviour.
Step two	Identify the events that trigger the behaviour.
Step three	Identify the reinforcers that are currently sustaining the problem behaviour.
Step four	Be clear and specific about what behaviour you want (usually the opposite to the behaviour you have got).
Step five	Work out how to change the triggers so that the problem behaviour is no longer triggered and the wanted behaviour is.

Step six	Work out how to change the reinforcers so that the problem behaviour is no longer encouraged and the wanted behaviour is.
Step seven	Check that your plan is feasible (that you really can put it into action and want to go through with it) and work out how to implement it.
Step eight	Finally, implement the changes and watch the problem behaviour decrease and the wanted behaviour increase.

Eight steps might strike you as rather daunting but once you have used the 'behaviour approach' a few times, the formality of these steps can be relaxed and the whole approach seems more natural.

Initially, the most difficult part of the 'behaviour approach' is the novelty of concentrating solely on the external events that surround someone's behaviour. It seems more natural (because it is a more familiar way of thinking about people's behaviour) to slip into speculation about underlying motives, attitudes and feelings. The 'behaviour approach' doesn't deny the existence of such things. It merely recommends that for practical purposes you solve the problem by changing the external circumstances in which the behaviour occurs. It is your responsibility to manage problem people. Since your behaviour breeds their behaviour, you get the people you deserve.

Keys to changing behaviour

In the previous sections we have talked about managing people, communication and motivation and we would recommend further reading on this subject. Chapter 5 on discipline and handling staff problems will help to focus upon the key areas. To summarise, we suggest the following procedure:

- *The manager owns the problem*
  Tempting though it always is to blame the other person, the plain fact is that it is the manager's responsibility to do something to solve the problem. The manager always owns the problem.

- *The manager's behaviour breeds the subordinate's behaviour*
  In these cases we have seen how the manager unwittingly did things to create or aggravate the very problems they were suffering from. The manager's own behaviour is *always* a significant factor since the subordinate's behaviour is a reaction to it. It follows, therefore, that if the manager's behaviour changes, so will the subordinate's

- *The events surrounding behaviour always hold the key to changing it*
  The very essence of the 'behaviour approach' is to concentrate on what is happening before and after the behaviour in question. Triggers happen before and reinforcements after. Change the 'befores' and 'afters' and you change the behaviour.

- *The effectiveness of positive reinforcement must never be underestimated*
  Positive reinforcement has an important part to play in all the cases we have looked at. It is as simple as being careful to notice people, involve people, thank and congratulate people. The more often such reinforcers can happen after the desired behaviour, the more likely it is that the problem behaviour will decrease and the desired behaviour increase. Everyone likes positive reinforcement.

- *Modifying problem behaviour is a gradual process*
  Problem behaviours take a long time to establish themselves and it takes time to disestablish them and replace them with more desirable behaviours. The 'behaviour approach' is not magic. It depends for its success on breaking the links between triggers, problem behaviours and reinforcers. This is a gradual evolutionary process, like water dripping on a stone.

4.5 Leadership styles

Many owners and managers in hairdressing have never considered the kind of style they adopt when managing staff and the potential advantages and disadvantages of each. If we really wish to get the best from our staff we need to consider the range of possible leadership styles available to a manager.

The quality of leadership is one aspect which distinguishes the successful salon from one that is performing poorly. Many business failures can be traced back to poor or weak management leadership. It is no surprise then that research into the key elements of successful leadership have been pursued for centuries and only now are being put together into a picture that seems to make sense.

Early beliefs that leaders were born and not made have been proven to be untrue but today it is generally agreed that successful leadership is a function of the manager's skills to diagnose the people and tasks needed in a situation and *the ability to modify this approach to suit the situation*. For a manager to be a good leader, it is not necessary to change our inner values but to be able to change the style of interaction to fit the situation. All leadership has three features in common:

- Leadership is an influencing process.
- There are two or more persons involved – a leader and a follower.
- Leadership occurs in situations when we are trying to achieve given, implied or unconscious goals and objectives.

It does not follow that the person with the most formal authority is necessarily the leader in any situation. A potential leader is anyone who tries to influence somebody.

4.5.1 The theories of leadership

Why should we bother to understand the theory behind leadership? The answer is so that we can have a greater understanding of where we obtain our ideas and beliefs. Much of it is passed on to us from the way we have been managed in the past – or we may have read a range of books on various aspects of leadership, some of which have worked and some of which have not!

(1) Trait approach

The early studies on leadership tried to identify whether successful leaders had common personal characteristics or psychological traits. If these could be identified, the search for good leadership and management in organisations would be simple. *However, very few common factors have come to light after over half a century of research, yet how many times have you heard a salon owner say 'Managers are born, not made'.*

(2) The behavioural approach

This approach recognised that attention needs to be paid to *interpersonal relationships at work as well as productivity levels*. The 'people approach' school of leadership considers that leaders provide an encouraging function – that is sharing power and authority with the group or, in other words, encouraging leadership. This approach claims that successful leadership is achieved when the leader's style *matches the demand of the situation*. In other words we need to be constantly adaptable depending upon the needs at the time. Whether the approach is successful will depend on three key elements:

(1) The leader/staff relationship
(2) The degree of structure of the task (is it clearly defined or open-ended?)
(3) The leader's formal power or level of authority (can he insist or impose instructions upon his staff?) or whether he requires their active co-operation, e.g. coercion *versus* co-operation

(3) Managerial decision making

This approach states that there are three alternative styles of decision making which are:

(1) Autocratic
(2) Consultative
(3) Participative

Which style should be used depends upon the answers to certain types of problems. For example, some decisions are not negotiable or open to discussion or debate (autocratic); some decisions require feedback in order to arrive at the best decision in a given situation (consultative); other decisions require the full co-operation and input from everyone in order to arrive at the best decision (participative).

(4) Situational leadership

This approach was based on the concept that good managers need to adapt their styles to meet the *needs and characteristics of individual situations*. It describes four leadership styles based on two aspects of task behaviour and relationship behaviour. *It claimed that the best manager is capable of adjusting his style to the pressures of the situation and the needs of the staff.*
   Task behaviour tends to be a one-way communication whilst *relationship behaviour* opens up two-way communication through encouragement, friendliness and recognition. This latter approach suggests that the leader matches his needs, the staff needs and the task itself to the situation.

Examples of task behaviour
'Please clean the floor immediately.'
'Will you go and unload the stock that's just arrived.'
Examples of relationship behaviour

'We seem to be having a problem with staff coming in late – what do you think is causing it?'

'The cleaning rota doesn't seem to be working very well – how can this be sorted out?'

Today's managers face demands at work which, though technically more sophisticated, show little difference from those faced by managers sixty years ago. They still have to achieve targets, they still have to organise work, and they still have to motivate, control and develop their subordinates.

They still are driven by the demands of short-term results at the cost of reflective thinking and long-term planning. The able manager seeks to change his situation and adopt a more *proactive approach*; leading and getting things done by other people is active behaviour, not re-active behaviour. Consequently the underlying assumption is that good leaders can be developed with an emphasis on interpersonal skills training; it is possible to help individuals to become more self-aware and to understand the consequences and implications of their leadership behaviour.

The manager must also recognise that he (as a manager) is only one of many factors influencing the staff's attitudes towards their job and the company. He must also identify the other factors which influence the way subordinates behave particularly in relation to their reaction and behaviour towards him and how this might be enhanced, e.g. what motivates them and how this might be improved. This means looking at how the manager generates higher levels of performance through procedural systems, organisational structures, jobs design, motivational approaches and inter-personal relationships.

Putting leadership theories into practice

Applying the theories in practice means adjusting our behaviour to meet the situation:

(1) When to be autocratic – as in giving instructions;
(2) When to encourage staff to give feedback;
(3) When to present the problems to staff and allow them to be fully involved in finding a solution.

This last approach is the one where many managers feel anxious and experience a fear of losing control. They tend to ask questions such as 'what if I don't like their suggestion', but the manager is also part of the team and it is his experience and knowledge that can often influence decisions. *It is important to speak last after listening to everyone's views instead of first.*

Concentrating your behaviour on clearly defined tasks, goals and objectives helps to diffuse the emotion and ensures that managers look at what can be changed in a particular situation instead of concentrating on personalities which cannot be changed.

The following are aids to putting the theories into practice:

(1) Job descriptions
(2) Clearly defined standards
(3) Achievable goals or targets can all help
(4) Regular staff meetings
(5) Brainstorming sessions
(6) One-to-one discussions
(7) Appraisal interviews

Finally, make the time to listen and involve staff. This is the difference between a successful leader and a dictator.

4.6 Understanding power and how to use it

Power is a key concept in understanding human behaviour within companies. It affects other approaches in managing people such as motivation, leadership and the organisational structure within salons. These approaches often leave unanswered certain questions but these lie through the analysis of power. This work was developed by French and Raven and later by Hersey, Blanchard and Nortemeyer (a guide to further reading is detailed at the back of the book).

There are different interpretations of power, but essentially it means a firm base from which to act. Does an individual have authority, money and contacts with influential people? Can this power be used to influence people? Does the individual have a role which gives him authority to carry out action or does clearance have to be given for every single action each day from the owner of the business – to buy light bulbs, to replace floor tiles?

Certain companies, particularly in the hairdressing industry, only value certain power levers. Using power in the most appropriate way, however, demands substantial thought. There need to be three such requirements if power is to be used as a springboard.

(1) *Resources* such as financial resources, people resources. This enables the person to influence the rewards offered, e.g. who orders stock, with which manufacturer, who recruits staff and controls budgets.
(2) *Dependency.* Dependency cannot be seen in isolation. It is coupled with the resource factor. For example, people are more powerful if they are in a position to promote others but also others depend on them to do so. Under such circumstances, not contradicting one's boss could become a vital consideration – possibly at the expense of not being as effective at work.
(3) *Availability of alternatives.* This could influence the power position of people. If an individual is able to use alternative resources it is possible to reduce dependency. An employer may have the resources to terminate someone's employment, however, but could be unwise to do so, as in so doing a skilled, experienced person could be handed over to a competitor.

Power levers

Having established that power does not function in isolation, it is now possible to explore the various power levers or strategies that an individual can employ. There are seven power levers.

(1) Reward power
    Reward power is used by people in a position to influence the rewards meted out to others. For reward power to be used successfully, the person must be able to control resources which are desired or required by others.
(2) Punishment-centred power
    As the term implies, an individual can adopt punishment-centred

methods. The source of such power may lie in the person's job, which may include the authority to fire people, organise them or move them around the company. The manner in which authority is exercised will determine whether other people view such action as the right use of authority or as a punishment, as may happen when an employee does not accept the new job offered and is moved to a less successful branch.

(3) Position power

Position power stems from the organisational position or role, e.g. manager or director. It is directly affected by authority and control and is based on how the job functions. *For example, managers may be able to delegate work and re-set priorities.* Individuals in any level of job can help themselves in three ways by:

(a) Access to information.
(b) Access to other people or various networks in the company.
(c) Being able to organise other people's work to ensure that they are more effective.

(4) Personal power

Personal power depends upon individual characteristics, loosely termed personality, and physical characteristics which make individuals attractive to others. These people are often described as charismatic, popular, having panache or flair. Equally, physical attributes such as height, size, weight, and strength would be considered aspects of personal power. Rather than using other roles such as rewards, coercion or knowledge the person influences others by emotionally stimulating them. Hence, personal power is based on an individual's ability to make others sympathetic towards him as a person.

(5) Expert power

A person who is perceived as possessing specialist knowledge or skills in a particular field is said to possess 'expert power'. Use of expert power depends a great deal on who is seen as an expert at the time and for what reasons. An individual is only seen as expert until a better 'expert' comes along.

(6) Information power

Information power provides an important power base. Raw data in itself means very little. *Information which is processed and interpreted and used to support a point of view or to downgrade other people's arguments can be a powerful base from which to act.* The skill is knowing the information necessary to suit the circumstances.

(7) Connection power

Connection power means having both personal and professional access to a large number of people within and outside the organisation. These people may or may not have information relevant to the situation but making large numbers of contacts who could be valuable is of primary concern. Making friends at conferences, getting to know people at conventions, and distributing one's business cards at meetings are ways of making contacts. The individual attempting to increase his connection power may not know what value each of his contacts has. Simply making contact, by joining artistic or business groups, golf clubs, women's organisations, etc., could be useful at a later date.

Complete Exercise 4.3 and identify which power levers you already possess.

Exercise 4.3 Which power levers do you use?

Tick

1. I have *reward power* to:

- award pay rises/bonuses.
- decide who goes on courses.
- decide who gets promoted.

☐
☐
☐

2. I have *punishment-centred power* to decide:

- who is allocated new clients or not.
- who is allocated low priced services, e.g. blow dries.
- who is allocated unpleasant tasks – cleaning of toilets, emptying the rubbish bins.
- who gets sent on errands.
- who gets transferred from one salon to another branch.
- who gets fired.

☐
☐

☐
☐
☐

☐

3. I have *position power* by:

- access to stock control figures.
- access to information on number of services/takings.
- access to performance figures of individual staff.
- being able to talk to my boss on a regular basis.
- being able to use the support services available within the company, e.g. secretaries, training services.
- being able to use support services available from product suppliers.
- being able to set targets or goals for the salon or individual staff.

☐
☐
☐
☐

☐

☐

☐

4. I have *personal power* because:

- I am popular with staff and colleagues.
- I am physically attractive, e.g. tall, petite, slim, well-proportioned, healthy, fashionable.
- I am well dressed.
- I am well-groomed.
- I can tell an amusing story.

☐

☐
☐
☐
☐

5. I have *expert power* in the following areas:

- I have successfully and profitably expanded by business.
- I have photographic work experience.
- I have show-work experience.
- I can produce high quality hair cuts.
- I have training skills in hairdressing
  - technical skills
  - selling skills
  - business skills.
- I have promotional skills.

☐
☐
☐
☐
☐
☐
☐
☐
☐

- I have marketing skills.   □
- Other.   □

_____

6. I have *information power*:

- I know where to obtain the information.   □
- I know how to collect *factual information* to support my
  viewpoint or argument.   □

_____

7. I have *connection power* by:

- utilising my personal contacts within the company. □
- utilising my contacts within the industry.   □
- utilising my social contacts through my hobbies/
  interests which may be of future use.   □

_____

You will be surprised at how many you may actually have but the question is *do you use them effectively?*

Handling the change

If you wish to change the power structure, do not expect it to happen overnight. It will require a *plan of action*. Figure 4.10 illustrates the cycle of handling the change. Note that change can take three weeks, three months or even three years for Stage One but certainly not three days.

Fig. 4.10
Handling the change.

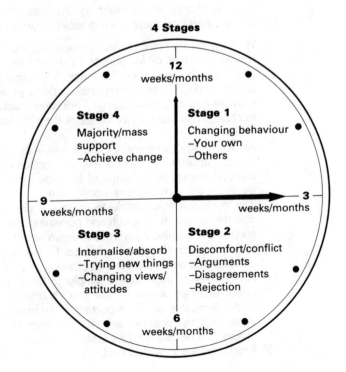

Stage One

To change the behaviour of individuals we need to change our behaviour towards them and *positively reinforce* the behaviour we want. Consistency is the key. By that we mean that the behaviour required of the leader must continue *every* day of the week, not just on less busy days. One approach may be to set up an induction programme to provide instruction in the new and desired practice and structure within the company.

Stage Two

This occurs after a period which may be six weeks or six months, or even six years. Attitude change will slowly come about as people adopt new behaviours and discard old practices. *Practising new behaviours reinforces the need to change one's approach.* If people see themselves succeeding with the new approach, then in time the attitude change will be successful.

It is common for staff to experience at this stage what is known as 'dissonance'. This is a state of discomfort that people experience as a result of different influences and changes which make them feel uncomfortable. This feeling is common when people may have been doing something for many years and then they are asked to change. There is a conflict within themselves about the change. An example of this is when you may have an opinion of something, and people whom you value, such as your friends, may have the opposite view. This then brings about the feeling as to whether you should stick to your own viewpoint or change to the opinion of your friends. If you value your friends then you may change but you will still experience the feeling of inner conflict. This is a normal feeling and we experience it in many areas of our life.

Managing change in organisations involves attempting to reduce inner conflict in others and there are a number of ways of achieving this:

(1) We may set up small project groups, e.g. maybe we wish everyone to handle long hair or for stylists to do all their own colouring work as opposed to having a specialist tinter. A feeling of dissonance (discomfort) is likely to result. Introducing small working groups in which those people who are happy to have changed are mixed with those that do not want to change has much more influence than the leader imposing his or her views.

(2) Re-designing jobs whereby certain people do not have to carry out all of the new approaches, only some, can reduce discomfort. Giving people the opportunity to do some of the new jobs well and getting positive feedback will increase their confidence.

(3) The company may decide to impose a rigorous training programme which is meant to be tough and punishing. *As long as sufficient people survive the training then the likely outcome is that those who succeed will value what they have achieved.* Outward bound courses are often used for this activity in selecting managers or sales staff.

(4) An alternative approach is simply to allow time for discussion. The opportunity for people to talk to each other and exchange their views and experiences can be important. If the majority of people in the group agree that the changes are valuable then those not in favour of the change will often alter their attitudes in line with the majority.

(5) Finally, asking individuals publicly to commit their support to the change

can be a powerful tool. This encourages a commitment of ownership that they will positively go forward with the new approach.

Stage Three

This occurs after nine weeks or nine months depending upon the extent of the problem or how much change is anticipated. The individual will now emerge with newly shaped values and practices which he or she tries to put into operation. This process is known as *internalisation*. A person at this stage is likely to find the changes acceptable and may willingly attempt to do more to bring about the change within the power structure. The person will clearly identify with the new approach and way of doing things.

Stage Four

Stage Four can happen after twelve weeks to twelve months. If sufficient numbers of people undergo *internalisation* then they are the *critical mass* (the majority) who are likely to support the changes of power structure within the organisation.

Chapter Five
Handling Staff Problems and Disciplinary Procedures

5.1 Discipline

Discipline involves two separate elements linked closely to ensure a reasonable and safe behaviour among staff so as to promote business success and to protect clients from injury or upset. The first is education and training to attempt to generate acceptance of and adherence to fair and reasonable rules and standards of work set by the organisation. The second is the procedure and response to be adopted when behaviour falls below these standards (the disciplinary procedure). This will also involve the punishments involved for repeated infringements.

In an ideal world we would have only self-discipline and there would never be any need for rules and procedures. But human nature being what it is, people need guidance and reminders as to what is expected of them, especially young or inexperienced staff. People often admit to having 'lazier selves' which if not checked get worse.

> 'I started being a few minutes late, then it was ten, then half an hour. Then I was told off. If they had said something at the beginning it would have been easier. Then you don't get into bad habits.'
>
> Interview with a Junior Stylist (London)

It is important not to see discipline as negative or punishment-centred. These attitudes are often symptoms of other staff problems and removal of the causes may make for better performance and improved profitability.

Staff are generally much happier when they know what is expected of them and the standards that they must meet as detailed in previous sections on managing people and job descriptions. They will gain security and confidence from knowing the boundaries within which they must act. This also protects them against victimisation and erratic treatment provided that the rules are fair and necessary.

An open approach to rules can be compared to police styles of traffic control. Which would you prefer?

(1) To receive a fine through the post for speeding measured by radar (unknown to you) and photographed licence plates.
(2) Noticing a marked police car on the motorway and having to slow down to avoid being stopped.

Which style of rules do you have in your salon? Which do you think your staff would prefer?

If you wish to ensure reasonable and safe behaviour amongst staff, the staff must know the following:

Fig. 5.1 The
disciplinary
process.

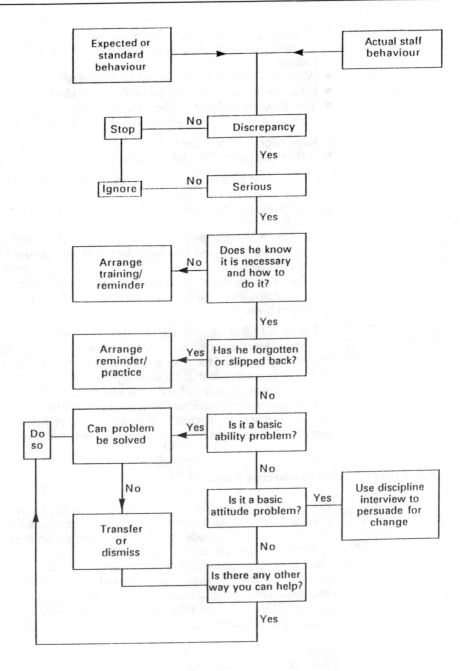

- What is expected of them and an indication of the standards as detailed in the sections on job descriptions (Chapter 3) and rules and regulations (below)
- What they are or are not allowed to do, and why
- What will happen if they fall below these standards or break the rules
- That these procedures will be applied equally and fairly to all staff for all infringements (not just the ones you do not like or the weakest ones)

Many salon managers and owners would ask the question, 'Why do I need to bother with all this?' We list below four reasons why all this is worthwhile:

(1) It promotes a better standard of work amongst staff and creates a better salon image.
(2) It increases morale and staff confidence and a positive attitude towards work.
(3) It reduces the amount of time spent in arguing the whys and wherefores of what is good and bad behaviour and encourages better working relationships.
(4) The salon will be better prepared for any complaints of unfair dismissal if you follow the guidelines and introduce the documents recommended in this book.

Figure 5.1 illustrates in diagrammatical form the whole process of discipline. Note that a disciplinary interview or dismissing members of staff is the last resort, never the first. If we have gone to such pains to advertise, recruit, select and train staff it is short-sighted to dismiss staff because we are, as management, unable to handle the situation.

If we wish to handle staff problems and to ensure that standards and codes of behaviour are fairly applied to all members of staff then we must introduce written rules and regulations so that staff know what is expected of them.

5.2 Procedure for producing rules

Rules may cover a wide range of activities but we provide a checklist of possible areas that rules may need to cover in salons (see Fig. 5.2). You may or may not wish to include all of these in your own set of rules.

It is essential to have a *clear reason* behind the rules and to explain why all these rules are necessary. Nothing causes more hostility than a bad or unfair rule or one which is clearly old-fashioned or stupid. Resentment can be avoided if adequate explanations are given and rules are based on logic and reason. Rules based on prejudice or emotion will simply encourage 'rule breaking' and 'beating the system'.

Standards of job performance

In addition to rules, staff need to know what standards are required of them and how these will be measured. The basic document for this is the job description. This has been explained in some detail in Chapter 3 which also gives some examples of specimen job descriptions for hairdressing jobs. The job descriptions supplied are an outline so that readers can identify the key areas in defining the job.

Fig. 5.2 Areas for rules to cover in salons.

(1) Protection of company facilities/safety
- Security
- Handling of money and valuables
- Treatment of equipment, furniture etc
- Smoking
- Weapons
- Handling hazardous chemicals etc.
- What to do in case of fire, bomb threat or holdups (robbery) or other emergency
- Health, hygiene and Safety Regulations

(2) Respect for company property
- Damaging or defacing property
- Use of company time
- Use of company resources (telephone, equipment, lotions etc.)
- Personal calls
- Valuables etc.
- Works areas etc., tidiness
- Uniforms and dress

(3) Completing company records (accuracy and truthfulness)
- Bookings
- Timesheets
- Expense claims

(4) Punctuality, absence, sickness, attendance
- Procedure to be followed
- Approval in advance
- Standards required

(5) Use of alcohol or drugs

(6) Gambling or other activities

(7) Respect for other staff/clients
- Distributing unauthorised material
- Abusive language, fights, arguments
- Eating, chewing, sexual harassment etc.
- Obeying senior staff
- Infectious diseases

(8) Confidentiality
- Documents of business
- Information about business
- Surveys (taking part)
- Financial performance

(9) Care and maintenance of stock

(10) Vigilance over theft
- What to do if you see this happening

Sample misconduct and disciplinary rules/procedure

The Company reserves the right to terminate employment in cases of misconduct or failure to comply with the Company's regulations, or when artistically or technically the employee does not reach or maintain the standard required by the Company in accordance with their job description. The Company's disciplinary rules are contained in this Company Manual.

(1) The employee will not normally be dismissed for a first offence, except in cases of gross misconduct. Gross misconduct is:

- Where an employee's work involves accounting for or handling cash and fails to comply with instructions as laid down by the Company.
- Drunkenness which would seriously endanger the salon, staff or clients.
- Items of equipment or stock belonging to the Company removed from the premises at any time, either intentionally or unintentionally.
- An employee approaches, solicits or accepts custom from any person who is a customer of any salon within the Company and undertakes services for them outside the premises.
- Any serious offence which has been finally warned to the employee previously.

(2) The following procedure will take place unless for cases of gross misconduct:

- Verbal warning by immediate superior, i.e. manager, in the *presence of a third person* and a file note forwarded to the administrator for record purposes.
- Second verbal warning, procedure as above, but the subject of the second warning *must be the same subject* as the first warning.
- Third and final warning resulting in possible dismissal. Details to be communicated to the managing director. Third and final warnings will only be carried out by the managing director. They *must* be put in writing to the employee stating the reason for the warning, the dates of the previous warnings and the time limit set before the warning is reviewed. Final warnings must be on the same subject as the two previous warnings, i.e. the three warnings cannot be given on time-keeping for first warning, technical ability for second warning.
  Accurate records of what was said, the date of the conversation, who was present and the time limit set before the next review must be forwarded to the administrator for safe keeping.

(3) The policy is such that disciplinary action will be taken only when:

- There is good and clear evidence of some offence.
- It will be demonstrably fair and consistent with the offence committed.
- A member of staff can be represented.
- Staff have a right of appeal (see below)

(4) All staff will have access to a set of up to date rules and regulations of the company.

(5) There is a right of appeal for any member of staff to the Directors of the Company. Appeals must be notified within 48 hours of disciplinary action. Management reserves the right to hold a disciplinary hearing when all interested parties will be invited to attend.

(6) The results of any disciplinary action will be held on file for no more than two years after the offence.

If in doubt on disciplinary procedures always check before speaking to the employee *not afterwards*.

5.3 The disciplinary process

Once a salon has the following two documents it becomes much easier to measure and identify if staff do not meet the standard expected:

- Written rules and regulations
- Job descriptions

You may now need to apply some kind of disciplinary procedure. Not every kind of organisation needs disciplinary procedures but the advantage of a written code resolves ambiguity and introduces good management practice.
  A disciplinary procedure should include all of the following features:

(1) Provision for both informal and formal warnings before disciplinary action is taken
(2) An indication of the range of disciplinary actions that may be taken
(3) A reference to any set of rules or standards which will form the basis of any decision to discipline, including those items of 'gross misconduct' rendering the employee liable to summary dismissal
(4) Any appeals procedure against the result of a disciplinary enquiry

Fig. 5.3
Guidelines on disciplinary procedures contained in the Code of Practice (20 June 1977 issue).

Disciplinary procedure should:

(1) Be in writing.
(2) Specify to whom it applies.
(3) Provide for matters to be dealt with quickly.
(4) Indicate the disciplinary actions which may be taken.
(5) Specify the levels of management which have the authority to take the various forms of disciplinary action, ensuring that immediate superiors do not normally have the power to dismiss without reference to senior management.
(6) Provide for individuals to be informed of the complaints against them and to be given the opportunity to state their case before decisions are reached.
(7) Give individuals the right to be accompanied by a trade union representative or by a fellow employee of their choice.
(8) Ensure that, except for gross misconduct, no employees are dismissed for a first breach of discipline.
(9) Ensure that disciplinary action is not taken until the case has been carefully investigated.
(10) *Ensure that individuals are given an explanation for any penalty imposed.*
(11) Provide a right of appeal and specify the procedure to be followed.

(ACAS published by DOE (HMSO): obtainable from local office)

(5) Indications of any written records kept about an employee and the length of time held before removal from the employee's file, e.g. absenteeism and lateness records

A sample disciplinary procedure is listed in Fig. 5.3. It is also advisable to check that:

(1) The disciplinary procedure does not conflict with the ACAS Code of Practice
(2) Staff have personal access to copies of rules and regulations, job descriptions and disciplinary procedures
(3) Disciplinary procedures do not apply where problems arise due to staff incapability rather than culpability
(4) All staff responsible for carrying out disciplinary procedures are aware of the ACAS Code of Practice

5.4 The disciplinary interview

The disciplinary interview is a problem solving interview whose aims are to:

• Establish facts and determine who is to blame
• Weigh up both sides of the issue
• Formulate action plans to try to achieve results and eliminate the problem

The purpose of a disciplinary interview lies in letting people know where they are falling short of the standards expected and of any breaches of rules. It also serves as a means of identifying other problems in the company which may emerge at the interview. It is for this reason that we must be aware of and understand the various communication techniques detailed in Chapter 4 and, in particular, the barriers to active listening. One of the greatest mistakes that managers make at disciplinary interviews is spending far too much time talking and not enough time listening. From an employee's point of view there is nothing worse than sentence being passed before all the evidence has emerged at the interview. The main stages of a disciplinary interview are shown in Fig. 5.4.

There are a number of approaches that an interviewer can take to a disciplinary interview:

(1) Conspiritorial
(2) Stress
(3) Tell and sell
(4) Tell and listen
(5) Joint problem solving

Professional interviewers would recommend (5) as the most realistic approach to disciplinary interviewing. Figure 5.5 compares these approaches and notes the pros and cons of each. A number of physical items need to be borne in mind when interviewing and we list these below:

(1) Avoid extremes of heat and cold and ensure adequate ventilation.
(2) Avoid extremes of light and dark, e.g. lights shining into eyes.
(3) Ensure that conditions of privacy exist – not in a corridor or public room.
(4) Eliminate interruptions, e.g. phone calls and other staff.
(5) Choose chairs which are reasonably comfortable and easy to sit in.
(6) Set things up so that you are facing one another.

(7) Provide water and an ashtray if appropriate.
(8) Ensure you have the interviewee's job description and all other relevant documents available.

5.5 Conclusions

In conclusion, therefore the principles for effective discipline are:

- Discipline as close to the offence as possible.
- Ensure there is a clear set of rules or standards and the staff know what these are.
- Never discipline in public, always in private.
- Do not have favourites – nothing undermines discipline faster.
- Discipline in a *calm and neutral frame of mind*. Shouting, yelling, swearing, throwing things, sarcasm and insults contribute nothing and are counter productive, leading to mistakes and apologies.
- The aim of discipline is primarily to correct behaviour and only in the last resort to punish when training or counselling have not been effective.
- Concentrate when disciplining on things which can be changed by the employee, not personal characteristics. We can never change a personality, therefore we must concentrate on the problem.
- Be fair, firm and *consistent*. Rules require monitoring and disciplining for every breach but ensure that the 'punishments' are suited to the 'crimes'.

Fig. 5.4
Disciplinary
interview – main
stages.

Preparation before the interview
(1) Ensure the interviewee knows the purpose.
(2) Collect as much evidence as possible before the interiew, e.g. job description/standards/rules and regulations/procedure etc.
(3) Examine employee's past record/performance.
(4) Determine your personal strategy (see text).

The interview itself
(1) Explain the purpose of the interview.

(2) Establish the facts as far as possible.
  - No evidence – no case.
  - Ask employee for his version/explanation.
  - Hear witnesses (if relevant).
  - Go over key points until you are clear.
  - Adjourn if insufficient information.

(3) Agree facts with interviewee.
  - Establish areas of agreement.
  - Explain reasons for required changes.

(4) Establish responsibilities.
  - Examine reasons for problems.
  - Examine special or mitigating circumstances.

(5) Agree future course of action.
  - Agree standards and changes to close difference.
  - Agree any support/help to be given.
  - Agree any sanctions/penalties applicable.
  - Agree review date for improvement.

Strategy	Description/example	Advantages (pros)	Disadvantages (cons)
(1) Conspiratorial approach	Conspiring with interviewee against the system. e.g. Let's solve this together in spite of them.	Helps reluctant interviewee to talk. Removes guilt from interviewer who hates doing it.	Can be easily misunderstood and cause future problems. Punishment necessary. Perverts the real objective of interview.
(2) Stress approach	Give interviewee a 'hard time'. e.g. You may as well confess – we know what you have been doing.	Interviewer feels powerful. Interviewee may confess and promise to improve. Young females find this difficult to take.	No real evidence of any real commitment to change. May disillusion staff. Encourages aggression, lying, dishonesty as defence.
(3) Tell and sell	Explain situation and consequences and reasons behind it and persuade employee to improve. e.g. If you could just remember to clock in/ out properly each time . . .	Useful for young people who may not link actions to their consequences. Also compensates for where staff are unclear about rules, procedures and punishments.	Requires persuasive skills on part of interviewer. Some rules may be difficult to sell to staff.
(4) Tell and listen	Explain as in (3) above then listen to interviewee's explanations weighing up consequences. Useful in clarifying areas of uncertainty. Usually leads into (5).	Wide application where manager wishes to stay friendly and acquaint staff with facts. Needs to be rounded off by agreeing course of action.	Many managers are all tell and no listen (as in (3)). Some staff may be over-zealous and not listen to you!
(5) Joint problem solving	Encourage staff to identify for themselves with your help what has gone wrong and what should be done. Requires a flexible approach to staff problems.	Useful for preventing staff becoming 'case-hardened' and habitual offenders. Often works where all other methods have failed.	Takes longer. Requires most skill and sensitivity to staff. Skill in open questions and listening absolutely essential.

Fig. 5.5 Disciplinary interviewing strategies.

- Follow a set of guidelines for disciplinary action as shown in Fig. 5.4.
- Do not carry private discipline into the open with snide references. When you have completed the interview, you should get back onto normal terms with the staff as soon as possible and not harbour grudges.

If you follow the above procedures then you will ensure that you do not have to:

- Reverse decisions
- Cope with increased staff resentment
- Lose tribunals or other legal actions, a strong motivator to ensure you get procedure correct

We can all improve and can find time to do so if we want. Many salon owners do so constantly but others all too frequently wait for events to happen to them. The barrier to improvement is always apathy, arrogance, and priorities placed elsewhere.

Chapter Six
Training

6.1 Introduction

Training is a systematic development of the knowledge, skills and attitudes required by an individual to perform adequately a given task or job. Training involves learning of various kinds and in various situations. Learning may be something that the trainee wants to do for him or herself, or it may be necessary to provide it for that person. If training is provided or offered, the individual may need to be given an incentive – in other words to be motivated – to learn and to apply the learning. Even if the trainee is self-motivated it may still be necessary to provide guidance and training which will help the person to channel or focus his/her enthusiasm towards a worthwhile goal.

Training can take place in a number of ways – on the job or off the job, in the company or outside the company. It can involve the use of many techniques such as:

- Demonstrations
- Practice
- Coaching
- Guided reading
- Lectures
- Talks
- Discussions
- Case studies
- Role playing
- Assignments
- Projects
- Group exercises
- Programmed learning
- The discovery method

These techniques can be provided by a wide range of people such as:

- Specialist company trainers
- Managers
- Supervisors
- Colleagues/stylists
- External trainers
- Educationalists

The step-by-step process towards training is as follows:

(1) Identification and analysis of training needs
(2) Defining the objectives
(3) Preparation of training plans and programmes
(4) Implementation of the plans
(5) Measuring and analysing the results
(6) Evaluation of training programmes and technique

6.2 Identification and analysis of training needs

The analysis of training needs aims to define the gap or difference between what is actually happening now and what should, or is expected to, happen in the future. Training needs should be analysed into three areas:

Fig. 6.1 The
training cycle.

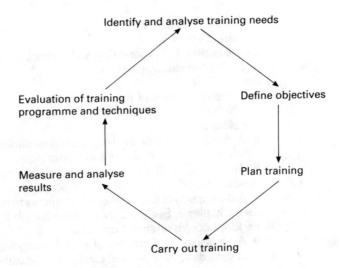

(1) The company or the salon as a whole

To analyse the company or the salon as a whole defining the salon's strengths and weaknesses and the salon or company's future requirements. For example the salon may be operating in a changing environment whereby more competitors are opening in the town or city. This may require the salon to adopt a different approach towards the services it offers, the pricing strategy of the salon and the range of work that the stylists may be expected to achieve. Computerisation on reception for client records may be an area where the company needs to develop its skills to offer a comprehensive service or to personalise promotional methods.

(2) Individual salons

The salon as part of a group may lack certain expertise or skills, for example the salon group as a whole may have a good knowledge of hairdressing, colouring or perming skills but an individual salon may be weak in one of these areas.

(3) Individuals

Certain staff within the organisation will need to be trained to develop their potential. They may be grouped together with a common training need, e.g. training in long hair work or men's hairdressing, or they may need to receive individual training.

Methods of analysis

There are three basic methods of analysing training needs:

(1) *Surveys*
  ● Client satisfaction survey
  ● Staff questionnaires

- Competitors' analysis
- Market street surveys

(See Chapter 1 on Marketing and promotions for further information regarding the examples given.)

(2) *Job analysis*
- A broad analysis of the needs of the job and any special problems which may be seen by the job holder, his/her manager and possibly colleagues
- A detailed study of the responsibiities, duties and tasks carried out which forms the basis for a job description
- An analysis of the knowledge and skills required by the job holder which forms the basis of a job description
- A description of the training requirements to meet the needs of the job

(See Chapter 3, Section 3.2 Analysing the job.)

(3) *Performance/assessment appraisal*
- Assesses the performance of individuals against agreed objectives and standards already set and clearly defined within the organisation and will consider potential for promotion
- Establishes the gaps in knowledge, weaknesses in doing the job and areas to be developed if the individual is to progress

(See Chapter 3, Section 3.13 Integration of new staff. See also the Appendix Sources of further information for further reading on staff appraisal.)

6.3 Defining the objectives

Training must aim to achieve *measurable goals* expressed in terms of improved performance by individuals, a salon as part of a group, or a company as a whole. The goals must be realistic and achievable and you need to remember that you cannot train people to change their personalities, you can only develop them by various training techniques to learn skills and to want to apply them.

As explained in Chapter 3, job descriptions must have clearly defined areas of responsibility and levels of authority with minimum standards which are measurable and achievable. Training objectives, like job descriptions, which are vague and woolly will result in the training being difficult to measure. The reason why many owners and managers of salons are not committed to training is often because the aims and objectives were not clearly defined in the first place.

Sending staff upon training courses without individuals knowing why they are attending or what they are hoping to achieve or, even worse, being sent on a training programme as a punishment to 'get their act together' tends to have a demotivating effect.

Implications of training

There are many long term benefits of training but it would be foolish to pretend there are no disadvantages. These disadvantages occur when owners or managers (or training experts!) have not clearly identified the real training needs. Detailed below are potential problem areas which may occur:

Cause	Effect
Staff sent on course as appeasement but not allowed to put into practice new skills and/or behaviour.	Frustration, demotivation, deterioration in performance.
No clearly defined responsibilities.	Frustration, demotivation, deterioration in performance and/ or behaviour.
No clearly defined authority.	Frustration, demotivation, deterioration in performance and/ or behaviour.
No involvement in decision making.	Frustration, demotivation, deterioration in performance and/ or behaviour.
Disruptive behaviour.	Deterioration in performance and/ or behaviour, staff leaving.
No consultation on decisions that directly affect the staff.	Frustration, demotivation, failure to contribute ideas in the future, staff leaving.
Authoritarian management style.	Frustration, demotivation, staff resignation.
Increased confidence by learning new skills.	Challenging decisions and superiors, questioning policy, potential resignation if staff not listened to.
Third party reinforcement of own views.	Challenging decisions and superiors, questioning policy, potential resignation if no change in operation of business.

Read Chapter 3, Section 3.2 Analysing the job and Chapter 4 Managing People for further understanding on why these problems may occur.

6.4 Planning the programme

Training programmes should be based on the analysis of training needs and should include:

(1) A definition of the objectives, describing the outcome of training in terms of the results or behaviour expected. In other words, what the trainee will be doing after having achieved the objective, e.g.:

At the end of a training course in selling retail products the stylist will be able to sell a range of retail products to 10 per cent of all clients visiting the salon.

(2) Details of:

- Timing/length of programme (days of the week and times during the day)

- Content of the programme – subject headings
- Methods of training – lectures, role playing, project work
- Who will train
- Venue or place of training – on/off the job, in or outside the company

(3) The method by which the training will be evaluated – one-to-one interviews, surveys.

(4) Estimate of costs.

Timing/length of programme

When planning the timing and length of the programme take into consideration the following factors:

- Operational needs, e.g. salon opening hours
- Individual's age and experience
- Barriers to learning, e.g. tiredness at end of the day, noise, interruptions

(See section 4.2 on Communication.)

Contents of programme

Plan the programme to take into account the following points:

(1) Logical structure. Define the programme into a logical structure with key subject headings.

(2) Context. Start by explaining the whole story or the whole picture. What is the objective or the goal of the training programme and where does it fit into the whole plan or story of their job or the salon or organisation in which they work?

(3) Explain why the job has to be done.

(4) Never just teach a process.

(5) Then teach the detailed process the trainee must learn to achieve the goal.

Digestible chunks

Present the information or training programme in amounts that the trainee can cope with. Read section 4.2 Communication, particularly on the process of communication, questioning techniques and active listening.

Know your trainees

Adjust your approach to meet the needs and ability of the trainee, e.g. hairdressing trainees, senior stylists, managers.

Link the training to the trainee's existing knowledge

Draw on the previous experience of the trainee and link this to the job to be learnt. Give illustrations and examples wherever possible.

Concentrate on positive instructions

Avoid negative instruction; talk about and demonstrate the right way to approach a job.

Give the trainee feedback on progress

Tell the trainee how they are doing and give praise and encouragement.

Allow the trainee time to practise

Practice reinforces understanding and learning.

6.4.1 *Training techniques*

The main training techniques available can be divided into three areas:

(1) On the job techniques
(2) Off the job techniques
(3) A combination of both

On the job techniques

It is essential to stress the importance of on the job training and how valuable this can be. Figure 6.2 shows sources of on the job training.

Advantages of on the job training:

- Immediate contribution together with a feeling of responsibility
- All the learning is immediately relevant and can be put into practice quickly (a distinct disadvantage when training off the job) and is perhaps a more

Fig. 6.2 Sources of on-the-job training.

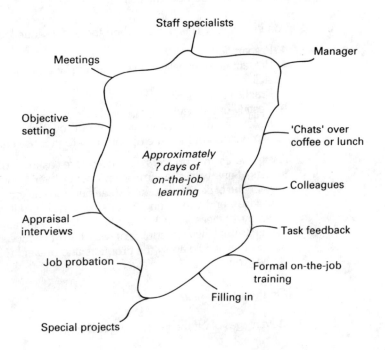

Staff specialists

Meetings

Manager

Objective setting

'Chats' over coffee or lunch

Approximately
? days of
on-the-job
learning

Colleagues

Appraisal
interviews

Task feedback

Job probation

Formal on-the-job
training

Filling in

Special projects

creative approach to what could be done in a hairdressing salon instead of the standardised, boring process that many trainees have to suffer

Problems of on the job training:

- Often a skilled person working on the salon floor is unable to communicate the skill being trained in simple, understandable steps
- The learner may be frightened by the gap in his or her ability in comparison to the skilled person and is unable to learn
- Bad practices and attitudes are passed on as well as good
- The skilled person is prevented from performing at his or her normal level or has to devote productive time to the trainee
- The trainee will make mistakes which may ruin materials or products

Demonstrations This requires telling or showing a trainee how to do a job and then allowing them to get on with it. This is the most common and effective method as long as it is done properly, i.e. by a trained instructor following a logical training programme based on job analysis and the practical application of it. It is also essential that the instructor has received training in training techniques and has preferably undergone a professional training course with recognised qualifications, has good communication skills and understands the psychological aspects of training.

Coaching In which counselling takes place, usually between the manager and staff and preferably based upon performance and/or assessment/appraisal.

Job rotation This method broadens staff experience by moving them from job to job. Many hairdressing trainees rotate on a regular three monthly basis to work with individual stylists whereby they can learn from each individual's techniques. This is an effective way as long as the learning experience is properly planned and controlled and the staff to whom they have been allocated have competent skills.

Job instruction This occurs when there is a sequence of:

- Preparation
- Presentation, usually involving an explanation and demonstration of the skill
- Practice of the skill
- Testing of the new skill
- Follow-up or evaluation of subject or skill learnt, e.g. hairdressing demonstration then the opportunity to practise and be evaluated

Assignments or projects Trainees are asked to complete tasks or investigations with the aim of improving their knowledge of a particular subject and of developing skills in seeking and analysing information, creating new ideas and presenting results, e.g. hair product knowledge training whereby trainees learn the products, their features and benefits, use the products until they feel confident with them, produce suggestions or ideas as to how they would apply the products and present their findings to the rest of the group.

Off the job techniques

Advantages of off the job training techniques:

- The possibility to learn skills in a step by step process with assessment and feedback at each stage
- The lack of distraction of everyday pressures of the job
- Time to reflect (an important part of learning)
- The opportunity to mix and talk with others doing similar or different jobs
- On external courses there is the opportunity to talk with people from other organisations
- The practical advantages of using outside training companies who are specialised in this field

Obstacles to effective off the job training include:

- The individual must want to learn. If there is no interest, or no belief that the individual needs it, or no belief that the course will provide it, then it is very unlikely that learning will occur.
- Learning is attached to the context in which it is learned and it may not be easily transferred. For example, good test scores may be gained at college or on a course but the learning may not be used on the job because the need or the opportunity to use it does not occur at the same time.
- Unless the learned material is used on the job it is quickly and easily forgotten.

Lectures/seminars Talks designed to transfer information to an audience using controlled content and timings. Lectures may appear to be the best way of increasing knowledge but they are limited by the capacity of the individuals to absorb what has been heard – which could be as little as 20 per cent. This can be caused by the size of the audience, the language and speed at which the lecturer delivers the material, the complexity or lack of visual aids or environmental barriers such as noise and interruptions.

In the author's experience, this is the least effective of training techniques as the audience often pick up and absorb what they want to hear without understanding how they may apply the information unless other training techniques are used to reinforce the objective.

Discussion Discussion techniques aim to get a group to participate actively in learning and to give people a chance to learn from the experience of others.

Discovery method This style of instruction allows the trainee to learn by finding out principles of a subject for him/herself but must be backed up with suitable guidance from the instructor.

Programmed learning/open learning A text which progressively feeds information to trainees, e.g. open learning, correspondence course. After each piece of information is delivered or given, questions are asked either verbally or through a computer or reading material which the trainee should answer correctly before moving on. Hairdressing open learning videos are now available.

Case studies These are descriptions of an event or situation which the trainees analyse in order to diagnose the cause of the problem and work out how to solve it.

Role playing Where participants practise skills by acting out a situation, assuming the roles of the characters, e.g. recruitment/selection techniques, disciplinary interviewing techniques, counselling techniques, assessment/appraisal.

Group exercises Trainees examine problems and work out solutions as a group, e.g. creative brain storming, group project work.

6.4.2 *Aids to training*

Visual aids

Visual aids have three main uses:

(1) To convey information
(2) To reinforce the spoken word
(3) To provide background information and atmosphere

To convey information They should be used whenever information can be conveyed more effectively by visual means especially:

- To give a breakdown or analysis of complicated information
- To show the stages in a process
- To provide evidence and examples of people, places or objects to support the discussion or presentation

Visual aids such as films or video tapes are the most interesting, but should not be allowed to play for too long as they can detract from the talk.

To reinforce the spoken word Visual and audio/visual aids can be used to introduce a spoken text, to link one part of a presentation to another, to summarise a sequence of ideas or pose or ask a question.

To provide background information and atmosphere Static visual aids such as photographs of a new company logo, posters, charts, product packs, can be set up beforehand and left throughout the presentation. They can provide an alternative subject of focus to the speaker, something else which the audience can look at to reinforce the theme.

Visual and audio aids can also help set the tone and mood of the presentation. The choice should depend not only on the subject, but on the venue as well as the size and nature of the audience, e.g. young hairdressers would require a different stimulus from a presentation than a 'long in the tooth' company of sales representatives!

General guidelines for visual aids

- Projected visuals, e.g. films, slides, overhead projectors, are easy to see because they are magnified.
- Too many types of visual aids in one presentation may be difficult to co-ordinate and may actually distract the audience.
- Never use existing visual material just because it happens to be available, e.g. an out-of-date photograph or poster. Making-do will probably hinder rather than help you reach your objectives.
- Order all materials at the earliest possible date. They often take time to prepare and should be available in time for checking and rehearsal.
- Make sure all the necessary equipment will be available at the rehearsal or training session, e.g. spare bulbs, leads, plug adapters.
- Keep a list of all the visual aids you plan to use and make a note of them in your training programme or script to jog your memory.

- If creating visual material during your training session, e.g. writing on flip charts or acetates, always remember the following:

  Have an outline of figures or notes pre-planned (so you are not left counting on your fingers!)
  Check the quality of the pens for the overhead projector or flip chart (keep the caps on until you need them). Only use this method if your printing is legible and you know how to spell any difficult words.
  Wherever possible use a flip chart or board you can stand beside *not one on the wall behind you.*

Audience capacity of visual aids

Remember the following statistics:

- Flip chart messages can be seen by 15 people and no more.
- Overhead projector transparencies will reach up to 50 viewers if you have a long 'throw' from machine to screen.
- Video cassette/TV will reach up to 20 people per 24 inch screen. Good quality, big screen video projection will reach up to 100 people.
- 35 mm slides can be magnified to reach 100 people.

How to use visual aids

Remember the '4 Ps':

(1) Plan
(2) Presentation
(3) Precaution
(4) Performance

Plan
- Don't use unnecessary slides.
- Make sure all the information you need is available.
- Use slides for impact when words would confuse the audience. We all listen at the same speed but read at different speeds.
- Introduce colour. Colour has more impact than black and white.
- Use large writing and very few words. The more information on the slide, the less impact it will have.
- Make sure that you use words on the slide to emphasise the main point.
- Make sure the diagrams are readable.

Presentation
- Check all the equipment and paperwork is available and in good running order.
- Check that the slides, films or diagrams are the right way up.
- Check that the visual aids are in focus.
- Check that the slides or diagrams are in sequential order.
- Check the room for electrical sockets, acoustics, window closing and blinds, visibility of the audience.
- Never make last minute major alterations in the presentation as this will confuse you and the audience.

Precautions
- If more than one person is taking part it is essential that a full rehearsal is carried out. Always expect the worst to happen and be prepared for it.

Performance
- Do not ignore the diagrams and slides.
- Do not stand between the audience and the screen so that they cannot see.
- Do not keep looking over your shoulder at every slide change.
- Do not talk to the screen.
- Do not hold the slide for too long – if you leave it on the screen it will detract from what you are saying.

Hints on preparing a notes system

Unless you are a very experienced speaker or trainer do not rely upon your visual aids as your only notes – what happens if the equipment doesn't work?

Bearing in mind that many people have difficulty in spelling it is essential to prepare a notes system and to familiarise yourself with the spelling of certain words. Use the following guidelines:

(1) Always prepare your notes or script yourself. Only you know how the information should flow and which parts should be set out with special emphasis.
(2) Avoid flimsy paper for scripts – cards are easier to hold. Write on one side only and number each one clearly in the top right hand corner.
(3) Do not staple sheets or cards together; put to one side each card when you have completed delivery of it.
(4) Use different colours to mark the places where you intend to use visual aids or invite audience participation.
(5) Attach photocopies of any transparencies to the appropriate notes.
(6) If you have difficulty with spelling use the following ideas when writing on a flip chart:

- Get a member of the audience to write for you so you can concentrate on the feedback
- Get the feedback and have a pre-planned list already written out
- Have a card system of common words which tend to be used in your training sessions

We have tended to concentrate upon visual aids used in a training session such as videos, films, slides and OHP transparencies but there are alternative methods of reinforcing training such as:

- Audio cassette tapes which can be used to reinforce the learning message at a later date when the trainee is on his/her own
- Diagrams as part of handouts
- Books for additional in-depth reading and to be absorbed at the trainee's own pace
- Games which can introduce the fun element to learning
- Competitions/quizzes which introduce the discovery method but in an amusing way

Venue or place of training

Check all the physical and environmental arrangements:

(1) Is there sufficient seating and is it comfortable to sit for long periods of time?

(2) Can everyone see and hear?
(3) Can interruptions be avoided including the telephone?
(4) Ensure the temperature is not too hot or too cold.
(5) Ensure the environment is quiet.
(6) Provide ashtrays for smokers and segregate non-smokers if they wish. Alternatively, ban smoking but have a 'smoke break'.

Estimate of costs

Many enthusiastic trainers forget that the first question a salon owner or manager will ask is 'How much?' The costs need to cover the following:

● Development of training programme
● Training aids, e.g. films, equipment, production of training handouts
● Cost of venue and refreshments
● Lost revenue

Training is always a long term investment but business owners and managers tend to focus on the short term lost revenue as opposed to the long term benefits of developing people. The hairdressing industry is no exception to this attitude. Many salon owners view training as negative on the basis that 'if I train them they will leave and become my competitors' but the question to pose is, 'Can I afford not to train?' Within the industry the most valuable resource available to make businesses grow and prosper is people. If we build our people, our people will build our business – without people we might as well become self-employed mobile hairdressers with hairdressing salons becoming a thing of the past.

6.4.3 *Training approaches: short term versus long term*

Many of the training methods that are applied within the hairdressing industry tend not to work long term. In this section it is crucial to understand how trainers affect others and learners are affected by them in learning situations. A simpler way of describing it would be to say the things we say and how we say them have an effect upon the outcome of training. Much of the training that is received and conducted within the industry has been *authoritative* for many years. This involves the trainer taking a dominant or assertive role, focusing on training activities and not the participants or learners. Three approaches are used:

● Influencing or directing behaviour
● Imparting new knowledge
● Challenging beliefs, attitudes or behaviour

These approaches seem to be a quicker way to achieve results by giving instructions, but whilst they may be helpful initially, they prevent learners from understanding and being able to manage on their own later. An example of this is when learners are shown how to neutralise a perm. If the outcome goes wrong they may have difficulty in identifying the cause, thus creating more problems in the long run. This in turn affects the learners' confidence to attempt the task again.

The same can be said for salon owners who attend training courses to be 'stimulated and wound up to perform' without understanding the theory behind what they have been shown to do. If events do not work out in practice upon returning to the salon they reject the new methods and approaches without the understanding of what went wrong or how to correct it. This prevents learners of all levels owning the learning and absorbing it permanently. This is one of the reasons why people often return to the same training courses or seminars – the training did not stick!

The alternative approach to training and learning can be achieved by a facilitative approach. The trainer is less obtrusive, allowing the trainee to learn and develop by self-direction and self-discovery. This is the difference between showing a toddler how to build his bricks and the order of building them, instead of allowing the toddler to discover the best route for himself while giving him your undivided attention when he gets into difficulty.

To enable learning to be absorbed permanently the following methods are required:

(1) Releasing tension in the learner, e.g. dealing with the barriers which prevent learning such as fear and anxiety particularly if the course is seen as a punishment. This can be achieved through laughter, time for constructive discussion, and facing the problems.
(2) Allowing time to reflect on what has been learnt either during the training session or for a sufficient lapse of time to be allowed between each training session to absorb the information.
(3) Recapping the key learning points either through the 'trainer' or by the trainee.
(4) Self-discovery training methods through group work or projects to 'discover' the key learning points. Avoiding telling trainees the answers.
(5) Understanding theoretical frameworks and concepts in order to help the learner to identify the cause of problems and/or the solutions. This is just as appropriate for business skills as it is for hairdressing skills.
(6) Analysing the variety of options available. It is crucial for the learner to realise that there is never one answer but several – the skill is deciding the pros and cons of each.
(7) Being supportive by praising the positive actions and helping the learner to value your contribution.
(8) Showing positive feelings, care and concern.

The greatest depth of learning occurs with the above training methods, where the learner – not the trainer – solves the problem in a supportive and non-threatening way.

If we can move our training towards these *self-managed learning methods* then we can start to reach the under-developed potential in the industry, our salons and within individuals. Harnessing the talents, potential and energy cannot, however, come about by training individuals on courses and seminars – it can only occur by learning throughout the whole company. *This means becoming a 'learning company'.*

A learning company is an organisation that helps the learning of all its members and continually transforms itself to meet the changing needs of the business, clients, the people we employ, our suppliers and the environment (see also Section 7.4).

6.5 Evaluating the training

Training is evaluated by comparing its objectives or goals with its effects or outcome to discover how far it has achieved its purpose. Evaluation can take place at a number of levels:

- *Reactions* The immediate reaction of trainees to the training – how useful they feel it is, what they think of individual sessions and speakers, what they would like to put in or take out.
- *Learning* The measurement of the skills or knowledge trainees have gained as a result of training, e.g. a greater understanding of communication techniques, a heightened awareness of how speed in technical training methods can increase overall profitability to the salon.
- *Applying the learning:* What skills will now be put into practice and the time span agreed as to when the improved performance or new skills will be in operation.
- *Job behaviour* The assessment of how trainees have applied their training on the job.
- *Impact* The extent to which the behaviour of trainees, after training, has improved the performance of the individual, the salon and the whole organisation, e.g. after retail sales training has the retail sales percentage increased?
- Monitoring performance resulting from the training and giving feedback as to the outcome.

Methods of evaluation

- Comparison of targets prior to and after training
- Comparison of job performance to job description
- One to one interviews
- Surveys (dependent upon the training received)
- Behaviour of staff who have attended training

Evaluation of the trainer

At the end of each training session all good trainers should be prepared to ask the following questions:

(1) Did I prepare well?
(2) Did I put the job into context?
(3) Did I advise the learner what to expect in terms of both the job and the training time involved?
(4) Did I break the job down into digestible chunks?
(5) Did I put the training over in the right sequence?
(6) Did I bring out the key points?
(7) Did I show confidence and enthusiasm?
(8) Did I get and maintain the learner's interest?
(9) Did I get the learner to participate?
(10) Did I ask the right questions?
(11) Did I make proper use of the equipment and material for demonstration and practice?
(12) Did I use my notes?
(13) Did I follow through my instructions to evaluate effectiveness?
(14) Did the learner know how he/she was getting on?
(15) Did I ensure the learner's final performance was up to standard?

Chapter Seven
Planning and Organisation

There are many reasons why clients visit a hairdresser – the majority of them are nothing to do with having their hair cut! This is covered in detail in the sections on promotions (Chapter 1) and motivation (Chapter 4). Equally important is the effect that bad planning and organisation have upon productivity which, in turn, affects the potential turnover and profitability of the business.

Planning can be categorised into the following key areas:

(1) Planning the salon
(2) Planning the work
(3) Planning your time
(4) Planning your staff's time

Points (1) and (2) are discussed in this chapter and points (3) and (4) in Chapter 8.

7.1 Planning the salon

Planning the salon layout is a key element in achieving a successful, profitable salon where the staff and clients enjoy the hairdressing experience. Salon owners often spend a substantial amount of time selecting the decor and image of a new salon as a kind of extension of their own personality but too little attention is paid to the work flow aspect and the effect it has upon:

- Client comfort
- Staff comfort and efficiency
- Productivity levels
- Marketing
- Meeting legislation requirements, e.g. Health and Safety at Work Act (see Chapter 9)

7.1.1 Client comfort

Clients perceive part of the image of the salon by its efficiency and comfort. This will affect whether they return to the salon because it has been an enjoyable experience and/or whether they will recommend it to their friends.

We need to consider the following points when planning a new salon:

- Access to reception
- Security of coats and belongings
- Comfortable seating in reception
- Comfortable seating at the backwash
- Comfortable seating at the styling position
- Access to backwashes and styling positions

- Heating and ventilation
- Lighting
- Access to toilets
- Conditions of toilet facilities
- Colour scheme

7.1.2 *Staff comfort and efficiency*

Staff will be more productive, particularly on busy days, if we consider the following points when planning a salon:

- Heating and ventilation
- Lighting
- Floor surfaces – easy to walk on, easy to clean
- Work surfaces – easy to clean, no sharp or dangerous edges
- Access to stock cupboard
- Access to dispensary
- Distance from backwash to styling position
- Access to coat and gown cupboard
- Access/distance to refreshment making facilities
- Optimum space for styling position
- Uncluttered traffic flow areas
- Colour schemes and their effect on the eye and psyche

7.1.3 *Productivity levels*

Reception area

When planning the layout of the salon how much thought is given to the size and space of the reception area? Is it too small making it difficult for staff to perform their jobs efficiently? Does it take up more than 15–20 per cent of the salon area? How much lost productivity area has been used by the reception desk? We must ask the question, 'Why do we have a reception area at all?'

The purpose of a reception area is to:

(1) Project the initial image of the salon
(2) Welcome clients and put them at ease
(3) Provide facilities for clients to enter and depart with ease (particularly on busy days)
(4) Provide facilities to house coats and gowns
(5) Provide waiting facilities
(6) Provide a consultaton area (optional)

How many salons meet all the above criteria?

Backwash/styling positions

From frequent visits to hairdressing salons we have come to the conclusion that backwash chairs were designed by men! Otherwise, why is there no allowance made for the fact that female clients are often between 5'3" and 5'6"in height and that we are not physically structured to have a straight shape from knee to shoulder! The shortcomings of chairs and backwashes are emphasised further when undergoing perming or colouring processes.

Why are backwashes positioned some distance from the styling position so that staff walk several miles each day between the two key areas in the salon? Even worse if they are up or down a number of steps. How much time is lost in productivity by the inefficient placement of key areas?

How much thought is given to easy access of equipment, e.g. trolleys, dispensary, electrical points and sterilisers, and the productivity time lost in reaching and using them?

Does the salon have adjustable styling chairs? Think of productivity loss due to absenteeism when staff are absent with bad backs or slipped discs when adjustable chairs would have solved the problem!

Refreshments

When offering clients refreshments, have the facilities available to supply them been considered? How long does it take to walk up a flight of stairs, wait for a kettle to boil and return with the drink? Has the time been costed into the pricing structure? Are there other ways of reducing the time element such as a thermostatic hot water boiler, a dish washer and a duty rota for staff to ensure that everyone helps keep the refreshment making area clean?

The average time to make a drink, including washing the cup and saucer, will be 6–10 minutes. Calculate how many clients have refreshments over a week and then a year! Think of the lost productivity time usually because this element of the service was not planned in the first place.

The answer to the planning and organisation of the salon layout is to adopt what is known as 'helicopter vision' and look at the traffic flow and stress points or to sit at key areas in the salon so that alternative ways of working can be achieved even in the smallest of spaces.

7.2 Planning the work

When planning work within the salon we often simply respond to the clients' wishes but, with a little forethought, we could ensure that the work flows easily and smoothly throughout the day instead of in the usual stop/go pattern.

7.2.1 Appointment systems

The majority of impulse visits to salons occur late morning or during the afternoon, very rarely at the beginning of the day. If we wish to maximise productivity we must fill up the appointment book systematically wherever possible. This involves booking clients into the salon by offering them the 'either/or' technique.

Example
Receptionist: 'When would you like to come Mrs Smith?'
Client: 'Tuesday.'
Receptionist: 'We can offer 9.30 a.m. or 10.00 a.m.'
If the client says can you make it later, offer 10.30 or 10.45 and so on – not 3.30 p.m.

This approach will then allow for impulse visits later in the day instead of salons turning potential customers away even though they were not busy earlier.

Staggered appointment systems

Staggering appointments is one solution to planning work more efficiently. It will:

(1) Avoid 'stop/go' working
(2) Increase productivity
(3) Distribute support staff evenly
(4) Reduce congestion at the backwash
(5) Reduce congestion at the reception area
(6) Reduce stress

Example
One trainee works with 2 stylists as follows:

Stylist one	Stylist two
9.00	9.15
9.30	9.45
10.00	10.15
10.45	11.00

Distribution of appointments makes for smoother use of trainees' or shampooists' time. It helps to avoid congestion at the backwash and reception area.

The purpose of three 30 minute appointments and a 45 minute appointment is to allow for extra services which may have been sold (e.g. colouring or perming), late clients, and slow working hairdressers. Some stylists who are very fast may only need four 30 minute appointments and a 45 minute appointment. Junior stylists, however, usually need two 30 minute appointments and a 45 minute appointment until their speed increases with practice.

The concept of staggered appointments means that two or three stylists work as a team with a trainee or salon assistant to ensure a smooth work flow. This is important for support staff who are often asked to carry out several tasks all at the same time!

7.2.2 Operational tasks

There are a number of areas in the running of a salon which, if planned in advance, can make the daily routine more efficient and cost effective and reduce stress levels for staff and clients.

Duty rotas

Many salons have duty rotas for trainees to ensure that the daily tasks are completed. Whether the salon has trainees or not – and in the future many will not – the daily tasks need to be completed. These should be split into: a.m. daily tasks, p.m. daily tasks; weekly tasks; monthly tasks.

It is important to ensure that rotas are:

- Fair – jobs are distributed to male and female staff equally (equality means fair distribution of work for both sexes)
- Reasonable tasks, i.e. not being asked to scrub the floor with a toothbrush!
- Achievable, e.g. equipment and cleaning materials are available to complete the task

- Rotated regularly so that some employees do not get all the boring or dirty jobs

Stock control

We have already identified in Chapter 2 Understanding money how important it is to control direct costs. Stock control is a key area. The main objectives are to ensure:

- Stock percentages remain constant
- Stock does not run out
- We do not over purchase

This means having systems and standards within our salon to ensure we control stock levels. Who is responsible for stock control and how often is it taken – once a week, fortnightly or monthly? Most major manufacturers will supply salons with stock control forms. One or two staff at most should be responsible for ensuring that the system is kept. The more staff involved in controlling stock, the more mistakes will be made. Stock levels rise for a number of reasons:

- Wastage
- Pilfering
- Purchasing methods

Wastage Salons must clearly identify in their training of staff the amount to be measured of:

- Tints
- Bleach/peroxide
- Perm lotion
- Neutraliser
- Shampoo
- Conditioners

What may appear to be small quantities of wasted products accumulates over a 12 month period into a substantial amount of lost product and money.

Pilfering Pilfering often occurs in salons because:

- The stock is not secure
- Staff are not allowed stock at cost or free
- There is no staff purchase book
- There is no stock control

Systems for staff purchases ensure that you control stock and monitor how much is being used, particularly by any individual member of staff. (We have all heard of staff with four grandmothers and 20 sisters!)
    If you expect staff to wear the products and styles of the salon you must offer products either free or at cost price otherwise you encourage pilfering.

Purchasing methods Many salons purchase excessive stock for a number of reasons:

- No stock control
- Smooth talking salesmen
- An attractive incentive scheme
- To obtain higher discounts

With most hair product manufacturers, the larger the order, the higher the discount. This does not mean, however, that you have to purchase a large quantity of one product, e.g. a brand-name perm, but to pledge that over a 12 month period you will spend £x. The higher the total spent the higher the percentage discount. This does not mean that all salons would benefit from a higher discount on products in purely financial terms. Some salons prefer to negotiate 'non-financial' discounts such as promotions, training or marketing expertise (see Chapter 1 on Marketing and promotions for further information).

The key to successful purchasing is always stock control coupled with putting 90 per cent of the salon's purchasing power with one manufacturer who can offer either attractive discounts or, alternatively, business support and expertise.

Client record cards

How many clients come through your salon during a week? One hundred, two hundred, five hundred? How many clients will come in next week and the week after that? Can you remember all of their names, where they live, what service was carried out on their hair on their last visit to the salon? You must have some method of recording information about your clients. There are three key reasons for doing this:

(1) Technical information
(2) Personal details
(3) Promotional aid

Obtaining information about your clients prior to the visit helps with planning and organisation because you can:

- Anticipate the client's needs
- Look efficient which creates a good image
- Reduce your own stress levels
- Reduce memory overload

Technical information You need some kind of record for perming and colouring to ensure that you know:

(1) How long it was since the client last had a technical service
(2) What products and/or colours were used on her hair

This is essential, not only to trace any potential problems or complaints regarding the service, but also to save time when recommending future technical work.

If you collect information accurately, then it is easy to recommend retail home care products for the client's use in conjunction with perm or colour. You can identify if she is having problems in handling her hair at home and make the appropriate recommendations.

Personal details Clients like to feel they are special, particularly if they have been visiting the salon for some time. They expect the salon to know their name, where they live and some information about their personal life such as whether they are married or single, have any children, or what they may do for a living. Information collected in this way helps to build up a picture of a client. It creates a personal relationship with them and makes it easier to sell our services.

Promotional aid If you collect information about the type of clients, their age group and the services they have received, then it becomes easier to identify what type of promotional activity would suit the client. It is *always easier* to sell to regular and loyal clients than it is to new clients. It makes promotional activity much more personalised so that you are likely to get a higher response rate than a 'hit and miss' approach. Without collecting information about clients you will find you either forget them or your memory goes into overload.

In conclusion, if you wish operational tasks in the salon to run more smoothly thereby creating a happier working environment, you must ensure you train staff not only *how to make the systems function but why they are important.*

7.3 Business planning

Now you have organised yourself and your staff you should have plenty of time to plan your business so that you control it instead of it controlling you! When first opening a hairdressing salon the owner and/or manager tends to be concerned with building a reputation in the locality and making money so that the business continues to exist. After the business has been operating for some years, many salon owners start to ask themselves such questions as:

- Why do I work?
- Is all the hassle worth it?
- Where am I going?
- What do I want?
- How am I going to achieve it?

For most people the key question is 'what do I want?' The answer often eludes us. What options are available? Failure to make time to think and plan for our personal future and the future of the business results in frustration, stagnation and demotivation. This in turn rubs off on the people with whom we may share our lives and those with whom we work. Once we have found the key to what we want by a process of analysis then our energies will be focused and channelled to achieve them.

What is business planning?

Business planning is:

(1) Thinking before doing. This means systematically examining alternatives.
(2) Collecting useful information and being aware of the competition in your locality and environment.
(3) Watching competition and 'getting them before they get you'.
(4) Predicting your performance by setting realistic targets and monitoring your actual performance identifying the differences and examining ways of controlling them.
(5) Deciding exactly where the business is going over the next few years and working to achieve this by planning in advance.
(6) Becoming efficient by running your business so that is economical in operation.

Fig. 7.1 Stages
in business
planning.

Stage 1 *Plan*		*Life planning*
		Who am I?
		What do I want?
		Where am I going?
		What do I want to achieve?
		What must I do to achieve this?

Stage 2 *Measure*   *Analyse opportunities*
How are we doing? Are we good/bad/indifferent?
What are the strengths and weaknesses of the
    business?
What is the competition doing?
Who are our customers?
What do they want? Do we meet their needs?

Stage 3 *Compare*   *Identify options and alternatives*
What are the options available to achieve our
    objectives?
Expansion? If so, how?
New products? Extra staff? Bigger salon?
Additional salon?
Reduce costs? Increase prices?
Retail sales? Motivate staff?
Bring in a consultant?
More promotion/advertising? Staff training/
    development?

Stage 4 *Act*   *Examine alternatives and choose most acceptable in
terms of*:
- Priority area
- Cost effectiveness
- Ease of introduction
- Quick returns
- Most flexible

This is a personal choice dependent on what you or
external 'experts' see to be the priorities.

Stage 5   *Formulate detailed plans for selected options*
- Capital investment and finance
- New equipment
- New materials
- Recruitment and training
- Timescale for changes
- New systems/procedures/rules
- Monitoring/control system for changes
- Communicate to relevant staff

Managing the changes in an effective way is a key
part of successful planning

Produce detailed budgets in terms of:
(1) Investments
(2) Costs/expenses
(3) Revenue/profits
(4) Non-quantified benefits

Communicate these to relevant staff and monitor
actual results with those expected/anticipated and
act accordingly.

(7) Controlling the business so that its performance is predictable and manageable, which in turn makes it easier to run.

What are the benefits for you?

Planning your business properly will achieve more of the following items than leaving it to chance:

Fig. 7.2 Business planning – plan of action.

Types of plans	Questions to ask
Level 1 – Purpose of the business	What is the purpose of the business? Why am I in the business? Why am I a hairdresser?
Level 2 – Major objectives	What purpose does the business serve for me? • An ego trip • A hobby • An income • A way of life What are its objectives? What do I need to do to achieve them?
Level 3 – Strategies	How am I going to achieve the objectives? How do I deal with competition? The environment? Do I ever think about it? (Or wait until it hits me)
Level 4 – Policies or major rules of conduct	What are the rules which will guide my decisions? What are the beliefs I hold which will govern my thinking and structure my decisions? e.g. pricing – I will always be the cheapest/dearest etc. Are these my greatest problems rather than assets?
Level 5 – Procedures and rules	What are the standards and guidelines for staff and management? What are the required standards of behaviour or conduct expected? Are these clear and properly understood?
Level 6 – Programmes or priority projects	What are the current key result areas, projects or activities I am trying to develop in? Have I allocated staff, money and expertise in the right proportion to achieve them?
Level 7 – Budgets	Do I budget ahead? Do I check my actual performance against my budgeted figures? How do I know whether I am: • Successful • Profitable and/or where I can improve?

(1) The business will be more successful financially.
(2) Reduced staff problems and miscommunication.
(3) Easier to manage and less hassle.
(4) More time to act – less 'fire-fighting'.
(5) Less 'chopping and changing'.
(6) More control and predictability over performance.
(7) Focus on achieving and rewarding rather than on punishing and scapegoating.
(8) Feel 'on top of the business' instead of 'the business is on top of me'.

In order to achieve business planning we need to look at the five stage process shown in Figure 7.1. Once we have answered these questions then we can consider a plan of action and the questions to ask (Fig. 7.2).

In order to help you to identify the options and alternatives available under Stage 3 in Figure 7.1 we have listed a range of objectives and how these may be achieved in a blow-by-blow approach (Figs 7.3–7.7).

If you have reached this stage in the book then how to plan your business becomes obvious because you now have a systematic approach to help you achieve it. You can begin to understand how the key areas of running a salon all fit together into 'the grand plan' or 'jigsaw'.

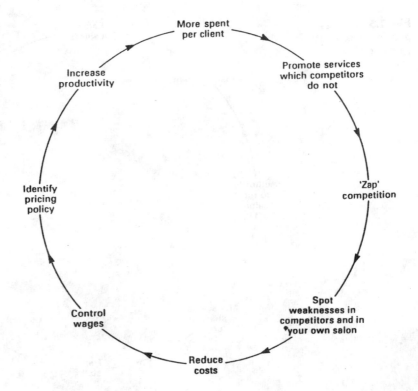

Fig. 7.3 Business planning objectives – how to become rich.

Fig. 7.4 Business planning objectives – be famous.

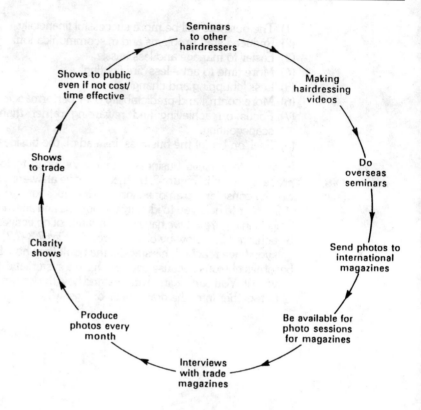

Fig. 7.5 Business planning objectives – retire/do less work.

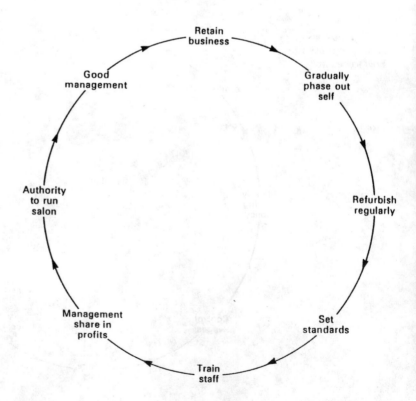

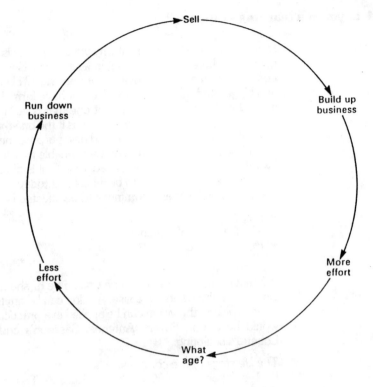

Fig. 7.6 Business planning objectives – retire.

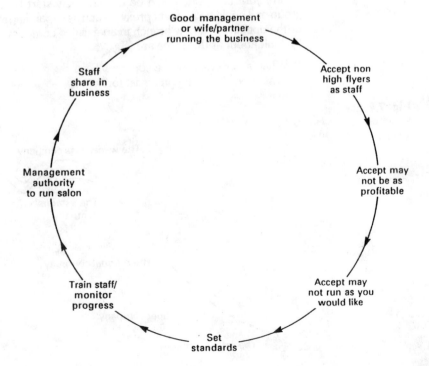

Fig. 7.7 Business planning objectives – hairdressing as a hobby.

7.4 Is yours a learning company?

Have you ever asked yourself why your company is the way it is? How did it get to be where it is today? Is it in its infancy? Is it a small and fast growing company with a central power figure driving it? Has it become independent and bigger and more complex? Does it have formal procedures? Has it lost its way and got out of touch? Is it one that is failing or bankrupt or has its original purpose been completed? Or is it the one that has decided that now is not the time to die and has found new purpose, new identity and new life?

If in the previous chapter you were unable to ask the questions 'What do I want?' and 'How am I going to achieve it?' it is often helpful to identify how the salon or company got to be where it is today – how did it evolve? Every company has been and continues to be affected by three key factors:

- Ideas
- The life stage of the company
- External forces

The ideas stage
When a salon owner opens a new salon he or she has a vision, an image of what he or she wants to realise. A salon can be anything the owner wants it to be provided the vision can be applied in a practical way. Examples of this would be Simon Forbes Antenna, Sassoon's cutting technique, Robert Lobetta's sculpting.

The life stage of the company
Each company has a *life stage* (see Fig. 7.8). This is the natural stage of the development of each company. Recognising where the company may be at the present time and what needs to happen within it to manage each life stage is an important function. Can you identify the life stage of your company?

An *infant company* could be a brand new start by an entrepreneur or group or it could be a parent project, such as expanding into beauty, retailing or the opening of a new branch in an existing company. The key questions to think about at this stage are

- What is our vision of the company?
- What does the company exist for?

Fig. 7.8 Life stages of companies.

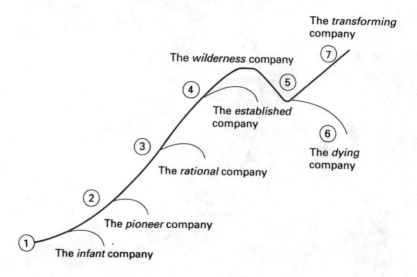

The *transforming* company

The *wilderness* company

The *established* company

The *dying* company

The *rational* company

The *pioneer* company

The *infant* company

- What is its purpose?
- How can the vision become reality?
- What people, money, equipment are required?

A *pioneer company* is a small and fast growing company with a central power figure or group driving it. Key questions to ask are:

- Do we stay small or get bigger? If we grow, what new systems do we need to cope with expansion?
- What new people do we need and how will we integrate them?
- Who can replace the leader and what plans do we have for succession?
- Do we need a new leadership style?

The *rational company* has outgrown its founder members and has become independent, bigger and more complex. Key questions are:

- Is the founder really in touch with the business needs now?
- Is the management style too authoritarian or too personal?
- How can we use systems to bring order, consistency and fairness?
- What new procedures are needed to manage people?

The *established company* is just that – well set up with formal procedures in most areas of the day-to-day operations. Key questions are:

- How can we encourage risk-taking and motivation?
- How can we minimise bureaucracy?
- What can be done about the barriers between departments and functions?
- How can we give more authority to some departments?
- Are we getting bored with our business?

The *wilderness company* has lost its way and got out of touch. Key questions would be:

- How can we change our relationship with our customers and suppliers?
- Do we have the right kind of clients?
- How can we change our view of our surroundings from seeing them as enemies and threats to one which is full of opportunities and potential?
- What are we here for?
- What should our new purpose be?

The *dying company* is one that is failing or bankrupt or where the purpose of its being has been completed. Key questions are:

- Is it time for the company to die?
- Should we make a good end or try to create new life through a merger, major surgery or management buy-outs?
- What are our moral obligations to employees, customers, suppliers and community?
- What new seeds can spring from the husk of the company?

The *transforming company* is the one that has decided that now is not the time to die and has found new purpose, new identity, new life. Key questions at this stage are similar to those for the infant company except that *they have an awareness and the experience of the past from which to learn:*

- What is our new vision?
- What is our purpose for being in business now?
- Who are our new customers?

- What new services are we offering our old ones?
- How are we going to work differently to accomplish our visions and goals?
- How can we learn from what we are doing?
- How do we organise ourselves for training?

All companies can be given new life and made to operate in such a way to move into the next life stage.

7.4.1 External forces

These are outside forces that directly affect our business. Identifying them is known as *boundary scanning*. There are five:

(1) The threat of new entrants (new salons).
(2) The bargaining power of suppliers (one or two main suppliers).
(3) The bargaining power of buyers (competing in a shrinking market place).
(4) The intensity of rivalry amongst the competition which tends to happen in a recession.
(5) The threat of substitutes or imitators copying the successful aspects of your company (your best promotional ideas, pricing policy, or benefits offered to your staff).

Action learning is therefore about all these things. Looking outwards, learning and acting upon it instead of being inward looking, being insular, and hoping that what is happening to ourselves and our companies will go away instead of putting into action what needs to be done. Action learning will enable your company to be truly *transformed* – revitalised to handle the opportunities emerging from the recession.

Chapter Eight
Managing Time and Priorities

8.1 Planning your time

'If only there were more hours in the day!' 'It is quicker to do the job myself.' 'I don't know where the time has gone.'

All of these statements will sound familiar to the overworked, run-off-his/her-feet manager in the salon. At least, that is often the description the owner or manager would give of himself. The staff probably wonder what the person in question is fussing about as we have all seen salon owners and managers who are 'busy being busy'.

What we are really talking about is the difference between *efficiency* and *effectiveness*.

- Efficiency is doing the job right
- Effectiveness is doing the right job

Effective managers are those who have managed to come to grips with two key issues:

(1) Organising themselves
(2) Organising other people

The two are inter-related because we cannot delegate until we have organised ourselves. What are the keys to a disorganised manager becoming an organised manager?

The first major point is *planning*. Initially, you may have to spend more time to make time, but that is a sensible, positive investment. This means taking control of the time at your disposal and deciding how you want to spend it. But you cannot decide on how you want to spend it until you know where the time has gone now. Then you can examine how you want to use your time and try to move the two things closer together.

Let us look at the ways time is lost:

- Unclear goals
- Lack of planning and organisation
- Unnecessary meetings
- Interruptions and phone calls
- Putting things off
- Too much routine work
- Insufficient delegation
- Lack of self-discipline
- Poor filing/record keeping systems
- Fatigue (lack of rest breaks)
- Long hours
- Physical unfitness
- Pet projects

- Unrealistic timing
- Too many outside interests
- Morale or personal worries

The first stage is to find out how you are spending your time *at present* by keeping some sort of diary or record for a period of at least two weeks but preferably a month. We have drawn up a time recording form which will be easy for you to follow in Fig. 8.1. At the end of each week simply record how much of your time you have spent on various items. We offer a list of

Fig. 8.1 Time recording form.

TIME RECORDING FORM

DAY   DATE   NAME

Time Started	Nature of Activity	Type	Duration	Note Interruptions which occur type/reason/time

USEFUL CATEGORIES

1. Working in Salon (Cutting/Styling)
2. Talking to Staff (Informal)
3. Talking to Customers when not cutting hair (Informal)
4. Dealing with Visitors/Salesmen
5. Ordering and allocating stock
6. Dealing with Correspondence
7. Book-keeping/Accounting etc.
8. Telephone calls—Analyse reason and time spent on the phone. (Personal/Business)
9. Personal Time (Breaks etc)
10. Travelling Time
11. Reading Magazines/Sales Literature etc.
12. Promotional work for salon
13. Promotional work for Manufacturers
14. Unallocated Time

NOTES FOR USE OF TIME RECORDING FORM

1. Begin as soon as you begin work or travel to work. Enter time you leave and not arrival time.
2. Each time you begin a **new** activity note the time and note the activity. If you are interrupted while tackling something note the type of interruption (phone call etc) and reason and how long it took to deal with.
3. At the end of the week analyse the sheets and code up the activities according to our scheme (or your own). Add up the total time spent on each category (or class) and also the time spent on all activities and express as percentages of the total.
   e.g. If the total time spent working was 40 hours and you spent 6 hours in the salon cutting/styling this would be:

   6/40 x 100 = 15% of your time

4. Check that all the percentages add to 100 and you have then completed the weeks analysis. Continue for 4 weeks and then calculate % of time over the whole period. This then is how you currently spend your time.

Also note the number of interruptions on average per week. This forms the first part of **your time** improvement plan.

categories we have found useful but you might like to modify this to suit your own needs.

Examine the information

The next phase is more difficult, to examine how you are spending your time and whether it is productive or not.

Look at the unallocated time. This is the time 'lost' – why? Can it be made more useful or cut out completely? *Examine the number of interruptions* – can they be reduced or eliminated? Can someone else answer the phone, take messages and arrange for you to ring back? Can people see you at prearranged times, such as first thing each morning rather than at different times during the day, except in emergencies?

Are you handling jobs following these principles:

- Do one job at a time
- Finish it before going on to the next
- Plan workloads and priorities

Are you clear about your *priorities*? How do you wish to spend your time? Can more routine work be delegated to staff? (Freeing your time and giving them job satisfaction.)

If you are spending too much time on paperwork – are your systems wasting time? Can you find things – have you a proper filing system? Do you have a desk to work at, a comfortable chair, quiet surroundings, a calculator and stationery or is it 'organised chaos'? Is your desk full of old letters, magazines and circulars which you are constantly moving around? Clear your desk of all rubbish – throw it out! Invest in some filing trays – in, out and pending – and use them.

Are you writing where you could phone? Do you use a desk diary for appointments and reminders?

Do you read everything that comes in? If you need it, keep it – if not throw it out.

Do you use a typist? If so, dictation is three times faster than writing things in long hand. It may be worth considering investing in a dictating machine. Do you read information slowly? Perhaps you need a speed reading course?

Now examine in further detail where you spend your time. Is it too much travelling? Would it make sense to live nearer or to travel less often to each shop? A well-run business will run for some of the time without you.

Are you spending too much time cutting hair and not enough time managing? Are you spending too little time talking to staff and solving problems? This can be seen by low morale and general lack of success.

Are you spending enough time *training* staff and maintaining standards through supervision?

Are you spending too much time playing golf? Have you lost touch with your business? This is OK provided you have good quality managers who have been given the responsibility and *authority*, otherwise the business will become neglected.

Figure 8.2 lists possible time wasters, their diagnosis and some suggestions for a cure.

Fig. 8.2 Time
wasters analysis.

Time waster	Possible diagnosis	Possible cure
Unclear priorities/ goals	Inadequate planning. Lack of belief in planning. Busy being busy!	Remember, only politicians redouble their efforts when they have lost sight of their objectives. Write down objectives and agree priorities.
Management by crisis	Inadequate forward planning and unrealistic deadlines. Staff bring problems too late.	As above. Allow reasonable time. Think the job through. Allow time for unavoidable interruptions. Be approachable. Encourage staff to bring problems when they occur, not later.
Paperwork overload	Too much paperwork. Failure to screen aggressively. Reluctance to tackle paperwork.	Examine systems and improve/streamline if possible. Be selective – throw away things you do not need. Change your attitudes or delegate to someone else who will do the work.
Too many interruptions/phone calls	Enjoyment of socialising. Inability to say no. Overkeen to be involved and informed. Lack of self-discipline. Too familiar. Use work to deal with work problems.	Do it elsewhere. Use lunches or after-work drinks. Be realistic – say no. Ensure staff understand their individual responsibility. Only be involved if essential. Manage by exception or delegate. Screen and group calls. Be brief. Decide what you wish to say before you dial.
Lack of delegation Too much routine work	Fear of staff's inadequacy. Fear of staff's incompetence. Fear of staff overload.	Assess it correctly. Train where necessary. Delegate properly. Give credit for success. Advise/ correct mistakes, don't punish. Balance up workload so everyone is working hard.

Where you want time to go

Identify active and reactive tasks. This means write a list of all the jobs you have to get done, not just today's but your long term tasks and priorities. It may not be in any order at this stage but just 'brainstorm' the list. It is likely to be a 'mishmash' of large and small tasks, urgent and non urgent, immediate and long term, boring and interesting. Start thinking about the items on the list and try to identify them into *active* and *reactive tasks.*

The active/positive tasks are the ones you must do to achieve the objectives of your job, e.g. make a profit in the salon, train the staff in order that they may function effectively as stylists, promote the salon to attract more clients. The reactive tasks are all the junk that hits you every day and has to be dealt with to keep things running. The danger, and this is the trap that most disorganised managers get into, is that we spend all the available time on reactive tasks – coping with the day to day jobs – and no time on positive tasks.

Examples of reactive tasks
(1) Dealing with clients
(2) Supplying clean towels
(3) Tidying the salon
(4) Visiting the wholesaler
(5) Answering the telephone
(6) Client complaints
(7) Staff absenteeism
(8) Broken light bulbs
(9) Burst water pipes

The more you plan your active/positive tasks the shorter will become the list of reactive tasks.

Schedule your work

From looking at the list you should now be in a position to schedule your work into the time you have available. To schedule a task you have to know two things:

(1) How long you want to spend on the task. This is determined by how important the task is, for example, promoting the business.
(2) How soon you have to get the task completed. This is determined by how *urgent* the task is. If we do not complete our stock control and order stock from the manufacturer then we will be forced to run down to the wholesaler to purchase stock or to borrow it from the salon across the road!

Importance and *urgency* are not the same thing. An urgent task is not necessarily important. It may be urgent but trivial, e.g. do we have fresh milk for clients' coffee, are the shampoo dispensers topped up? Deal with this kind of task straight away. Do not procrastinate and don't spend all morning on discussing the whys and wherefores of the problem. In that way you will leave yourself lots of time for the important tasks.

Aids to planning your time

(1) *The Diary* The diary is an important aid to helping you to become more

organised. You can schedule chunks of time in the diary or appointment sheet so you can achieve positive tasks. This means setting time aside for preparing and writing reports, seeing sales reps, having regular meetings with your staff, training staff. You cannot expect that all of these tasks should be completed prior to the salon opening or after the salon closes. Why should you, for example, expect staff meetings to be held at 7.00 p.m. on a Wednesday evening? How about holding them at 8.45–9.30 a.m. one morning? The result would be a more attentive, positive reaction from the staff because the owner or manager has seen that the meeting is sufficiently important to book out the first two appointments on that day.

Use your diary to jog your memory about telephone calls that have to be made. Allocate time twice a day for receiving and making telephone calls instead of constantly excusing yourself from your clients every time a call comes into the salon.

Use your diary to remind yourself of the letters and correspondence which need to be followed through. The diary will help the organised manager to achieve his/her objectives.

(2) *Visual planners* Other devices to help managers are such things as wall charts, year planners and 'bring forward' files. Why search through a mountain of paper when a simple bar or line chart which is updated weekly or monthly can demonstrate sales targets, service targets, training needs and staff holidays? The chart can show you comparisons with previous years and once set up becomes a useful document in managing your business.

Now you have organised your own time you are in a position to organise other people.

8.2 Planning your staff's time

Now you have organised yourself how can you organise the team? In Chapter 4 on Managing people we talked about clearly identifying staff's responsibilities and levels of authority and the standards you expect. We discussed that job descriptions must state the minimum standards required and the goals you expect staff to work towards which would, in turn, allow you to manage and motivate your staff further.

Now you have clearly identified where time is spent in your own jobs, can any of these tasks be delegated? Often we hold on to tasks because:

- We enjoy doing them, e.g. photographic work/organising shows
- We can do them more quickly ourselves
- It will be to the standard we expect because we have done it ourselves
- We feel anxious about letting go

Some of the tasks we do ourselves may be very boring and not stretch our own potential but they can be used to stretch and develop others. This will give us more time to spend on the important active tasks.

Delegation does not mean abdication – the buck still stops with the manager/owner even if someone else has been selected to do the actual job. Delegation should be seen like the process of teaching someone to swim or drive a car. When they first start they think they will never get the hang of it and they need constant support, training and *the manager's time* to help them grow and become more confident when performing the tasks.

Unfortunately, some managers believe staff should be thrown in at the deep end to 'sink or swim'. This method of delegation does nothing to help their confidence – some people never swim again! Delegation will ensure that you do not lose overall control – it is the detail which bogs us down so that we fail to perform the key areas of our own jobs.

Areas for possible delegation

(1) Appoint a head trainee responsible for trainees
(2) Allocate stylists to be responsible for the day to day training of trainees
(3) Give receptionists responsibility for bookkeeping and paperwork procedures
(4) Allocate a senior stylist or assistant manager to run stock control procedures

The key to delegation is setting the standards you expect from all staff and discussing and agreeing the goals they will work towards.

Plan of action to delegate

When deciding to delegate a part of your own job, you may well select a candidate and inform him of the decision. To you this will often mean it should all 'just happen'. But unless your candidate is very able, prepare yourself for a shock. We detail a suggested plan of action:

(1) Decide which tasks to delegate
(2) Decide the staff to whom you will delegate
(3) Brief and train the individual
(4) Inform other people
(5) Be available for discussion/encouragement on key areas of the job
(6) Monitor key areas of the job

In conclusion, by delegating tasks effectively you will gain a considerable amount of time as well as gaining more motivated and interested staff. Staff who, in time, will be able to take more responsibility leaving you time for active, positive tasks. The key points in organising yourself, therefore are:

(1) Make a list
   - positive/active tasks
   - reactive tasks
(2) Establish priorities
   - importance
   - urgency
(3) Schedule your time
   - schedule active tasks
   - allow time for reactive tasks
(4) When organising other people remember to:
   - delegate (which task and who does it)
   - brief people and train them
   - inform others
   - be available for advice
   - check on key points

Chapter Nine
The Law

9.1 Legislation affecting employment of staff

A number of pieces of legislation, dating mainly from 1963, have changed the emphasis with regard to the employer/employee relationship. In consequence, many areas of employing staff are now directly affected by law. The list that directly affects employing staff is outlined below but it is essential that owners and managers refer to the legislation itself, and in cases decided by industrial tribunals, obtain legal advice in relation to their own particular case. The purpose of this summary is to provide a guide as to the areas which need particular attention. We have already detailed in Chapter 3 information regarding contracts of employment and in Chapter 5 detailed the importance of job descriptions, written rules and regulations, grievance procedures and disciplinary procedures which are all part of good employment practice and which considerably reduce the likelihood of an industrial tribunal case.

The legislation directly affecting employment of staff is:

- The Race Relations Act 1976
- The Sex Discrimination Act 1986
- The Employment Protection Act 1982
- The Industrial Training Act 1964
- Employment and Training Act 1973
- The Payment of Wages Act 1960
- The Equal Pay Acts 1970 and 1983
- The Health and Safety at Work Act 1974
- The Redundancy Payments Act 1965

Law, whether it is civil or common law, is a complex issue and just as we have recommended that specialists are consulted for certain aspects of running the business, such is the case with legislation.

One of the most useful reference guides in this area is Croner's *Reference Book for Employers* because it constantly updates the subscriber on any new legislation directly affecting the employment of staff.

9.2 Recruitment

In principle, an employer is free to choose whomsoever he/she wishes for employment provided two main categories of legislation are taken into consideration. (See Fig. 9.1.)

(1) Selection on grounds of sex and/or marital status could be held to be discriminatory under the provisions of the Sex Discrimination Act 1986.
(2) Selection on grounds of the race or ethnic origin of the person would be considered unlawful under the provisions of the Race Relations Act 1976.

Fig. 9.1 Sex and racial discrimination in job adverts.

> Sex discrimination (applies if you employ five or more staff)
> (1) Avoid words like storeman, salesgirl etc. If these are used make sure the advert clearly offers the job to both sexes.
> (2) Make sure the job is not understood as being offered to only one sex.
> (3) If the advert uses he, him etc. ensure alternatives are used he/she, him/her and these are consistent throughout.
> (4) If pictures are used, show men and women in equal size and prominence *or* a disclaimer (equal opportunities) is needed.
>
> Racial discrimination
> (1) Job adverts must not discriminate on racial grounds, i.e. colour, race, nationality, citizenship, ethnic or national origins.
>
> A fine of up to £400 in either case is possible.
>
> In short do not specify: sex, marital status, colour, race or nationality in adverts.

9.3 Servicing the employment

The employer must perform certain duties imposed by legislation as follows:

(1) Payment and amount of wages governed by the Payment of Wages Act 1960 and Equal Pay Act 1983.
(2) Health and safety of employees whilst employed or *on the employer's premises* affected by the Health and Safety at Work Act 1974.
(3) Maternity leave affected by the Employment Protection Act 1982 which gives the pregnant employee four rights:

  - The right to time off for ante-natal care
  - The right not to be dismissed if the employee has accumulated two years' continuous employment by the beginning of the 11th week before the expected date of the birth
  - The right to maternity pay
  - The right to return to work within the same position or similar position, if the employee has stated in writing that she intends to do so. The pregnant employee will have up to 29 weeks leave after the date of confinement provided she notifies her employer in writing at least 21 days in advance of her intention to return to work.

For further information regarding this Act, read the Act itself, Croner's *Reference Guide* or contact the DHSS.

For salons employing five staff or less maternity leave does not apply.

9.4 Health and Safety at Work Act 1974

There is much legislation regulating health and safety at work. The legislation falls into two categories:

(1) That which is general laying down broad outlines.
(2) That which is specific and detailed applying to particular types of premises.

The Health and Safety Executive produce a number of free leaflets and Codes of Practice and we have found them particularly helpful in clarifying how to apply this law to hairdressing salons.

It is the duty of every employer, as far as is reasonably practicable, to ensure the health, safety and welfare at work of all staff. This includes, in particular, the following:

- Maintenance of equipment which should be safe and without risk to health, e.g. sterilisers, mixing of chemicals.
- Safety in connection with the use, handling, storage and transporting of articles, substances (products) and equipment.
- Provision of information and training and supervision to ensure that employees understand health and safety at work.
- Provision of access and exits from the place of work which are safe and without risk.
- Provision of adequate facilities and arrangements for staff's welfare at work (staff rooms!).

Again, we would strongly recommend that the Health and Safety Executive and Croner's *Reference Guide* are consulted. We have already suggested in Chapter 5 areas which rules should cover and these have incorporated the requirements of the Health and Safety at Work Act.

Chapter Ten
The Future of the Industry

One of the advantages of being a consultant is being able to observe the industry from a wider perspective, whether from the viewpoint of the single salon owner, mobile hairdressers, multi-site salons, franchise organisations, hair product manufacturers or managing agencies. As we move towards the next century, the industry will be forced by market and economic factors to change its approach and attitude if owners/managers wish to make a good living from their businesses.

Threats/opportunities facing the industry

- An ageing population
- Franchising
- Shortage of young people
- Home hairdressing
- Skill shortage – stylists/managers/trainers

10.1 An ageing population

By the year 2000 half the population in the UK will be 40 or over – by the year 2040, 80 per cent of the population will be pensioners (source: OECD, Henley Forecasting Centre)! This raises a number of issues:

Ageing clients

When we begin to get older we are looking for a range of sevices with a different emphasis. Often, the older we get and the more experience we have of life, the more discerning we are in terms of what we expect in return for our custom. Until we have a fixed income we may not be price conscious but will certainly expect value for money.

Ask anyone over 35 who visits a hairdressing salon what they expect from their hairdresser:

- Personalised service
- High standards of cleanliness
- Quiet background music
- Convenience – e.g. parking facilities or for the hairdresser to visit them
- Hairdressing/technical services to make him/her younger and desirable
- Hair care advice
- Selection of refreshments (not just tea or coffee)
- Hours to suit the client
- Staff who understand how it feels to be older

In a recent market survey carried out by major manufacturers the typical profile of a hairdresser showed 'an age of 24', 'stays in the industry for five years', 'reads the Daily Mail' and 'shops at Next'! We can see how this can instantly create a communication barrier!

Ageing hairdressers

Where do all the old hairdressers go? There has always been a fear among many hairdressers of the thought of getting old, but in fact, with an ageing population, older stylists will come into their own. Older stylists for older clients – so they are able to communicate and understand the client's needs. Where does this leave the present day practice of employing young people as trainees in hairdressing?

There is already a shortage of young people in the industry which will continue through the 1990s. In 1987 there were 27 000 school leavers, half of them employed by just 20 large companies. The rest were fought over by all the remainder of the service sector.

Why do we bother to compete? Why not be more selective about the employment of trainees by learning recruitment/selection skills, training them intensely during the day over a 12/18 month period instead of the traditional 2/3 years and paying them a realistic salary whilst training?

The remainder of the hairdressing and support staff could be employed from two other sources:

(1) Women returners who may have previously been hairdressers, now needing refresher courses.
(2) Women returners who have not previously been hairdressers but who could be trained as either hairdressers or salon assistants.

This would meet the needs of an ageing population/clientele. They would be able to understand and communicate with their clients because they will know how it feels to be older and what clients will expect. What prevents this happening?

(1) Attitudes/resistance to change
(2) Low pay

The apprenticeship and YTS scheme have created a false market for a number of years whereby we have paid staff slave-labour wages on the pretext that we cannot afford an alternative. This is rubbish! If owners and managers spent more of their time in running their salons as businesses and developed their skills to be more successful and profitable they would not need to worry about the shortage of school leavers.

New skills needed by owners/managers

(1) Recruitment/selection skills
(2) Understanding money and pricing strategy
(3) Planning and organisational skills
(4) Man-management skills
(5) Training to train
(6) Promotions/marketing
(7) Computerisation

Owners and managers who do not take this path to solve their problems will need to take alternative action such as:

(1) home hairdressing, or
(2) franchising

In 1989 approximately 40 per cent of hairdressers were either employed as home hairdressers or self-employed. It is our prediction based upon these marketing and economic factors that this figure will continue to increase throughout the 1990s to 60 per cent if we do not attract or harness this growing sector of the industry. Not all home hairdressers are unprofessional. They do meet a demand. The market research surveys we have carried out show that clients, particularly those with families, want the convenience of home hairdressers. These clients are saying we do not meet their needs. Hairdressers have tended to discourage children from visiting salons – but this action discourages the parents too. In the mid-1980s there was an increase in the birthrate – children have become a 'fashionable accessory' (although this is not necessarily the authors' view) and we need to rethink our approach to the family as a 'one client unit' in terms of service and pricing strategy.

10.2 Franchising

During the 1980s a number of companies developed into the franchising market, each with their own strengths and weaknesses. These companies were the pioneers in this industry and as new companies move into franchising they will learn from the mistakes of others.

The strengths of franchise companies are often the weaknesses of many small salons who need to compete with them to survive. Small businesses lack resources – this means they have to do all their own paperwork, training, recruitment and stock control as well as come up with promotional and marketing ideas. Work like this is usually carried out at weekends or in the evenings and experience is often gained through costly mistakes.

This is where franchising comes into its own. Franchising companies are able to offer their franchisees organised promotional back-up, both locally and nationally, to attract clients. A franchise salon uses the reputation of a large company and offers support systems and controls to help a franchisee become successful more quickly. Franchise companies may offer:

- Induction training
- Hairdressing training
- Management and career development training
- Paperwork systems
- Discounts on stock
- PR/promotional back-up

These are the franchise companies to join – but at what cost? What kind of percentage should franchisees be paying for this range of services? It could be anything from 5–10 per cent depending upon what the franchisee gets in return. When thinking of this market it always pays to shop around and compare as much as possible like with like.

How does the small salon owner who wants to 'go it alone' compete with a large, well organised company? The answer is to beat them at their own game. This means becoming organised, delegating to staff, setting up training and career structures and setting standards of what you expect from them. In fact, the salon owner or manager who reads this book will have the clues as to how to make these things happen for them.

10.3 Home hairdressers

Why does a stylist become a home hairdresser? Some of the reasons for this are:

- Increased flexibility in working hours
- Less responsibility
- More money
- No salon politics

In the previous section we suggested that we need to attract this growing sector of the industry. There are many disadvantages to being a home hairdresser, as a number discover after two to three years, which is the average time that home hairdressers stay out there on their own. Many of them would be interested in working within a structured organisation where there is stimulus and creativity and greater job security. But the rewards must be great too. We have another reason for suggesting we consider harnessing this market and using home hairdressers as part-time staff.

Professor Charles Handy, who is visiting Professor at the London Business School, predicted in his book *The Age of Unreason* (Century Hutchinson) that part-time work will be normal by the end of this decade. He put forward his 'shamrock' theory whereby the work force would be made up of three types of workers.

At the moment there are 24 million people employed in this country. Some 16 million of them are full time, meaning that one-third of the entire population work part time. He predicted that within the next ten years half of the entire working population would be employed on a part-time basis. He suggested that employment trends over the next few years will change so dramatically that the working population will fall into three sectors:

(1) A core of highly paid professionals
(2) A flexible workforce
(3) A contractual fringe

He considered that the core of highly paid professionals would enjoy high pay, long term contracts, good benefits and expensive company cars. The flexible workforce would be employed, he suggested, on an annual hours agreement so that they worked to meet the demands of the business and to fit in with their own domestic commitments. This type of workforce will be ideal for salons who open 12 hours a day, seven days a week, and for those busy periods at Christmas and Easter. As some two-thirds of the country is now developing towards the service industry as opposed to manufacturing, which requires people to work a wider variety of hours and days of the week, how can the hairdressing industry meet this change in people's working patterns? The answer is that hairdressing salons will have to respond by opening longer hours and more days of the week.

An alternative approach to looking at the trend of home hairdressing is to use it as an opportunity – to expand your business into the home hairdressing market. For example, why is it that there is a home hairdressing market at all? Women who have children and domestic commitments often find that salon hours from 9 a.m.–6 p.m. are not compatible with feeding, shopping, delivering and collecting children from school. Yet, many of these women are experienced workers who would work extremely hard at the salon but who have other priorities in their lives. If we do not consider attracting these people back into the fold then we create another rod for our own backs.

The third area of the workforce, the contractual fringe, would be made up of specialists and consultants such as training consultants, PR and marketing consultants and accounts and legal consultants whom it would not be financially viable to employ on a full-time basis but who could be used as and when required. Professor Handy did stress, however, that unless companies start to develop their own *training staff*, training would never be continuous and would restrict the future growth of many organisations. Bearing in mind that there is a shortage of highly skilled stylists and managers in this country due to the lack of investment in training, then the industry will continue to have the problem it has today which is a shortage of skilled staff.

10.4 Shortage of skilled staff

As an industry, we have failed to invest our time and money in the development and training of people at higher level and failed to reward them accordingly. Some of the larger companies have, over the years, trained and developed staff who are then attracted either to the prospect of 'cash in hand' employment, or wish to start their own salon by either funding it themselves with their own name over the door or deciding that franchising is an alternative option. The industry continues to create its own weakness, with a shortage of high quality hairdressers, lack of hairdressing training standards and almost non-existent management training. The UK invests less money in training, particularly management training, than any other country in Europe and that is not just in this industry. Out of the 165 000 people employed in hairdressing, only approximately 4000 people have ever been on any kind of management training course or seminar. A sad state of affairs by anybody's reckoning. In many European countries, hairdressers are unable to open hairdressing salons unless they or at least a member of their staff has passed a Master's Certificate. This certificate ensures that they understand how to train people and understand the financial aspects of the business and how to market their salon. In many of these countries, staff are paid five or six weeks' holiday pay, sick pay and high salaries because they charge more for their services. Will this be the answer to the skills shortage? How many Europeans will want to work in our companies if we do not offer the benefits that they are used to in Europe? What is much more likely to happen is that European companies will come to this country and open up in competition, particularly European franchise companies. Will these companies pay UK staff five or six weeks' holiday pay, sick pay and high basic wages? Will UK salons be able to compete with this?

The solution is that we must learn new skills and we must recognise and acknowledge that many people in the industry who started at 15 or 16 need to learn new skills. What is wrong with acknowledging that we do not have a skill? We cannot be experts in everything – but if we want our businesses to grow and develop then we must move into new realms of operating our businesses in a professional way.

10.5 Hair product manufacturers

If we are looking at the future of the industry then it is reasonable to look at the professional hair product manufacturers and the way in which they have offered their support to hairdressers over the years.

The objective of a manufacturer, like all businesses, is to make a profit but as the needs of the industry change, manufacturers must respond to this need if they wish to gain or retain their share of the professional haircare market. It is not enough to sell products at advantageous discounts. Hairdressers will look to manufacturers for a wider range of support and knowledge if they use their products. This means that the sales force needs to rethink its approach to the industry by offering what hairdressers need such as:

- Technical back-up and training
- Expertise in promotions, marketing and advertising
- Business support services
- Information on computerisation for stock control, client records and mail shots
- Man management training courses

A salesman will need to become an expert, knowledgeable not just in the product range to help salons use the products professionally, but to offer a wider range of support services in return for their custom. If we are an ageing population then we will have ageing salon owners who will expect value for money, personalised service and who, because they have many years' experience in the industry, will expect a more sophisticated support system.

We are not advocating that these services should be offered free but that they should be costed into the 'package' just as we have recommended that the salons cost into their pricing package an all-inclusive service for certain basic services with 'specialist' services charged at realistic prices!

This raises implications for the way in which the sales force and technical staff employed by manufacturers are trained in the future. Do manufacturers need to have a sales force who, within their area, have a particular specialism in marketing, training, computerisation? It is the manufacturer that recognises this shift or change in emphasis in the way in which it services its clients that is likely to be the winner during the next decade.

Appendix
Sources of Information

Marketing and promotions

Small Firms Advisory Bureau.
Institute of Marketing, Moor Hall, Cookham, Berkshire.
Kotler, P. *Managing Management: Analysis, Planning, Implementation and Contract*, Prentice Hall, 1988.
Peters, T.J. & Waterman, R.M. *In Search of Excellence*, HarperCollins, 1982.
Porter, M.E. *How Competitive Forces Shape Strategy*, Harvard Business Review, 1979.
Porter, M.E. *Competitive Advantage*, Free Press, 1985.

Understanding money

Parker, R.M. *Understanding Company Financial Statements*, Penguin, 1972.
Puxty, A.G. & Dodds, J.C. *Financial Management*, Chapman Hall, 1991.
Sizer, J. *An Insight Into Management Accounting*, Pelican, 1973.

Finding and keeping staff

Belbin, R.M. *Management Teams*, Heinemann.
Equal Opportunities Commission. Head Office: Overseas House, Quay Street, Manchester M3 3HN.
Institute of Personnel Management, 35 Camp Road, London SW19 4UX.
Kakabadse, A., Ludlow, R. & Vinnicombe, S. *Working In Organisations*, Penguin, 1988.
Sisson, K. *Personnel Management in Britain*, Blackwell, 1990.

Managing and motivating staff

Handy, C. *Age of Unreason*, Century Hutchinson, 1989.
Handy, C. *Understanding Organisations*, Penguin, 1979.
Hershey, P. & Blanchard, K. *Management of Organisational Behaviour*, Prentice-Hall, 1982.
Huczynski, A. & Buchanan, D. *Organisational Behaviour*, Prentice-Hall, 1991.
Lupton & Gowler, D. *Selecting A Wage Payment System*, Kogan Page, 1969.
Pedler, M., Boydell, T., Burgoyne, J. *Learning Company Project Report*, Manpower Services Commission, 1988.

Training

Kenney, J. & Reid, M.A. *Training Interventions*, Institute of Personnel Management, 1987.

Management Charter Initiative, Russell Square House, 10–12 Russell Square, London WC1B 5BZ.

Pedler, M. *Action Learning in Practice*, Gower, 1991.

Pedler, M., Boydell, T. & Burgoyne, J. *The Learning Company*, McGraw-Hill, 1991.

Index